D1564039

The Anthropology of Ireland

The Anthropology of Ireland

Thomas M. Wilson and Hastings Donnan

Oxford • New York

DA
925
.W55
2006

First published in 2006 by
Berg
Editorial offices:
1st Floor, Angel Court, 81 St Clements Street, Oxford, OX4 1AW, UK
175 Fifth Avenue, New York, NY 10010, USA

© Thomas M. Wilson and Hastings Donnan 2006

All rights reserved.
No part of this publication may be reproduced in any form
or by any means without the written permission of Berg.

Berg is the imprint of Oxford International Publishers Ltd.

Library of Congress Cataloging-in-Publication Data
Wilson, Thomas M., 1951-
    The anthropology of Ireland / Thomas M. Wilson and Hastings
Donnan.
        p. cm.
    Includes bibliographical references and index.
    ISBN-13: 978-1-84520-238-5 (cloth)
    ISBN-10: 1-84520-238-4 (cloth)
    ISBN-13: 978-1-84520-239-2 (pbk.)
    ISBN-10: 1-84520-239-2 (pbk.)
    1. Ireland—Civilization. 2. National characteristics, Irish. I. Donnan,
Hastings. II. Title.

    DA925.W55 2006
    941.5—dc22   2006017170

British Library Cataloguing-in-Publication Data
A catalogue record for this book is available from the British Library.

ISBN-13 978 184520 238 5 (Cloth)
ISBN-10 184520 238 4 (Cloth)

ISBN-13 978 184520 239 2 (Paper)
ISBN-10 184520 239 2 (Paper)

Typeset by Avocet Typeset, Chilton, Aylesbury, Bucks
Printed in the United Kingdom by Biddles Ltd, King's Lynn

www.bergpublishers.com

67375355

For Katharine and Anahid

Contents

List of Figures

Acknowledgements

Grateful acknowledgement is due to Rosellen Roche for permission to quote from her unpublished doctoral dissertation, to Gill Alexander of the School of Geography at Queen's University Belfast for drawing the maps, and to Pat McLean of the Ulster Museum in Belfast for help in selecting a cover image. Thank you also to Justin Dyer and Mary Warren for their careful work on the copy editing and index, respectively, and to Queen's University Belfast for a contribution towards the cost of reproducing the painting by Hans Iten. A particular debt is owed to Helena Wulff for her detailed reading of the whole manuscript, to Denis O'Hearn for his comments on chapter one, and to Fiona Magowan for her suggestions on chapter five. We also thank our colleagues throughout Ireland and around the world who over the years have offered advice, supplied information about their research, and supported various publications of ours, alone, together and with others. The Centre for Border Studies of the University of Glamorgan, and in particular its co-directors, Professor David Dunkerley and Professor Hamish Fyfe, generously allowed Thomas Wilson time and space to write while he was a Visiting Professor in spring 2005, and Teodora Corina Hasegan provided needed editorial assistance in Binghamton University. We are grateful for the continuing support and constant pressure we have received, as always, from Kathryn Earle of Berg Publishers, and we acknowledge also, with thanks, the patience both she and Hannah Shakespeare have shown us over the course of this project.

Preface

For over eighty years Ireland has proved attractive as a research locale for anthropologists, and can lay claim to being one of the first European locations to be the site of what we would recognize as a modern anthropological study, that by Conrad Arensberg and Solon Kimball in the early 1930s. It would not be too much of an exaggeration to suggest that those early field researchers in Ireland and the influential ethnographies they produced became a stimulus for a subsequent generation of Europeanist anthropologists, who continue to explore issues and themes many of which were first considered in the Irish context. One of the aims of this book is to appraise such contributions, and to consider ways in which an anthropology of Ireland is increasingly well placed to contribute further to central anthropological debates. In this respect we hope that the book will be of interest not just to researchers with an interest in Ireland, but also to anthropologists wherever they research.

We do not attempt to cover in detail everything that has been written by anthropologists about Ireland, even if such a task were possible. Instead, for each of the chapters we have selected some of the best and most representative ethnography to provide a substantive focus and illustration for our discussion around issues that continue to be of concern to Irish society and culture. Some ethnographies thus receive rather more extended consideration than others. Nevertheless, throughout all of the chapters we identify related work in parentheses as a guide to those who may wish to follow up the history of the study of a particular topic, as well as more contemporary work of relevance. In this regard, we have sought to be as comprehensive as possible, and trust that what this practice might apparently lose by encumbering the text with references is more than offset by what is gained in offering the aspiring ethnographer of Irish society – or anyone seeking an overview – just the kind of guidance and direction that they seek.

We should add, too, that ethnographers have not written about everything that is of contemporary concern to Irish people. Indeed, part of our aim is precisely to identify gaps in our ethnographic knowledge and understanding of the island and its inhabitants. Anthropologists largely chose the topics on which they work on the basis of personal interest, theoretical topicality, possibility of research access, and so on, rather than working to some master plan that would result in total ethnographic coverage of a particular locale or population. The book that is before you consequently draws on research that anthropologists have published, rather than, obviously, on that which is waiting to be done, sometimes urgently. This means that on some pressing issues we have had less material to draw upon than we might have wished, though rather than detracting from what is said here, we hope that this might encourage someone to do the field research that would fill the gap.

One issue that arises when using other anthropologists' ethnography to write about a place that one knows well is whether to disclose the actual location of their research. There has been sporadic debate in anthropology about the value, use and misuse of pseudonyms, and, cynically, about whether they protect the anthropologist more than they do the people studied. While we would prefer to identify the actual names of the places and communities studied by anthropologists, in this book we honour the published wishes of the authors cited and refer only to the community and location pseudonyms which those authors have given them. It might seem odd, then, to include in the book maps of the field sites referred to in the text. We have done so in order to offer a synoptic perspective on the distribution across the island of most of the major ethnographic field sites over the last century or so. Even though in many cases we are able to indicate only the county or city location of fieldwork, we believe the maps provide a rough guide to field sites in Northern Ireland and in the Irish Republic and a ready cross-reference to research cited in the body of the text. Readers should note, however, that in our view this is the only itinerary which these maps might allow one to plot.

We would also like to note that this book, as in all of our jointly authored and edited publications, is a shared project, and that both of us should be considered as principal authors regardless of the order of names on the cover. Moreover, despite its title, we obviously do not see this book as *the* definitive statement on what anthropology has to offer, or has offered, the study of Ireland. Our view is rather that there are many anthropologies of Ireland, and the book's contents strive to make this clear. We suggest throughout the book that there is not just one Ireland, but many Irelands; more even than the two Irelands of Northern Ireland and the Irish Republic. But a book called *Anthropologies of Irelands* would have been hard to get by our publishers. Our title notwithstanding, we ask that our readers approach this book as an examination of the many anthropologies of the multiple Irelands displayed within, and we hope that they will come away from its reading with the conclusion that they got rather more than what was promised on the cover.

Thomas M. Wilson and Hastings Donnan
Binghamton and Belfast, 10 May 2006

–1–

Anthropology Ireland
Identity, Voice and Invention

If Ireland had never existed, the English would have invented it.

Declan Kiberd (1995: 9)

Who invented Ireland? This is the question with which Declan Kiberd (1995) begins his analysis of the cultural roots and transformations of Ireland and the Irish. Kiberd quickly considers three answers to the question: Ireland was invented by the Irish, by the English, and by the peoples of the Irish diaspora, in an exile that is the 'nursery of nationality' (1995: 1–2). All of these peoples helped to name and identify the place, its territory, its landscape, but they also contributed to the idea of Ireland, to its many and changing manifestations, in ways which simultaneously invented 'the Irish', and their 'society' and 'culture'.

Historical and contemporary inventions of Ireland, the Irish and Irish culture and identity are all of critical significance to anthropologists, and have been since modern anthropology was born in the nineteenth century. Ireland was one of the first sites in the development of modern social anthropology worldwide, based as it was on the experimental and evolving notions of ethnography, which began to take shape in the 1890s, and which culminated in the so-called 'Malinowskian' model of anthropological fieldwork that dominated the discipline for most of the twentieth century. Ireland was also the location of a first attempt to marry the theoretical and methodological tenets of British social anthropology to those of American cultural anthropology, in ethnographic studies done in the West of Ireland in the 1930s. Thus, Ireland historically has been important as a site of research, but also as a domain of, if not also a trope in, significant leaps forward in anthropological thought. At least, that is how it was until the 1980s, when both Ireland and its anthropologies changed, in processes of reinvention that still impel us today. Anthropology, like Ireland and the Irish, is also an invention, an intellectual construction and professional body of scholars and research that adapts to fashion and historical forces as much and as quickly as other social and cultural entities. As such, it is also proper to ask: who invented the anthropology of Ireland?

There are many answers to this question too. The anthropology of Ireland has been moulded by multiple local and global forces. Among them are the developing intellectual and academic traditions and concerns of both American cultural anthropology and British social anthropology. But the anthropology of Ireland is also the product of local forces, developments in Ireland in universities and other centres of learning, and also in wider and sometimes dissident intellectual, scientific and technological domains. As we shall see in the pages that follow, the anthropology of Ireland has often been seen to be driven by scholarly interests and scientific paradigms with origins in Britain and the United States, particularly in the years leading up to and just after the Second World War. But by the 1970s this anthropology was directed and invigorated as much (if not more so) by internal intellectual change, both in the Republic of Ireland and in Northern Ireland,[1] as it ever had been by external forces. These alterations in anthropology within Ireland were reflections of social, economic and political change throughout the island, but they also mirrored changes that were transforming anthropology worldwide. These transformations in the method, practice, theory and professionalism of anthropology had a quick impact in anthropology in Ireland, and on the anthropologists who travelled to Ireland to conduct research. The growing theorizing of postcolonialism, postnationalism, post-modernity, transnationalism and globalization, beyond anthropology as well as within it, was leading all of the social sciences and humanities to re-think their approaches to identity and culture, which had long been prime areas of investigation for anthropologists.

In our view, the anthropology of Ireland has much to offer anthropologies elsewhere, and has contributed much to the intellectual and professional development of anthropology in the United Kingdom, in the United States and beyond. It has been a global anthropology, since its inception, and has figured prominently in much comparative anthropological research. These roles are not surprising, because of the global and comparative nature of anthropology as a professional discipline and an intellectual pursuit. But this global reach of the anthropology of Ireland is also due to Ireland's role in world society, economy and culture, a role that took on dramatic if not epic proportions as a result of the mass migrations of the mid-nineteenth century which resulted from the Great Famines. Ireland's global character has continued and been born anew since then, in ways including but not limited to the Irish diaspora, which in many countries across the globe has had a major impact on national politics (for example, in the ethnic politics of Irish-Americans in the United States); the rise and impact of the Celtic Tiger; the role of Ireland in almost all United Nations (UN) peace-keeping missions since the end of the Second World War; and Ireland's successes as a member of the European Union (EU).

In this book we recognize and address many aspects of Global Ireland, but we also recognize that the bulk of the anthropology we summarize and proffer here is in relation to the anthropology that has been conducted, debated, transformed and created in Ireland itself, on the island of Ireland. In this book, our Ireland is in the first instance a geographic Ireland. We accept that contemporary Ireland, the Irish and Irishness were invented in a global space, and that the anthropology of Ireland is incomplete without a consideration of the anthropology of the Irish, worldwide. Nevertheless, in these pages we primarily focus on what in the past has been seen to be, and what today constitutes, the anthropology of the island of Ireland.

The book has three principal overlapping themes. Taken together, we intend that these themes will provide both a historical and a contemporary record of anthropological ideas and practices in Ireland, about Ireland and its peoples. We also examine these themes in order to provide windows on Irish life for students of anthropology elsewhere, to enable the anthropology of Ireland to be framed in ways which will allow productive comparison. Through both of these engagements, with Ireland and with anthropology, we hope to offer the opportunity to non-anthropologists, in Ireland and beyond, to see how anthropologists have constructed Irish society and culture, in what we call 'Anthropology Ireland', and in so doing have contributed to a distinct discourse on Ireland which both sets Anthropology Ireland off from other scholarly and intellectual pursuits, and contributes to widespread consideration of the increasing importance of the notions of culture and identity to the economics, politics and societies of Ireland. Not all of these themes are addressed directly in each chapter that follows, but all implicitly inform each chapter's main and secondary concerns. Thus, this book is about the following:

1. It is about the anthropology of Ireland, in contemporary and historical form. It provides an overview of the history of anthropology in Ireland and a history of the anthropology about Ireland. It does so through a focus on the concerns, practices, theories, methods and professional evolution of social anthropology, which has historically been the arena of British scholars (including those of the Commonwealth and the post-empire, as well as many continental European countries), and of cultural anthropology, which developed principally in North America. But this focus is not in aid of presenting a critique of these major anthropological schools of thought, by using Ireland as a prism. Rather, we seek to use the frames provided by a historical perspective on these two world anthropological domains in order to elucidate the changing shape of the anthropology of Ireland and of things and people Irish, especially in terms of how that anthropology developed and changed in Ireland. We do not present an exhaustive and definitive review of all of the anthropological research that has been conducted in Ireland over the last century, nor do we summarize all of the major anthropological publications that have resulted. On the contrary, we explore certain continuities and discontinuities that we trace in the history of the anthropology of Ireland, in order to set the scene for our review of more contemporary trends and concerns in anthropology as it is practised and received in Ireland today. We also use this emphasis on Ireland to

touch briefly upon some of the ways in which the anthropology of Ireland has had an impact at home and abroad.

In this approach we also seek to examine how the history of the anthropology of Ireland has changed in line with transformations in Irish society, polity and economy, in both the North and South, though these have not been the only, and sometimes not even the principal, motors of the changing nature of Ireland's anthropology. The history of the anthropology of Ireland is also a product of the changing anthropological fads and fashions that shape intellectual and professional concerns and that have fundamentally transformed anthropology over the last century. From structural-functionalism to world-systems perspectives, and to the interpretive and multi-sited approaches of today, worldwide anthropological transformations have been transformative in Ireland's anthropology as well. The roots of this external professional influence are clear: most anthropologists who have conducted research in Ireland did not come from there originally, and most were trained in universities where the major theoretical developments of the day were the inspirations for novel research designs and professional advancement.

2. This book is about how Ireland has been constructed in anthropological writing and professional practice. It is about how anthropologists have contributed in their own distinctive ways to 'Writing Ireland', where writing about Ireland is about inventing Ireland in a manner that distinguishes the Ireland of anthropology from those Irelands constructed by other academic disciplines, and from those invented and reproduced in political institutions and other social bodies. This anthropological narrative of Ireland and its peoples and customs is distinctive in at least two ways: anthropologists generally ask different questions from those asked by other scholars, and they often ask them of people who are seldom the prime subjects of research outside of anthropology. This 'bottom-up' approach to people, ideas, behaviours, institutions, places and spaces is not the sole domain of anthropology, but, due to the field's reliance on ethnography as the principal framework for the collection and analysis of data, anthropology has relied on longer case studies of people who are often seen to be peripheral, or at least less significant, to the research designs of our cognate disciplines. This has changed mightily in the last two decades, but for most of the twentieth century, and even into this century, anthropology has been known best as the science of culture, where culture is seen as the combination of values, actions and structures that order social life. And to anthropologists culture is to be found, and found to be significant, in all levels and locations of society.

3. As we have just suggested, both the historical and contemporary anthropology of Ireland have been fashioned, in varying ways and to varying degrees, by international and global anthropologies. In this book we seek to contribute to the continuing

importance of comparison and the exploration of diversity and difference, which remain at the heart of anthropology. We thus strive to present, within the confines of a short book, something of the richness of research experience and ethnographic writing that have characterized the anthropology of Ireland since its origins. Inevitably, we have had to be selective, and there has not always been space to present as fully as we might have wished the ethnographic material that constitutes Anthropology Ireland. Nevertheless, we set out in the pages that follow many of the ethnographic case studies conducted in Ireland that have been the bases for clear and consistent contributions to anthropological theorizing for almost a century, in ways that have often brought world anthropological attention to the island. The breadth and depth of anthropological practice in Ireland today stand as exemplars of how empiricism, comparative social science, sensitivity to the ethics and politics of field-work, and provocative theorizing can all contribute to anthropology's increasing role as a creative and applied enterprise. Thus we seek to open up some windows on Irish life for the students and practitioners of anthropology elsewhere, to help locate the anthropology of Ireland within broader global frames.

One thing has become clear to us in the preparation and writing of this book. Over the last century, and most certainly today, there has been no single anthropological template that has driven or structured whatever might be seen to be the anthro-pology of Ireland. The theoretical and methodological models that have informed the various and overlapping, even sometimes successive, anthropologies that have investigated Ireland, and helped to define it in academic and intellectual ways, but often also in political and policy ways, have been in dialectical relationships with each other. These feedback relations have resulted in often contested versions of what Ireland is all about, of who the Irish are (or, most often, who the people of a locality are, and how that does or does not tell us something about the larger social entities of which they are presumably a part, such as the 'nation' or the 'church'), and of what they do in various events, institutions and seasons. Throughout all of this construction of Ireland and the Irish, though, the anthropologists who have crafted what we are calling the anthropology of Ireland have most often seen it within wider international and global contexts. This remains true today, when the anthropology of Ireland increasingly seeks to address matters of immediate concern in the lives of Irish people, often by contributing to the creation, imple-mentation and critique of social, economic and cultural policy, but in ways which may also speak to anthropology globally. Yet to achieve what might be possible, at home and abroad, the anthropologists of Ireland, and the anthropologists in Ireland, must clarify their anthropological identities and voices.

A Quiet Anthropology

As late as the early 1990s, anthropologists were facing certain questions of professional identity due to the generally accepted notions in Ireland of the discipline of anthropology (Wilson 1994a). While it may be too strong to assert that this was an 'identity crisis', it certainly was a malingering residue of years, generations even, of fostering the notion that anthropology was the academic discipline that studied primitive peoples in faraway exotic places. As the generally accepted story went, anthropologists did not study 'at home'; that was the domain in social science reserved for sociology, or perhaps politics and geography. But this stereotype of anthropological interest and practice – which often involved mythic imaginings of pith helmet, mosquito netting and long and solitary treks into the bush –was not just the product of popular media and other forms of non-academic culture. Some anthropologists were complicit in this view, in large part as they attempted to carve out or maintain a professional niche for themselves,[2] and there were those in the UK, the US and beyond who continued to foster the view that anthropology is about the study of non-Western 'primitive' peoples, despite the almost universal professional anthropological agreement that all peoples, in all societies, are the subject domain of the field.

As we shall see in the next chapter, Ireland had been one of the first sites for the ethnographic study of a modern nation, in field studies conducted in County Clare in the 1930s which helped to redirect the course of world anthropology to the study of rural communities in the developed Western and Northern hemispheres. But this important achievement, which put Ireland on the map for anthropologists training everywhere in the world, seemed to have only a minor impact on the popular consciousness of anthropology in Ireland. In the early 1990s it was still clear that 'anthropologists have not been very successful in removing stereotypes, making anthropology more popular … or making it relevant to decision-makers in the public and private sectors' (Wilson 1994a: 4).

If this was not an identity crisis, it was certainly a public relations problem, a case of not being heard, or perhaps not saying enough, clearly and loudly, to be heard. This was the case despite the public academic debate that developed in the 1970s, and which carried over into the Irish media, about the past and future directions of the anthropology of Ireland. By that time it had become obvious that an important and seemingly irreparable division had developed within Irish anthropology, between those who concluded that Irish rural culture and communities were in almost irreversible decline, and those who believed that such communities were representative of a long and vital history of the Irish people and their traditions and culture (this debate is discussed in chapter two). This professional difference of opinion was about the veritable core of a modern Ireland and its relationship with its past, as well as its reconstructions within the free-flowing conditions of post-modernity in which it found itself at the tail end of the twentieth century. Nevertheless, in the midst of the debates about Irish culture and identity and their roles in Ireland's reinvention of itself, the anthropology of Ireland continued in its quiet way, barely participating in the processes of policy-making, economic planning and elite, political and popular culture until the mid-1980s (Wilson 1994a: 6).

But if anthropology's voice in Ireland was muted for a long time, that time is now up. By the late 1980s, a body of work had begun to emerge with explicit and direct public policy engagement (Donnan and McFarlane 1989a; Jenkins 1989), some of which helped not only to inform but also to transform wider political understandings of, for example, the ethno-religious conflict that characterized Northern Ireland (Crozier 1989a, 1990a, 1991). Such work readily demonstrated how anthropology *in* Ireland and the anthropology *of* Ireland have much to contribute to the important concerns of public life on the island, and as such should, perhaps must, contribute to the political and civil discourse that informs all social and political process at home, and in those arenas of public culture that carry Ireland beyond its physical borders. Indeed, these engagements with public policy were subsequently described as 'cutting edge' (Sluka 1999: 450), and were widely recognized as more extensive 'than in any other region of Britain, and probably Europe' (Grillo 1999: 203).

Why, then, was anthropology's voice so 'soft'[3] for so long in public discourse? There are a number of historical and contemporary factors to be considered[4] as to why anthropologists have played such a minor role in the production of Ireland's public cultures: anthropologists often study people without particular public power and prestige; they often research communities and public arenas, and just as often more private local arenas of social life, that are distant from centres of decision-making; the discipline of anthropology was not one studied by, or even available to, policy-makers in their formative educational years; many anthropologists who research Ireland go back to university jobs in their home countries, and, while in Ireland, their intellectual concerns often have more to do with scholarly theory than with the practical concerns of a relevant and applied social science, particularly in an Irish context that may not coincide with public cultural contexts at work back home; and 'anthropology does not have a publicly sanctioned role as a player in the production of intellectual culture anywhere in the anglophone world' (Wilson 1994a: 6), which is a lingering problem in anthropology globally.

There is another reason why anthropological analysis is often seen to be less relevant to and more distant from the concerns of decision-makers in public life: anthropology's fundamental interests, and to some extent defining methodologies, take so much time, and so much commitment to the complexities of social and cultural life, that anthropological results have often been seen to lose their immediacy. Anthropological outputs, in fact, have for almost a century depended on long and deep research, where trust among one's hosts is built up after a great deal of time and social investment, and where the principles and assumptions of the anthropologist are queried by the people who are the subjects of the research as often as, and sometimes with greater intensity than, they are queried by the anthropologist, who is frequently alone in a new, sometimes strange, social environment. Furthermore, when anthropologists relate their findings, they are often insistent that simple answers, and certain cause–effect relationships, do an injustice to the complexities of social and cultural life; they prefer the intricacies of the 'thick description' (Geertz 1973) that has so motivated anthropologists for a generation and more.

What is this methodology that has been at the heart of what anthropologists do? The answer to this question is not as clear-cut today as it was in previous decades, as anthropology, in its own continuous internal debate over the subjects and objects of our field, recently has moved away from long-term field research, which in the past had demanded a sense of social and cultural holism, linked to a theoretical framework that required empirical data collection that was firmly within the intellectual traditions of comparative social science. This methodology was most often referred to as *ethnography*, which at the least involved 'total' immersion by anthropologists in the lives of the people who were their hosts, respondents, subjects and informants. This immersion in the public and sometimes private lives of groups of people was of course not total; ethnographers are constrained by many forces, such as language, gender, age, sexuality, class and access, whether that be physical, geographical or social. But the goal was, and to some extent still is, the Janus-like *participant observation*, where the anthropologist was meant to observe, record, relate and participate in all manner of social life, political action, economic practices and cultural meanings. Anthropological ethnographers are meant (although we accept that some anthropologists today would prefer the past tense here: *were meant*) to master the details of ordinary and everyday life, which at a minimum should entail learning, to a degree that made one as inconspicuous and as integrated as possible, the language, food, dress, drink, rituals, kinship and social structure, class, ethnicity, politics and economics, along with the myriad symbols and meanings of the great and mundane, of a people's culture.

But anthropology's historic and traditional methodology and methods do not in themselves define anthropological practice and anthropology's own culture of values, actions and institutions. Ethnographic field research relies on the gamut of social science methods, including formal and informal interviews, archival research, surveys, biographies, genealogies and audio, film and electronic recording (Gulliver 1989; Wilson 1994a: 5). In fact, 'everyone within the discipline is aware that fieldwork is a gloss for a promiscuous blend of all sorts of quantitative and qualitative research styles, none of which is the exclusive property of anthropology' (Donnan and McFarlane 1997b: 2). Rather, in addition to the professional and intellectual demands that long-term fieldwork requires (or used to require[5]), anthropology has had other important defining characteristics, which still give shape to the intellectual and professional dimensions of the discipline in Ireland, and as such have much to offer to the reinventions of 'Ireland' today. To us, anthropology is

> globally comparative, concerned with worlds of meaning as they are constructed by people; it is fundamentally humanistic and reflexive in its attempt to deconstruct or analyse these worlds of meaning and the social action connected to them; and it is perpetually rethinking how it uses its concepts, especially its central concepts like society and culture. (Donnan and McFarlane 1997b: 2)

It is our view, however, that these characteristics and methods, and the time and commitment needed to understand the complexity of local, everyday, even mundane social life, are among the best reasons why anthropology has a great deal to offer Ireland and its many avenues of regeneration, reconstruction and reinvention, especially in the arenas of public policy. This is because culture and identity are not just residual factors in political and economic life; they are the stuff of social action. They are the ways we approach meanings in life, and the meanings that motivate individuals and groups to move forward, in both positive and negative ways, within political and civil society. They are the lifeblood of heritage, tradition and social memory, which in and of themselves permeate all aspects of policy formation, implementation and reception. Anthropologists study, compare and wrestle daily with the messy and complex aspects of culture and identity; it is our job to make the minutiae of cultural experience in Ireland accessible, understandable and relevant to policy-makers, intellectual elites and the leaders in the cultural production of the nation, to allow culture and identity, as they are practised and believed in Ireland today, to be part of the reinventions of public culture. 'Social movements, after all, begin and end with the people and communities of the localities of Ireland. To understand the everyday lives of the so-called powerless in Irish life is to understand the source and impact of political, social and cultural power' (Wilson 1994a: 7).

Anthropologists of Ireland have increasingly begun to generate just such understandings and to tackle issues on which they were silent for so long, like nationalism, ethnic conflict, racism and sexism. Certainly there has been a growing reflexivity in Irish ethnography about the role anthropologists have played in constructing an Ireland of a particular kind, one with its own particular 'zones of cultural invisibility' (Rosaldo 1988: 79) that omitted key public issues from the ethnographic gaze. While this book celebrates how anthropologists 'Write Ireland' in ways that differentiate their field from that of others, and in the process constructs an Ireland different from the Ireland of others, it also stands as a reminder of the dangers of any discipline becoming too enthralled with talking to itself.

Reflecting trends within the discipline more generally – which for over a decade have emphasized the role of the ethnographer in the production of culture – so too anthropologists of Ireland have become more keenly aware of their own role as potential agents of change and of the audiences to which they do (and do not) speak. Like anthropologists elsewhere, they increasingly debate not only who should be their audiences, but also how best to communicate with them, all the while agreeing that at least one audience must be the people with whom they live and study, making them participants and partners in research rather than subjects and objects.

This is why we set out in this introduction our commitment that this book is not only intended for professional anthropologists and students of the subject. Its audience is also anyone who wishes to understand the transformations which Anthropology Ireland has undergone, due to the transformations that Ireland itself has experienced, but which are also the product of profound changes in the field of anthropology worldwide. Because the people of Ireland are enmeshed in multiplying levels and arenas of governance emanating from the region, the state, the European Union and from even more distant centres of decision-making, we also hope that this book might further encourage the opening up of anthropology in Ireland to the political concerns of policy. With regard to the major public issues in Ireland today, anthropology in Ireland can no longer afford to speak with that quiet, some might say all but silent, voice that characterized its past.

Policy, Practice and the Anthropological Voice

As we shall discuss in more detail in chapter seven, Ireland has undergone various important changes since it became part of the European Union. These changes, aspects of a broader process of Europeanization, have affected all levels and places in society and polity in Northern Ireland and the Republic. One of these effects is in the area of social policy, particularly in the arena of social partnership, wherein civil society and other non-governmental organizations participate in governmental decision-making. For the EU this sort of social partnership can lead, for example, to equality and parity between nationalists and unionists in Northern Ireland policy-making. But social partnership is also an arena of national construction, and the Republic of Ireland has been a leader in this form of consultative politics for some time.

Social partnership is a new form of governance throughout Europe, but it has been developed and widely adopted in Ireland since the late 1980s, at the same time as both the flourishing Celtic Tiger economy in the Republic and the developing peace process in Northern Ireland. Social partnership, a mix of governmental and non-governmental actors in a mutually agreed effort to meet the economic, social and political needs of their communities, has been widely perceived at home in Ireland, but also beyond among the other twenty-four members of the EU, to be a curious but important mix of home-grown Irish (and British, in Northern Ireland) solutions to the problems of social divisions and economic peripherality, which also have been stimulated and influenced by European values of social justice and political order. But what concerns us most here, and why this is relevant to anthropology in Ireland, is that this is a new form of governance that has been necessitated by radical transformations in the economies and polities of Northern Ireland and the Republic (and elsewhere in Europe and beyond), where old-style forms of government, and the non-governmental provision of order, often no longer hold.

In a process that is affecting all of the continent, Ireland has had to reinvent the means whereby localities are articulated within changing relations of regions, states and the Europe of the EU. In fact, social partnerships are representative of new forms of local and national governance that are adaptations to the globalization of international order. As such, '[t]he emergence of partnerships is a recognition of the multi-faceted nature of public policy and administration and the interconnectedness of regeneration decisions taken at the local, regional and international levels' (Hughes et al. 1998: 49). This attempt at repositioning power within various levels of Irish life is a response to the growing perception that Ireland must adapt to a 'no-one in charge' world (cf. J. M. Bryson and Crosby 1992: 4; see also Hughes et al. 1998: 49) in which no single institution, or even groups of institutions within a national frame, can provide the solutions to the changing problems of society and politics.

Social partnerships are thus an increasingly important facet of public culture in Ireland that, as a new form of governance, also direct the anthropological gaze to other forms of power-sharing and decision-making, many of which have been longstanding in both North and South, and many of which also have connected localities, regions and the nations of Ireland to similar entities within and beyond the island. Partnership is a useful metaphor to explore the organization of influence and power in Ireland, within local and national frames of course, but also within the global frames of capitalism, empire and diaspora that have involved the Irish for centuries. The concept is not without critics, however. To some, 'social partnership' is a rhetoric that offers the illusion of consultation to civil society groups and trade unions when policies are actually made somewhere else. Moreover, transnational corporations have played the major role in the formulation of the Celtic Tiger yet they are not a part of social partnership. Thus, one could argue that partnership is a mechanism that is intended to create the social stability that is necessary for the continuation of inward investment and economic growth, while not really shifting power to civil society or labour (cf. K. Allen 2000). In fact, with the recent reduction in economic growth and the return of higher unemployment in the Republic, trade unions have been demanding a redefinition of social partnership.

Partnerships, along with many other types of local politics, in many easily recognized forms but also in some less recognizable guises, figure prominently in the
analysis of the past, present and possible futures of the social anthropology[6] of
Ireland that follows, which may startle those readers who do not see the connections between policy-making and anthropology, the latter being the academic study
of what in most cases amounts to small-scale analyses of slices of everyday life
and patches of local societies. In the pages which follow, we seek to clarify some
of the connections between culture and identity, on the one hand, and the politics
and economics of power in Ireland, on the other hand.

At this juncture, however, it is important to highlight the role which the social
partners have played in what scholars in Ireland have labelled the 'reinvention of
Ireland'. This notion of the 'reinvention' of Ireland not only draws attention to how
changes in Irish life frame issues of Irish culture, but shows too how the anthropology of Ireland is changing, as it writes its version of what is being reinvented. The
'reinvention' of Ireland is a notion that is perhaps best represented in the works of
Irish economist Rory O'Donnell, and is an idea that was appropriated widely by government and the public and private sectors in the Irish Republic (for a review of the
impact of O'Donnell and of this concept, see Kirby et al. 2002b; see also Laffan and
O'Donnell 1998; O'Donnell 1999, 2000). As Kirby et al. (2002a: 1) have indicated,
the architects of policy in the Republic of Ireland, as represented in the Irish National
Economic and Social Council (NESC 1999: 21), have proclaimed that 'Ireland reinvented itself during the 1990s', in large part due to the economic upturns captured
in the accolade of 'Celtic Tiger' (a title which may not suit well the Irish economy in
general, or sit easily on the shoulders of the social partners in particular; cf. O'Hearn
1998). Whatever one thinks of the handle of 'Celtic Tiger', and however one assesses
accounts of its demise (Coulter 2003; O'Hearn 2003), it is clear that the economy
was a force for great social and political change in the Republic of Ireland for almost
two decades. It is easy to see why. Since 1993 the Republic's economy has grown at
an average rate of 6 per cent a year, and in 1997 its GDP per capita was for the first
time greater than that of the United Kingdom (Collinson 2005: 290). This is a startling turn of events in a country known up to the 1990s as one of the peripheral and
poorer areas of the European continent, last stop in the Celtic Fringe on the way to
the industrial might and social freedoms of North America.

What concerns us most here, in this brief consideration of the changing governance of Ireland, is how the ideologues of this reinvention of Ireland have turned
their attention to the relations between the economic and the cultural. Influenced
no doubt by Kiberd's (1995) analysis of the invention of modern Ireland, which in
his view occurred in the cultural revivals of the late nineteenth and early twentieth
centuries, O'Donnell (1999) has specifically viewed changes in the public life of
the Irish Republic which are due to Europeanization, social partnership and global
economic processes as a new culture tied to the new economy. [7]

But if there is a new culture to match the economy and society of the globalized and more multicultural Republic of the Celtic Tiger, wherein lies the difference between the old and the new? Is it just different according to the structural changes necessitated by the new service and informational economies of scale which have fashioned the South's economy as one of the strongest in Europe? If this is so, how do changes in production result in changes in consumption and distribution? And how do these have an impact on social structures and other economic relations, some of which were long seen in Ireland to be part of the domestic sphere or of informal broker economies? What is the stuff of this turn to the cultural in Irish life? Does culture play only a passive role, or does it figure as a causative factor in the reinvention of Ireland? And, as we shall examine in much of this book, have these changes in economy, society and culture made any impact in Northern Ireland, a constituency beyond the frontiers of the reinvented Republic of Ireland, but a cultural space at the core of the reconstructions of Irish and to a lesser extent British nationalism over the last century?

As Kirby et al. have concluded, the social partners (and, we suspect, some scholars) have approached the 'new culture' of Ireland with 'an adulatory and uncritical tone ... which often fails to trace the new culture's historical develop-ment or to identify the forces which have shaped it. Instead, it is seen as marking a break with the past and the coming-of-age of an enlightened, tolerant and liberal Ireland' (2002a: 2). They ask that analysts of this reinvention of Ireland look beyond the façade of greater prosperity, and the uncritical linking of this new wealth and national satisfaction with the perception that there has been a burst of cultural creativity, in order to investigate how 'the precondition of Ireland's eco-nomic success, namely subservient integration into a radical free-market or Anglo-American informational capitalism, has shaped values, attitudes and forms of cultural expression' (Kirby et al. 2002a: 2). In fact, in a call to scholarly arms with which we heartily concur, and which we suspect that anthropologists far and wide might view sympathetically, Kirby et al. go further, to ask that scholars 'explore ways in which culture could inspire political resistance and alternatives, using an engagement with Ireland's past to identify resources for reimagining and rein-venting a different Ireland of the future' (2002a: 2).

Multiplicity and Alternatives

Our book is in part about the Ireland of resistance and dissidence, of continuities and discontinuities, and about anthropological alternatives. We examine past and contemporary anthropological research and writing which seek to recognize and understand these alternatives and forms of resistance. This book is also about forms of integration and community, but even these demonstrate remarkable breaks with the past and show the diversity that has characterized Irish social and cultural life in recent years. This diversity, of behaviour, values and attitudes, as expressed through the idioms of tradition, culture and identity, represents a dramatic divergence from the images of Ireland as portrayed in the pages of anthropological texts written from the early years of the last century to the waning days of the 1970s, and maybe still persisting today, in select quarters, in some remarkably resilient forms of traditional and perhaps myopic anthropologizing. We agree with the new architects and the new critics of a reinvented Ireland that there have been sea-changes in Irish life over the last generation. Anyone who has lived through these changes knows this, and knows it in so many diverse ways that it can be difficult to determine where to start to describe them and to understand them, even for a native or long-standing resident such as each of us. How much more difficult it will be for a visiting anthropologist, new to Ireland, intent on a year-long journey of intellectual discovery and understanding.

This book is based on the supposition that so much has changed in Ireland over the last twenty-five years that we may indeed see it as a self- and other-generated reinvention, but this constitutes a simultaneous reinvention both of self and of others, that is, of the peoples of Ireland, at home, both in the North and South, and of their relations with each other; and with the United Kingdom; and with other peoples, nations, states and polities in the EU and the global beyond. In this reinvented Ireland there is much that will attract anthropological and other scholarly investigation (as in the anthropology of Britain; Rapport 2002). There are new forms of Irish culture, and new idioms of communication and interpretation. There are new ways in which culture marks the traditional domains of territory and identity. There are new ways of performing and demonstrating Irish culture and identity at home and abroad. There are new strategies of resistance to and subversion of both old and new structures of power, as well as new ways to preserve and perhaps contain old structures of power and domination. At the same time there are new arenas of political and social action, in the EU of course, but also through new technologies and new forms of economic and cultural integration within a global terrain. These arenas are not only agents of change, for example in the ways in which they stimulate the importation of new ideas and new peoples into Ireland, but also the means to deal with such changes, as we shall see in our examination of minorities in Ireland and of the changed roles of women.

To keep up with these changes the anthropology of Ireland must also reinvent itself, in ways which have already become part of the practice of anthropological reflexivity and self-awareness throughout the globe. By the anthropology of Ireland we mean anthropology as a professional practice within Ireland, as well as the scholarly investigation of Ireland and the Irish from whichever quarter it emanates, including those many visiting scholars who have come, studied, and returned to their home lands in order to use Ireland as part of their own personal professional reinventions. This anthropology must reinvent itself to keep up with the critical approaches to ethnography and culture which have marked major developments in American, British, French and other traditions of anthropology worldwide. It must reinvent itself to match the turn to culture which has characterized all of the social sciences over the last few decades, and which has required anthropologists to reconsider their methods, theories and own roles in the production of anthropological knowledge. The anthropology of Ireland must reinvent itself to keep pace with the social, political, economic and cultural changes which, while in some cases originating in Ireland but which are just as likely to be caused by factors external to the island, in Europe or in the global domain, characterize Ireland itself as both reinvented and refashioned, reformed and re-tooled. Anthropologists must re-tool themselves so as to better formulate research problems and questions, so as to ask the best (informed, insightful and felicitous) questions, so as to understand the answers in the midst of field research, and, in what we consider perhaps the most important aspect of this new anthropology of Ireland, so as to report and write anthropology in ways which inform the Irish and their own attempts to reinvent themselves. In short, the new anthropology of Ireland must make sense in Ireland, and for the Irish; its secondary goal, and only a secondary goal we assert, will be to fuel global anthropological and other scholarly concerns.

This reinvention of the anthropology of Ireland may not be so formidable a task. Since the beginnings of an anthropology of Ireland, the field has had an impact on Irish notions of themselves, and, in varying ways and times, on the inventions of Irishness and Irish ways. It has often been based on sensitive and nuanced portraits and understandings of Irish everyday life, understandings which initially focused on the diverse and, at the time when the first anthropological studies were done, distant locales of Clare, Tyrone and Kerry. It is to this earlier Ireland, and earliest anthropology, that we now turn.

–2–

Locating the Anthropology of Ireland

What a bloody awful country: get me a scotch, someone
                          Reginald Maudling (British Home Secretary, 1970–2)

The anthropology of Ireland began with the ethnographic research of C. R. Browne and A. C. Haddon in the 1890s (see Haddon and Browne 1891–3), but its modern period dates from the field research conducted from 1932 to 1934 by Conrad M. Arensberg and Solon T. Kimball in a rural and peripheral area of County Clare, on the western coast of Ireland (for a county map of Ireland, see Figure 2.1). The publications which resulted from this anthropological research (most notably Arensberg 1937; Arensberg and Kimball 1968) focused on social and cultural stability and change in the lives of poor farmers and their neighbouring townspeople. These books became so influential in the general anthropology and sociology of Ireland that they set the standard by which much of the anthropology of Ireland was judged up to the 1980s, and their work still inspires many Irish social scientists (warranting an Irish-produced third edition of their jointly authored analysis of social and economic relations in the town of Ennis and its hinterlands, *Family and Community in Ireland* [2001]).

The impact of these classic works in anthropology continues to be felt today. This is because the community-based model utilized by Arensberg and Kimball became the template for rural ethnographic research in Ireland, in which kinship and social structure were examined as a means of testing the theoretical model of structural-functionalism and its usefulness in combining the ethnographic interests of American and British scholars (Wilson 1984). It was also a template for community studies research globally, especially as this kind of research developed in subsequent British and American anthropology (see Arensberg 1961 for the clearest description of how the community study was both the object and the method for more than a generation of anthropologists' research). But Arensberg and Kimball's studies were also in themselves ethnographically sound, resulting, in *Family and Community in Ireland*, in a portrait of rural and urban Clare that provides 'insights into a way of life of which many fragments persist still, some remain vivid in memory, and others would have been forgotten without their book to recall them' (Byrne, Edmondson and Varley 2001: ii).

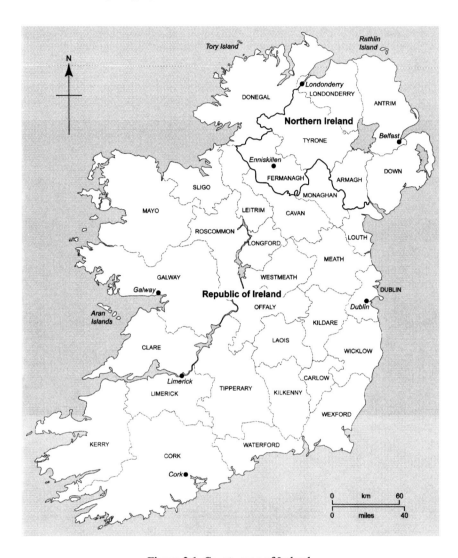

Figure 2.1 County map of Ireland.

This theoretical paradigm of community study had been slowly developing among British anthropologists who had conducted fieldwork in the far-flung and exotic locales of the early twentieth-century empires, among 'primitive', small and non-centralized populations and societies. By the time of Arensberg and Kimball's research it had been applied in the 'modern' and 'civilized' worlds only through a few community studies in North America, most notably those organized and led in the late 1920s by William Lloyd Warner in Newburyport, Massachusetts, which became known as the 'Yankee City' studies, and those conducted by Robert and

Helen Lynd, in the 'Middletown' studies. These research projects revolutionized social anthropological theories and methods in the 1930s, and widened the scope of acceptable research design among anthropologists, opening up anthropology to the study of modern and industrialized societies.

This turn to the ethnographic analysis of the modern was as influenced by developments in sociology as it was by those in social anthropology. Arensberg and Kimball were in fact undergraduate researchers in the Yankee City study, recruited by Warner, who at that time was their professor at Harvard University. When Warner was brought in to design the social anthropological component of a Harvard-led three-field anthropological analysis of modern Ireland, he asked his young assistants, who had participated in research in Yankee City among the ethnic Irish-American community there, to be the principal investigators in a social anthropological study of representative communities in a representative county in Ireland. The overall Harvard Irish Study was led, from 1931 to 1936, by Professor Earnest Hooton of Harvard (to whom Arensberg and Kimball dedicated *Family and Community in Ireland*), who sought to oversee biological, archaeological and ethnological research throughout Ireland in what was to be the first comprehensive anthropological study of a small modern nation (for an insightful and informative analysis of the entire project, see Byrne, Edmondson and Varley 2001). As it happened, Arensberg and Kimball would use this research as the basis for their doctoral degrees at Harvard.

As part of this exciting collaboration, among various social and physical scientists from the United States and Ireland, Arensberg and Kimball embarked in 1932 on what was then perceived as the first ethnographic anthropological study of social change in a modern nation in Europe. Ironically, unknown to them, Charlotte Gower Chapman (1971) had completed a study of a rural community in Sicily in 1930, but the results of her study were delayed so long that Arensberg and Kimball are still roundly considered the first great social anthropological ethnographers in Europe due to their studies in West Clare. In this fieldwork Arensberg and Kimball sought to bring an anthropological perspective, designed and largely 'tested' in non-Western settings, to a modern nation which, if not quite industrialized or modernized in terms of elsewhere in Europe in the 1930s, was clearly a literate and renowned land at the fringe of that continent.

It is worth noting that although many later scholars and Irish intellectuals criticized these publications as intentional portraits of an unchanging and traditional Ireland and of communities in stasis (see, for example, Gibbon 1973), the research and writings of Arensberg and Kimball intended no such thing. In fact, these scholars were drawn to Ireland as a place which was experiencing the transition from the traditional to the modern. While still predominantly an agricultural economy and rural society, many parts of the island had been industrialized for some time, and its growing urban centres of Dublin, Belfast, Cork, Derry, Galway,

Waterford and Limerick, among others, had been part of wider global commercial networks for hundreds of years. Belfast alone had been one of the key cities in the expansion of the British Empire. Hooton, Warner, Arensberg and Kimball were in Ireland to witness and chronicle the changes which derived from a marginal island nation's increasing modernization. As a result, Arensberg and Kimball were interested in both tradition and change, in the social structures and relations which either sustained or subverted traditional and historical Irish society, as witnessed in a market town and its surrounding rural townlands in the West of Ireland, in County Clare, in a region touted in many areas of intellectual production as representative of the 'real Ireland and the Irish' (as can also be seen in the comparison of political rhetoric, cinematic documentary images and ethnographic portraits in Wilson 1987). Thus 'Arensberg and Kimball were inclined to see Ireland as a transitional society that was neither wholly modern nor wholly traditional' (Byrne, Edmondson and Varley 2001: v).

This perspective on Ireland as a transitional society in the 1930s mirrors somewhat the situation in Ireland today that we reviewed in chapter one. In the 1930s the effects of the modern were being felt and studied in the West of Ireland by Arensberg and Kimball, whereas in the first decade of the twenty-first century we are concerned with the effects of the post-modern in Ireland. Both times were and are periods of reinvention and contest, and each begs us to reconsider our notions of the traditional and the modern, to allow us to discern what is truly different about what has been conceived of as post-modernity. At the least it is ironic that in the Ireland of the 1930s the Irish state was intent on creating and disseminating a national culture (in sports, language, parliamentary politics and education), and on developing an independent and strong economy and polity, yet it was beset by the conservative forces of the Roman Catholic Church, charismatic *gombeen* broker politics in rural and urban constituencies, and the inequalities of class and gender, all of which persist in Ireland today. Some might argue that if modernity was achieved in Ireland in the decades after the 1930s, then why are these forces so potent in the reinvention of Ireland as a global, transnational and post-modern entity? Perhaps answers to such questions can be found, at least in part, in the definitions and analytical categories we employ to conduct our research. For example, in Arensberg and Kimball's terms, and to many other scholars today, modernity might best be seen as a manifestation of a period of organized capitalism, industrialization and secularism. In this sense,

> modern societies are liberal democratic in their political organisation, market-led and industrialised in their economies, and have cultures that tend to be individualistic and pluralistic. Pluralism implies a separation of church and state and a range of beliefs and practices that are respectful of differences in a way that moves in the direction of what would nowadays pass for multiculturalism. (Byrne, Edmondson and Varley 2001: vi)

In their own view, Arensberg and Kimball were investigating the social forces which effected or prevented the Irish transition to a modern society. In so doing, and following in the footsteps of Warner and others, they were also pushing anthropologists to approach modern societies as their research sites, in order to show the utility of anthropological methods and theories for the sociological understanding of modern society and culture. In our view, we must question to what extent sectors of Irish society have achieved modernity, even while we address the concerns of a global and transnational Ireland (in chapter seven). We wish to avoid any question of Ireland and its localities being either traditional or modern. This 'either–or' lends itself to the polemic rather than to social science. As our review of the anthropology of Ireland past and present shows, Irish people, in the countryside and in the city, recognize, perceive and believe that various aspects of their lives are traditional, or modern, or a mix of the two. Anthropologists and other social scientists are charged with discovering how and why these distinctions are drawn.

Ironically, the attempt by Arensberg and Kimball to modernize the fields of social and cultural anthropology (which, at that time, were respectively British and American anthropology) resulted in a long period of sustained reproduction of theory and method, in what we might label an era of dormancy, in which the majority of anthropologists researching in Ireland 'felt the need to explain their research as an extension, validation, contradiction or variation of the work of Arensberg and Kimball' (Kane et al. 1988: 97). To do this they generally adopted the same unit of analysis, the community, the same focus on social relations, namely that of family and kinship, and the same model of research, that of structural-functionalism (Wilson 1984: 1; see also Byrne, Edmondson and Varley 2001: lxii). In sum, up to the early 1980s, with a few exceptions mentioned below, anthropologists persisted in testing the theory, methods and empirical findings of the path-breaking research in Clare, and in so doing seemed to confuse the issues at hand. As a number of scholars in Ireland concluded in 1988:

> Far from being coherent, the follow-up to Arensberg and Kimball has simply been repetitive, or fitfully genuflective. Rather than examining their theoretical approach and ethnography, researchers interested in Ireland have experienced the classic work initially as a centripetal force; their own findings are then presented as centrifugal extensions of the touchstone. (Kane et al. 1988: 98)

This focus on the works of Arensberg and Kimball – some might have concluded that at times it was a scholarly obsession, a figurative stalking of the giant intellectual ancestors – has led to numerous debates and misunderstandings in the past and contemporary anthropology of Ireland, many of which 'have been caused by misinterpreting [Arensberg and Kimball's] intellectual intentions, reading their work without reference to its historical context' (Byrne, Edmondson and Varley 2001: iv).

This chapter reviews the major themes in the anthropology of Ireland which emerged from this touchstone, and it begins our review of some alternative anthropologies which, although they may have had their roots in the more traditional bases of social and cultural anthropology, in Ireland and elsewhere, struck out in new directions. We also seek to problematize the nature of the rural and urban research that was conducted by anthropologists up to the 1990s, especially in terms of two dominant models which in our view have characterized the different but complementary general tone and scope of anthropological ethnographic writing in the Republic of Ireland and in Northern Ireland for much of the last century. The model of research and writing which has been so prevalent in the anthropology of the Republic we label as the 'dying peasant community', and in Northern Ireland the ethnographic model which was so dominating in anthropological research was that of 'tribal conflict', most notably between Northern Ireland's two 'tribes' or communities.[1]

These perspectives in the ethnography of the Irish Republic and Northern Ireland have served as gate-keeping devices, where these two political and territorial entities have taken on the character of ethnographic and cultural regions, with particular characteristics and features which construct for ethnographers the reasons and methods for study there (in ways similar to past anthropological interest in culture regions, such as sub-Saharan Africa, the sub-continent of Asia and the Mediterranean, where the ethnographic record provided a blueprint for subsequent lines of inquiry, which often did not allow for easy inter-regional comparison of the ethnographic cases between regions; see Fardon 1990). These two ethnographic motifs, of the dying communities of traditional Ireland in the Republic and the warring tribes of Northern Ireland, have been especially potent ones for getting past the gates of funding agencies, PhD and tenure committees, and publishers, particularly outside of Ireland (see Curtin, Donnan and Wilson 1993a). As a result, Ireland continues to be on balance a net importer of anthropological theories and methods, but not exclusively so. Much that involves ethnographers in Ireland today is driven by what is happening in Ireland today, providing anthropologists and other scholars with a remarkably rich environment in which to marry the intellectual interests of academic theorists and innovators with the applied and policy concerns of Irish people, along with the needs and interests of related academic, governmental and social institutions. In the following sections of this chapter we review the development of the two ethnographic themes which dominated so much of the anthropology of Ireland in the twentieth century.

'Anomie and the Disappearing/Dying Peasantry': The Template for the Republic

For over a generation after the seminal Clare study, anthropological research in the Republic of Ireland was dominated by the analysis of family roles, generational relations, inheritance, marriage patterns and a range of aspects of formal and informal kinship and social structure. These studies were almost exclusively done in rural settings. From the early 1970s, however, there began to appear a series of critiques of the methods and theory of the Arensberg and Kimball type of community study. Their common theme was the notion that anthropologists should not generalize to any great extent from the Clare study, which in their shared view was rooted in the time and place of Clare in the 1930s (for a discussion of the debates regarding the theoretical intentions of Arensberg and Kimball, see Wilson 1984).[2] As the post-Second World War research in Ireland began to be published, anthropologists, while analysing their locales in terms of the findings of their two anthropological ancestors, began to make tentative criticisms of Arensberg and Kimball's data and methods. The simple departure point for this mild, but growing, criticism was that the Clare study did not seem to account for behavioural variations and disparate social structural formations throughout the island. Thus, Gibbon (1973) criticized Arensberg and Kimball's historical methods, John C. Messenger (1964, 1968, 1969, 1983) identified a host of cultural values and political factors which were to be found on the Aran Islands off the west coast of Ireland, but which were not mentioned or were not emphasized in the Clare research, and Brody (1973) reviewed the many ways in which traditional farm life and rural community values were breaking down in the face of modernization and economic marginalization in the West of Ireland. These critiques notwithstanding, the majority of anthropological studies conducted in the twenty years after the Second World War took the Arensberg and Kimball study as their baseline. Even as some questioned the community model set out by Arensberg and Kimball, other anthropologists and sociologists simply tested the conclusions of the Clare study, either by chronicling social change in Clare itself (in essence updating Arensberg and Kimball's findings; see Cresswell 1969) or by following Arensberg and Kimball's 'Irish countrymen' to Dublin, where the effects of urbanization and modernization on the traditional relations of formerly rural families might be examined (see Humphreys 1966).

In the Republic, Arensberg and Kimball's work provoked a series of studies of rural communities, to test hypotheses on the stability of small-farm life and the durability of family structures and relations on those farms and between families in a wider community. The urban dimensions to Arensberg and Kimball's work, which were not fully realized until the second edition of *Family and Community* was published in 1968, attracted much less notice, which was one of the causes for a relatively late start to the urban anthropology of Ireland (for a review of this rural–urban dichotomy, see Curtin, Donnan and Wilson 1993a). In fact, the first major published collection of case studies in urban anthropology did not appear until 1993 (Curtin, Donnan and Wilson 1993b). In general, the anthropology of Ireland in the three decades after the Harvard study was an anthropology of rural life, with ethnographers seeking to test Arensberg and Kimball's notions of family and community (see Figure 2.2 for a map of anthropological field sites in the Republic of Ireland).

It did not take long for these 'tests' to prove that the elements found in the Arensberg and Kimball study were unstable, even though a quick reading of their original publications would show that they were not intended as a portrait of an unchanging social condition, as we already mentioned. Nevertheless, by the 1970s both the ethnographic and theoretical bases of the Clare study were being increasingly criticized at home and abroad; the concept of 'community' seemed to have diminished explanatory power, and the changing nature of Irish life, due to the related forces of modernization, economic development, secularism and integration within a wider Europe of the nine member states of the European Common Market (Ireland and the United Kingdom both became members in 1973), made people both more mobile and more involved in new relations of class, status and culture (Wilson 1988). As a result, ethnographers began to focus increasingly on the negative dimensions of community life, in part to explain why the precise structures of Clare social life were not to be found elsewhere in rural Ireland, and only thirty years later!

> By the 1970s the search for 'community' had proved futile and even the status of the ethnographic base of the original study was questioned (Gibbon 1973). Attention was subsequently focused on rural decline, anomie and communal demoralisation. The theme of the dying peasant culture of the remote rural west (Brody 1973; Scheper-Hughes 1979) came to dominate anthropological research in the south, almost to the exclusion of everything else. (Curtin, Donnan and Wilson 1993a: 9)

Much of the anthropological fieldwork conducted in the Republic up to the 1980s resulted in writings which caricatured 'Ireland as a dying society, a culture in demise, a social system characterised by pathogenic tendencies' (Peace 1989: 89). It was a place where the elderly were 'warehoused' and where the younger either emigrated or became alcoholic and mentally ill (Scheper-Hughes 1983a). The Irish of the so-called 'Celtic Fringe' became for American and European scholars alike some sort of home-grown exoticized Western 'other', in Robin Fox's terms the veritable 'vanishing Gael' (Fox 1975: 116–22). The subjects of this research became in large part its objects: 'classic' traditional, repressed, anomic, ignorant and sexist peasants, whose local community life and culture were out of control and out of their hands. While we would not presume to question the data

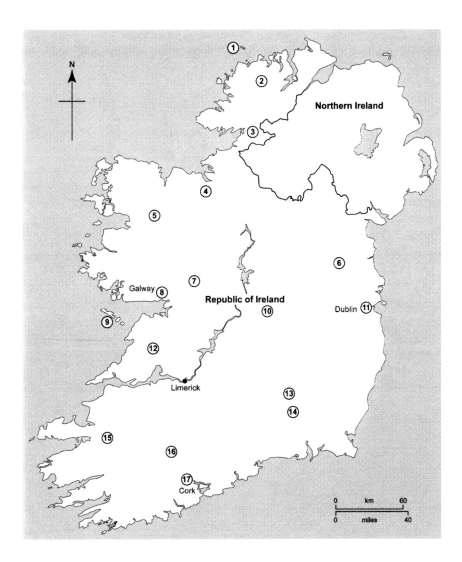

Figure 2.2 Anthropological field sites in the Republic of Ireland. (See page 26 for key.)

Key to Figure 2.2

1. Fox 1978, 1979
2. Collinson 2005; Kane 1968, 1979a, 1979b; Sacks 1976
3. Shanklin 1980, 1982; Taylor 1980a, 1980b, 1981, 1989a, 1989b, 1990, 1992, 1993a, 1995; Tucker 1989
4. Saris 1996, 1997, 1999, 2000
5. Curtin and Varley 1989; L. Harris 1984; Kneafsey 2003; Salazar 1996, 1998, 1999
6. Wilson 1988, 1989a, 1989b, 1990, 1991, 1994a
7. Haddon and Browne 1891–3
8. Basegmez 2005; Helleiner 1993, 2000, 2003; Helleiner and Szuchewycz 1997; O'Sullivan 1993; Szuchewycz 1989
9. Haddon and Browne 1891–3; J. C. Messenger 1964, 1968, 1969, 1971, 1983, 1989
10. N. D. Smith 1998
11. Bartley and Saris 1999; Basegmez 2005; Bradby 1994; G. Gmelch 1977, 1985; S. B. Gmelch 1986; Humphreys 1966; Komito 1984, 1989, 1993; LeMaster 1993; Maguire 2004; B. O'Connor 1997; Saris and Bartley 2002; Saris et al. 2000; Sheehan 1991, 1993; Throop 1999; Varenne 1993
12. Arensberg 1937; Arensberg and Kimball 1968; Casey 2003; Cresswell 1969; Peace 1986, 1992, 1996, 2001; Ruane 1989
13. Conway 1989
14. Gulliver 1989, 1992; Gulliver and Silverman 1995; Silverman 1989, 1992, 1993, 2001; Silverman and Gulliver 1992a, 1992b
15. Birdwell-Pheasant 1992, 1999; Breen 1980, 1982, 1984; Scheper-Hughes 1979, 1983a, 1983b, 1987, 2000, 2001; Shutes 1989, 1991, 1993
16. Bax 1973, 1975, 1987; Brody 1973; Eipper 1986, 1989; Peace 1993, 1997
17. Gaetz 1992, 1993, 1997

Multi-sited research
We have not attempted to incorporate the following multi-sited research into the maps:

M. Allen 2000; Brody 1973; Curtin and Varley 1982, 1986, 1987; G. Gmelch 1986; S. B. Gmelch 1989; S. B. Gmelch and G. Gmelch 1976; Haddon and Browne 1891–3; Kane 1978; Wulff 2002, 2003a, 2003b, 2003c, 2005, in press

contained within the anthropological accounts which gave rise to this caricature, we would dispute a good deal of the theorizing, comparative frameworks and conclusions reached. Certainly we can attest that in some parts of rural Ireland, at the same time as some of the dying peasantry research was being done elsewhere in Ireland, very different types of people and social formations could be found, as witnessed by Wilson (1988, 1989a) in County Meath and by Rosemary Harris (1972) in County Tyrone. At the very least such data and analyses called into question any attempt to use local ethnographic studies to stand for the whole of the Irish and Ireland, as representative of greater collectivities which are only presumed, and not demonstrated, to share culture. As Peace concluded in his review of this literature, 'the essential problem lies not with Irish society but with the anthropology of the ethnic Irish' (1989: 105). For decades, ethnographers, mostly drawn from outside Ireland, but not exclusively so, sought to prove or disprove the perceived basic tenets, and wisdom, of the Arensberg and Kimball study; to do so they had to find rural 'communities', with the right combinations of traditional farming, family size and structure, and relative isolation, in order to assess whether they were stable or in decline. Before we review the strengths and weaknesses of this popular style in ethnographic research and writing, we turn to the Northern Ireland equivalent.

'Tribal Conflict and Accommodation': The Template for Northern Ireland

The contradictions developing in the anthropology of Ireland in this period perhaps can best be illustrated by the different tradition in ethnographic research which began to emerge in Northern Ireland's anthropology in the years following the resurgence of 'the Troubles'[3] in 1969. This divergent trend was also based on community studies in the mould of that of Arensberg and Kimball, but although the initial community studies of Northern Irish villages and cityscapes focused on networks of kinship and social organizational relations, much like their counterparts in the Republic, different results were being obtained precisely because the cultural values and social structure of Northern Ireland were, at least on the surface, markedly different. No matter how hard they may have tried, no ethnographer of Northern Ireland's localities could ignore the facts of social class, nationalism and sectarianism. As a result, the community studies of Rosemary Harris (1961, 1972), Leyton (1966, 1970, 1974, 1975) and Bufwack (1982), among others, attempted to describe the social structure of local village life in Northern Ireland, but at the same time account for the divisiveness and friction which crosscut all levels of Northern Irish society. In the anthropology of Northern Ireland it was, and it remains, impossible to understand local rural and urban communities without understanding ethnicity, sectarianism, national identities, class, and the

overall importance of history in everyday life (the distribution of field sites in
Northern Ireland is indicated in Figure 2.3).

Because of this ethnic and religious landscape, ethnographers in Northern
Ireland had no interest in portraying societies and cultures in decline, even if a bad
sense of history suggested to them that Northern Irish societies had existed in a
stable and relatively unchanging condition for some time. This relative lack of
interest in or avoidance of issues of social change, of course, had something to do

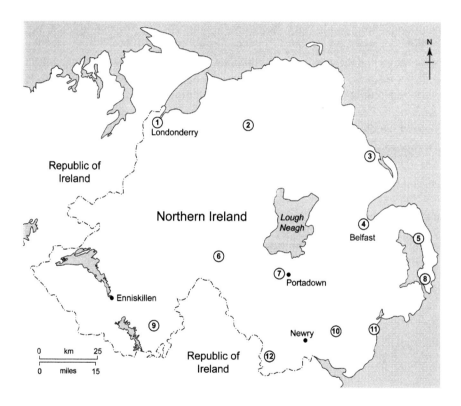

Figure 2.3 Anthropological field sites in Northern Ireland. (See page 29 for key.)

with the rather atemporal approach in early structural-functional studies in British anthropology, which on the whole tended to eschew historical and evolutionary perspectives. But it also had a great deal to do with the nature of Northern Ireland life, where the clear fact of the matter is that there were, and are, two populations divided by religion, ethnic and national identity, history, traditions, customs and political ideologies. These populations, identified in various ways and at different times as Protestant, British, unionist and loyalist, on the one hand, and as Catholic,

---

Key to Figure 2.3

1. D. Bell 1990; Butler 1985; Finlay 1987, 1999; Ingram 1997; McLaughlin 1989, 1991, 1997; Roche 2003
2. Cecil 1989, 1993
3. Blacking, Byrne and Ingram 1989; Buckley 1983; Shanks 1987, 1988, 1990
4. Aretxaga 1995, 1997, 2001a; Bairner 1997, 2001; Bairner and Shirlow 1998, 2003; Bryan 1998, 1999, 2000, 2003; Buckley and Kenney 1995; Burton 1978; Cairns 2000, 2001; Carter 2003a, 2003b; Donnan 1991, 1994; Donnan and McFarlane 1997d; Donnan and O'Brien 1998; Feldman 1991; Howe 1989a, 1989b, 1990, 1994; Jarman 1997, 1998a, 1998b, 1999, 2000; Jenkins 1982, 1983; Lanclos 2003; Murphy 2000, 2002; Ogle 1989; O'Reilly 1998, 1999, 2003; Shirlow 2003b; Sluka 1989, 1992a, 1992b, 1995; Taaffe 2001, 2003
5. McFarlane 1979, 1986, 1989
6. R. Harris 1961, 1972; Kelleher 1994, 2000, 2003
7. Bryan 1998, 1999, 2000, 2003; Buckley and Kenney 1995; M. Cohen 1993; Donnan and O'Brien 1998
8. Buckley 1982a
9. Glassie 1982; Vincent 1983, 1989, 1992, 1993, 1995
10. Bufwack 1982; Crozier 1985, 1989a, 1989b, 1990a, 1990b
11. Dilley 1989; Larsen 1982a, 1982b; Leyton 1966, 1970, 1974, 1975
12. Donnan 1999, 2005; Murtagh 1996, 1998; Wilson 1993b, 1993c, 1994b, 1995, 1996, 2000

Multi-sited research
We have not attempted to incorporate the following multi-sited research into the maps:

Carter, Donnan and Wardle 2003; B. Messenger 1975; Milton 1990, 1993, 1994, 1996, 2002; Wulff 2002, 2003a, 2003b, 2003c, 2005, in press

Irish, nationalist and republican, on the other – identifications that do not always and everywhere neatly map on to each other – have learned to live together, in relative tolerance, for hundreds of years. This tolerance masks some diametrically opposed positions in public and private life, divisions which resulted in an armed conflict that raged from 1969 to 1994, with violence continuing within and between these two 'communities' up to today.

The apparent contradiction whereby one side could tolerate and even cooperate with the other side in some situations yet murder them in others was the focus for much of the ethnographic work on rural Northern Ireland in the 1970s and 1980s, which sought to understand the structural and cultural bases for this seeming paradox by exploring the tensions between such opposed pairings as 'prejudice and tolerance' and 'opposition and integration' (R. Harris 1972; Leyton 1974). The question was starkly put by Elliott Leyton, who early in the Troubles suggested that the 'true enigma' in Northern Ireland was 'not why so many have died' but 'why so *few* have been killed' (1974: 185, emphasis in original). Even where the intensity and likelihood of violence was low, as in the villages that were the subject of ethnographies entitled *A Gentle People* and *Village without Violence* (Buckley 1982a; Bufwack 1982), the overriding and predominant concern was with how peaceful coexistence was possible in a region otherwise apparently irreconcilably rent by warring 'tribes'. Everything in Northern Ireland was dichotomized, and anthropologists described how Catholics and Protestants led parallel lives; they not only attended different churches and schools and held competing political views, but engaged in different sports, shopped in different shops, and married endogamously (Donnan 1990, 2000; McFarlane 1979; for an overview, see Donnan and McFarlane 1983). Largely living in different areas, Catholics and Protestants rarely mixed socially, and when they did, relations between them were heavily structured and characterized by avoidance of potentially inflammatory or offensive topics of conversation. To some external observers it seemed that Northern Ireland was a dual society composed of two competing tribes which periodically met in ritualized and seemingly irrational warfare. While not all ethnographers at the time set out to understand the pattern of tolerance and tribal territory – there were those, for instance, who sought to explain the violence in and between communities (e.g. Feldman 1991; Sluka 1989) – the prevailing image of Northern Irish ethnography drew on this 'tribal' model with its 'sectarianism and traditional cultural incompatibility between disputing clans' (Curtin, Donnan and Wilson 1993a: 10).

This relatively clear divergence in ethnographic focus between research conducted in Northern Ireland and that done across the border in the Republic was not just the result of the meteor-like intellectual impact of the original Arensberg and Kimball study. There were theoretical and professional dimensions to this divergence. British social anthropology has been the dominant articulating principle in the development of anthropology in Northern Ireland since its establishment. Throughout its formative years, British social anthropology emphasized cross-cutting ties of kinship and social organization, political networks, and disputes in communities, while the American perspectives of cultural anthropology were more interested than the British in historical and culture change, culture contact and acculturation, and culture and personality. As a result of the general theoretical differences which emerged in the 1930s and later between these two main discourses in anglophone anthropology, in the Irish context since the Arensberg and Kimball research more Americans have conducted research in the Republic than in the North of Ireland, and, conversely, more British anthropologists have done their fieldwork in Northern Ireland than in the South.

These theoretical and methodological interests later informed the development of professional and institutional anthropologies: the first anthropologist to hold an anthropology lectureship in a university in the Republic was an Irish-American who was trained in the USA as a cultural anthropologist. Eileen Kane began the professional study of anthropology in what was then called St Patrick's College, Maynooth; today the Department of Anthropology in the National University of Ireland, Maynooth, is the only such department in the Republic, and its chair and many of its staff are Americans, who also completed their doctoral training in the USA. In Northern Ireland the only department of anthropology, and the largest on the island, is the School of Anthropological Studies (incorporated since 2005 into a new School of History and Anthropology) in Queen's University Belfast, where its first chair was the Cambridge-trained ethnomusicologist and anthropologist, John Blacking. Most of its teaching staff have been trained in British universities, predominantly within the intellectual and methodological interests of social anthropology.[4] These differences in training and research interests aside, these two departments of anthropology have become important forces in the transnationalization of professional anthropology in the two constituencies of Ireland. Between them they have helped foster an inclusive approach to the intellectual and applied concerns of anthropologists that has been at the centre of the Anthropological Association of Ireland, which holds two annual academic conferences, one in Northern Ireland and one in the Republic, and publishes a peer-reviewed academic journal, *The Irish Journal of Anthropology* (at present, based in Maynooth). Not only has cross-border anthropology flourished in this changing academic environment, but both departments of anthropology have been instrumental in inviting scholars from Europe and North America to attend conferences and as visiting fellows. Anthropologists based in Ireland have also played key roles in international professional bodies: members of staff of the two Irish departments have been on the executive boards of the European Association of Social Anthropologists and the Society for the Anthropology of Europe (the latter a unit of the American Anthropological Association), while anthropologists in the sociology departments of universities in Galway, Cork and Coleraine have fostered international collaborations that have led to research projects in Ireland, continental Europe and further afield.

These international developments excepted, it is also clear that, as in many other national and wider regional contexts, localizing strategies in the past and continuing today have created conditions which both support and impede international appreciation of, and access to, professional anthropology and ethnographic research in Ireland. As Fardon (1990: 24–5) has concluded, national traditions of research and writing often affect wider regional representations which then inflect the full range of anthropological practices in that locality. This regionalization is in itself a strategy of professional power and knowledge, with its own impact on 'authoritative presentation, the stamping of professional credentials, the peripheralization of interlopers, the creation of clique-ish mystiques and the sustenance of regional stereotypes' (Fardon 1990: 24). One result of this in Ireland has been the creation of research blind spots and zones of invisibility and exclusion, as in the anthropology of 'culture areas' elsewhere. Just as the anthropology of India became associated with the ethnographic investigation of caste, Papua New Guinea with kinship and exchange, and the Mediterranean with the social values and practices of honour and shame, so too Ireland for anthropologists became a domain of urban sectarianism and political violence, on the one hand, and of rural peasant and small farm life, on the other. This association of Ireland with the bomb and the bucolic in effect made it little different, in form if not in content, from other parts of the globe studied by anthropologists. And it also established intellectual interests and professional practices which resulted in a generation, at the least, of continuity in ethnographic modelling and hypothesizing. In the next sections we look at this research design durability, and the beginnings of the changes which began to test the edges of these models.

Paradigmatic Durability

Although the 1980s ushered in a number of new developments in the anthropology of Ireland, the strong traditions in methods, research interests and theories begun by Arensberg and Kimball continued apace, if perhaps for no better reason than to provide straw men to be destroyed. Much of the ethnographic research of the 1970s began to appear in print near the end of that decade and into the first years of the next (although some scholars continued to express concern that the majority of anthropological research projects conducted in Ireland in the 1970s had not resulted in publication, see Kane et al. 1988). The themes of some of these publications represented major departures from the themes of the 'sacred texts' of Arensberg and Kimball, but nonetheless most researchers in this period continued to focus on the same type of questions and analysis as had been outlined in Clare.

While many anthropologists began to examine how the small peasant communities of the West of Ireland were unlike those of Arensberg and Kimball's day, and in so doing tended to characterize rural Ireland as declining, or even dying (see, for example, Brody 1973; Scheper-Hughes 1979; J. C. Messenger 1983), just as many continued to look at the structures and functions of kinship, social organization, marriage and the family, and the conditions of work and production which kept villages stable, peaceful and relatively traditional in their concerns (see, for example, Buckley 1982a; Bufwack 1982; Kane 1979a; Leyton 1975; Salazar 1999; Shanklin 1982; Taylor 1981). The only lively scholarly exchanges to appear in print in the anthropology of Ireland that attracted international notice revolved around issues of family form and function (see, for example, Gibbon and Curtin 1976, 1983a, 1983b) and rural social and political patrons and clients (see, for example, Gibbon and Higgins 1974, 1977; see also Shanklin 1980), which were clearly related to the intellectual groundwork set by Arensberg and Kimball.

Much of this debate on the history and structure of Irish families is significant beyond Ireland, and it provides one of many areas in the anthropology of Ireland which demonstrates the usefulness of anthropological research for discovering and comparing the wide range of social formations to be found elsewhere in Europe (see Goody 1983). In particular, the debates in Irish social history and ethnography over the changing form of the family since the early eighteenth century can inform wider discussion of the historical depth and cultural constructions which compose 'family' units everywhere in Europe. In fact, the mechanization of agriculture, patterns of emigration, and suburbanization and urbanization have been contributing factors in the changing definition of families throughout Ireland. This transformation in the structure and function of Irish families does not mean, however, that larger extended families are no longer an important force in Irish social life, but rather that the local and regional patterns of family and residence are factors of which all scholars and policy-makers of contemporary Europe must be aware. Since the 1930s, anthropology has been at the forefront of efforts to describe and explain family variations in Ireland, efforts which highlight the shifting and contested nature of all notions of 'normal' European family structures. While the intensity of this scholarly debate may have waned somewhat, anthropological interest in Irish familism and domestic relations remains one of the most important contributions which the anthropology of Ireland has made to intellectual concerns beyond the island (for an introduction to various aspects in the evolution of anthropological interest in Irish family structures and relations, see Birdwell-Pheasant 1992, 1999; Breen 1982, 1984; Gibbon and Curtin 1978, 1983a, 1983b; R. Harris 1988; Kane 1968; Leyton 1976; Shanks 1987; Varley 1983).

However, this attention to the structures and functions of family life in rural Ireland is not only evidence of the durability of the paradigms tested by Arensberg and Kimball and reproduced by many of their successors. It is also indicative of the vitality of the two revisionist models developed in contradistinction to those of Arensberg and Kimball, models which we have referred to above as dominant templates in the anthropology of Ireland. It would be wrong, though, to suggest that the time and focus of Arensberg and Kimball's research, and those of their critics, map neatly on to any clear-cut chronology. There are many successful anthropologists today, in the twenty-first century, who still stalk the Irish peasant family, and the rural peasant or post-peasant economy (see Salazar 1996, 1998, as examples of the most consistent voice in this regard), just as there are many who continue to utilize the templates which we have reviewed above, and which in our view need to be problematized in what we might label a post-revisionist stage in the ethnography and comparative anthropologies of Ireland. This post-revisionist stage might be better approached as sets of alternative concerns and often conflicting agendas and research problematics, rather than as a coherent body of revisionist scholarship. Our point is a simple one: the anthropology of Ireland may not have been instrumental in any major revisionist movement in anthropology elsewhere, or in the overall social science of Ireland. But the anthropology of Ireland, and its related concerns with ethnographic research and writing, was not static. It was, and continues to be, as dynamic as the societies in Ireland it seeks to document and understand.

These concerns and approaches are the subjects of the remainder of this book; they might very well be seen as the transformation, continual reassessment and relocation of both anthropology, as a practice and body of knowledge, and its subject, Ireland. Like their forerunners in Ireland, the new and not-so-new developments in the contemporary anthropology of Ireland owe a great deal to international and more global forces of change in anthropology. As a result of this global reach in the discipline, which is one reason for our call in this book to see Ireland more globally, it is maybe not surprising that some of the anthropologists most famous for creating and re-creating the templates we have set forth here have been mindful of changes in worldwide anthropology. This has been especially apparent in regard to reflexivity and the critical approaches to writing ethnography and the politics of the production of knowledge which seemed to escape the attentions of earlier generations. Thus, Nancy Scheper-Hughes returned to the site of her original Irish fieldwork, to meet, perhaps even confront (certainly and not surprisingly to be confronted by), her former hosts, some of whom had felt betrayed and saddened by her portrait of them (see the Prologue and Epilogue in Scheper-Hughes 2001).

In our view, the anthropology of Ireland today is becoming as diversified as the populations of Ireland in recent years. This diversity reflects the transformations in ethnography which have been the primary forces behind the reinvention of ethnographic research over the last two decades. These transformations have stimulated new research topics and agendas in Ireland, North and South.

Emergent Agendas

The continuities and discontinuities in research in the late 1970s and early 1980s which we have reviewed above were in effect the beginnings of new research agendas, which paralleled the new interests of scholars in North America, Britain and the rest of Europe. Some of the research interests of those decades are still vital in Irish, British, American and other scholarly traditions in anthropology, but some have been superseded by more recent changes in the structure of professional academic anthropology, and in the theoretical and methodological interests of ethnographers, anthropologists, sociologists and scholars in the cognate disciplines in the social sciences and humanities. This book is concerned with tracing the continuities and new developments in these interests. Here, we review the scholarship which developed after the 1960s, when anthropology became one of the most popular and growing academic disciplines in North America and Europe.

A series of critiques and overviews began to appear in the 1980s; all in essence were attempting to reset the research agenda for Ireland (see, for example, Curtin and Wilson 1989a; Donnan and McFarlane 1986a, 1986b; Jenkins 1986; Kane et al. 1988; Peace 1989; Wilson 1984). The changes in anthropological interest and research design were partly a reaction to the transformations which both Northern Ireland and the Irish Republic had experienced. Much of the Republic had become urbanized and suburbanized. The conflict raged in Northern Ireland. Both Irelands had joined the European Community on the first day of 1973. Economic recession had led to the return of emigration as a panacea for Ireland's social ills (a cure that was obviated in the South by the economic boom of the 1990s). National communication and entertainment services expanded, as did local (county and town) radio and television. Each night the images and events of Europe and beyond were brought into the kitchens and sitting rooms of Irish households, thereby seemingly encouraging secularization, modernization and internationalization. Leaders of other European countries and the European Union itself became as familiar to the Irish as their own politicians (which in some quarters might not be very familiar at all!). National educational reforms, access to new markets in continental Europe, and advances in information and communication technologies weakened the traditional ties of church and politics, increasingly forcing Irish people onto the European and world stages, and opening up their society to the twin forces of secularization and modernization.

As a result, it became unthinkable for some ethnographers to characterize rural villages as socio-cultural isolates (even though some continued to do so, and persevere even today in this circular vein of research). Thus, the revisionist trends in the anthropology of Ireland focused on how rural communities were tied to social formations and economic and political structures external to the locality, in terms of international and supranational relations, within Europe and the world-system.

Political economy approaches (see Roseberry 1988 for a review of this body of work in anthropology) became especially apparent in the historical anthropology which developed in a burst of intellectual activity in the 1980s and 1990s, becoming one of the most impressive bodies of Irish anthropological research, and one which has increasingly engaged scholars outside of Ireland. Among the notable contributions to this approach in the anthropology of Ireland have been the works of Marilyn Cohen (1993), Marilyn Silverman and Philip Gulliver (1992a; 1992b; Silverman 1989, 2001), Lawrence Taylor (1992, 1993a) and Joan Vincent (1983, 1989, 1992). Overall, in fact, this political economy approach represents a two-fold reassessment in the anthropology of Ireland. Not only did it contribute to the transformation of contemporary anthropology in both Northern Ireland and the Republic, helping it to keep pace with scholarly interests in the history of culture and power which have so inspired anthropologists elsewhere, but it has also contributed to Irish social and cultural historiography.

This political economy concern with Ireland's role in global capitalist development, the integration of the British state and world-systemic relations of commerce and state relations was symptomatic of the concern anthropologists increasingly had with the boundaries of traditional structural-functionalist community studies. In the last quarter of the twentieth century few anthropologists held to the fancy that local societies were self-contained and self-regulating. Instead, most researchers began to investigate how the people of Ireland's farms, villages, towns and cities were linked to local, national and global institutions, and they began to examine the regional and national processes of social change. As a result, a boom in anthropological writing occurred, which included studies of government and politics (Bax 1973, 1975; Conway 1989; Komito 1984; Wilson 1989a); religion and churches (Eipper 1986; Taylor 1989b); colonialism (Taylor 1980a, 1980b); urbanization (G. Gmelch 1977); migration (G. Gmelch 1986; G. Gmelch and S. B. Gmelch 1985); rural industrialization and development (Curtin and Varley 1982, 1986; Kane 1978; Ruane 1989); social and economic history (B. Messenger 1975; Vincent 1983); ethnic boundaries (Larsen 1982a, 1982b); and minorities (G. Gmelch 1986). Anthropologists also began to utilize Irish locations in order to test and expand models in anthropology which had their origins elsewhere, and in some senses had little to do with changing Ireland, but a lot to do with a changing anthropology in a transforming 'globalizing' world.

The wide range of anthropological research interests in Ireland today, which mark a break with many of the models which so dominated the field for sixty years, can be found in four collections of ethnographic case studies which in our view capture the letter and spirit of the new agendas in anthropology which came to the fore after the 1970s. These books, which deal with Ireland-wide social, political and economic change in the countryside (Curtin and Wilson 1989b) and in towns and cities (Curtin, Donnan and Wilson 1993b), and investigate new approaches to governmental administration and policy in Northern Ireland (Donnan and McFarlane 1989a, 1997a), include the work of anthropologists from Ireland, the United Kingdom, Canada, continental Europe and the United States. They are intended as university textbooks, and have been adopted in Irish and American universities. Their chapters are a persuasive if only a partial answer to the questions regarding relevance and applicability which were posed by scholars in the past (for example, in Kane et al. 1988; Wilson 1984) and which we reiterate in this book. The books' contributors and many other European and North American anthropologists have created many new research agendas in Ireland, squarely placing the anthropology of Ireland within a variety of mainstream concerns of the various fields in anthropology today.

As these books attest, anthropologists researching in Ireland over the last twenty years have been concerned with issues of urban unemployment (Blacking, Byrne and Ingram 1989; Donnan and McFarlane 1997d; Howe 1989a, 1989b, 1989c, 1990; McLaughlin 1989); ritual and religion (Crozier 1989b; McFarlane 1989, 1994; Murphy 2000, 2002; Szuchewycz 1989; Taylor 1989a); international frontiers and sovereignty (Vincent 1991; Wilson 1993b); women's roles and rights in society (Aretxaga 1997; Curtin, Jackson and O'Connor 1987b; Gaetz 1993; LeMaster 1993; McCann 1994; McLaughlin 1989); the symbolic definitions of nation and state (Shanks 1994; Wilson 1994b); political violence and interpersonal conflict (Curtin 1988; Feldman 1991; Kelleher 2000, 2003; Sluka 1989, 1992a, 1992b; Vincent 1989); political rituals and symbolism (Bryan 2000; Cecil 1993; Jarman 1997; Jenkins 1993; Wilson 1994b); suburban life and globalized culture (Varenne 1993); tourism and rural development (Michael Cronin and O'Connor 2003; Curtin and Varley 1989; Kockel 1994, 2002; B. O'Connor and Cronin 1993); landscape and environment (Kockel 1995; McLean 2003; Milton 1990, 1993, 1994, 1996, 2002; Peace 1997); ethnicity and minority rights and movements (Donnan 1991, 1994; Donnan and O'Brien 1998; Vincent 1993); intellectuals and the constructions of national culture (Sheehan 1993); consumer culture (Curtin and Ryan 1989; Wilson 1993c); social class (Crozier 1990b; Leyton 1975; Shanks 1988, 1990); the ethnography of gender and workplace politics (L. Harris 1984; ; Kelleher 1994; McLaughlin and Ingram 1991); and local and national history and historiography (Gulliver 1992; Gulliver and Silverman 1995; Silverman 1989, 1992; Silverman and Gulliver 1992; Vincent 1992; Wilson 1990).

As impressive a review as this compendium of interests and achievements is, it is not complete. In the chapters which follow we visit some of this newer research and their themes, placing them within the thematic contexts of older ethnographic research in order to demonstrate the theoretical and methodological vitality of past and present anthropology in and of Ireland. We also address in the chapters that follow some of the research concerns of ethnographers who have recently completed their doctoral fieldwork, or have just begun to publish, as partial evidence of the intellectual, academic and political interests of our students in Ireland and elsewhere.

While this chapter has served to introduce the historical and contemporary depth and breadth of anthropological scholarship in and on Ireland, this is still only a bare-bones introduction. In the remainder of this book we seek to put some weight on this framework. Anthropological research in Ireland has had its ups and downs, but it is alive and well, and willing and able to be involved in the scholarly effort to understand cultural behaviour and values in every walk and level of Irish life (for a longer review of the stereotypes and revisionist positions in Irish anthropology than this chapter allows, see Curtin, Donnan and Wilson 1993a). There is no better example of the relevance and contemporary value of anthropological research for Ireland, and by extension for Europe as a whole, than in the anthropological analysis of social and political problems and policy, in what amounts to new alternatives for the future direction of anthropology *of* Ireland, and *in* Ireland. One theme with which to begin our examination of recent and past inventions of Ireland, and their related inventions of anthropology, is to focus on relations of resistance and dissent which are created and sustained when the institutional structures of local and national government, and of church and state, seek to arrange, if not impose, social and political order.

Alternative Anthropologies

The reinvention of Ireland that we reviewed in the introduction to this book has led to remarkable changes in the political structures and relations internal to Northern Ireland and the Republic of Ireland, and between them. There is no better illustration of this than the Belfast Good Friday Agreement of 1998, and the subsequent referendum in the Republic which removed that state's territorial claim to sovereignty over the six counties of Northern Ireland. Furthermore, in this age of instant and incessant communication and media access, the role of citizen is changing throughout Ireland, leading to new notions of civil society, civicness, and political and legal rights and responsibilities.

New social actors are changing the configurations of policy-making in Ireland and Northern Ireland, where top-down decision-making is being challenged by a wide range of interest groups, lobbies, concerned community councils and new issue-orientated political parties. Traditional forms of politics are being transformed precisely because many local communities and groups of citizens are aware of alternative avenues in the construction of the social policies which directly affect them. The social partnership model of national policy-making in the Republic and the local district partnerships begun as part of the experimental Peace and Reconciliation Programme in Northern Ireland are examples of alternative strategies of public accommodation and resistance to past structures of governmental power.

There are many reasons for this relatively recent awareness of the issues and roles of public policy in the daily lives of Ireland's citizens, and in the research agendas of Ireland's anthropologists, but one of the most important agents for change in this regard has been the European Union. The EU is clearly a source of much political change through the processes of Europeanization, which will concern us in chapter seven, but here we would like to indicate that local, regional, national and supranational levels of policy-making are clearly in dialectical relationships with each other. As Ireland North and South reinvents itself along the lines considered in this book, it is also inventing new forms of political and civil society, some of which rely on tradition and accepted avenues of policy and political practice, and some of which chart new courses. Anthropologists have been investigating these new convergences of power, culture, identity and economic change for the last generation, in what certainly amounts to a vital and serious counterpoint to the authoritative narratives of conflict and peasantry outlined above. In the research represented in the edited collections by Donnan and McFarlane (1989a, 1997a), for example, we can see the range and depth of ethnographic investigation into public policy in Northern Ireland

Contemporary anthropology in Ireland has begun to address many of the concerns that involve anthropologists worldwide. This has been especially true in Ireland's towns and cities (Curtin, Donnan and Wilson 1993b), where a variety of forces have brought the problems of poverty, homelessness, disease, racism, sexism, the environment, urban sprawl and increased levels of violence to the forefront of everyday cultural consciousness. Anthropologists in Ireland were slow to react to the ways in which people have adapted to these problems, partly for the reasons outlined above and partly due to the general nature of the field everywhere, but they are now investigating the impact and development of these problems in a variety of local contexts throughout the island. Although it may be fair to say that anthropologists in Northern Ireland have been focused longer on issues of social disintegration and their relationships to public policy formation (for a review of this, see Donnan and McFarlane 1989a, 1989b, 1997c), the anthropological concern with matters of policy is now an all-island one. As we explore in chapter three, one of the longest-studied issues in urban life, and still one of the most serious in Irish towns and cities, has been the pressures young people face because of their rapidly changing economies and polities. Desmond Bell (1990), Richard Jenkins (1983) and Rosellen Roche (2003) have chronicled youth culture in urban Northern Ireland, where young adults not only have to face the day-to-day dilemmas of unemployment, peer pressure, sectarianism and deteriorating cities, but are also victims and agents of war.

It is in the study of youth and their problems that anthropology yet again can provide valuable insights into policy construction, implementation and administration. Although Northern Irish young people, especially in the ghettos of Belfast and Derry, seem superficially different from youth cultures elsewhere in Europe, largely because of extreme religious sectarianism and the violence which has been part of their daily lives, these differences may be illusory. Ethnic and racial prejudice and the violence of drugs and organized crime which are commonplace in many of the capitals of Europe may be little different in form from the patterns of urban street culture in Northern Ireland (see Jarman 2005). Ethnographers in Northern Ireland can provide the information to social policy-makers regarding both the national and the international dimensions to youth cultures, and the ways in which Irish young people have specific local needs, pressures and desires. For example, unemployment is a common cause of youth unrest throughout Europe, but Irish and British nationalism are variants of identity among Northern Irish youth which are peculiar to Ireland. Nevertheless, they are aspects of youth identity which can be addressed in modified and integrated educational environments (see Irwin 1997). The ways in which national and European social welfare policies have an impact in neighbourhoods in Belfast, and are understood and accepted or rejected by locals, is one of the principal avenues by which anthropologists can aid in the building of a general and applied social science of the European Union (see, for example, Cecil 1989; Ogle 1989).

The violence that is an everyday aspect of youth culture in Northern Ireland does not seem to be as pervasive in the Republic of Ireland, although this remains a matter of empirical inquiry. Nevertheless, the debilitating pressures of being educated, then unemployed (or under-employed, in terms of training and expectations), in a transforming national society such as the Republic, which itself may quickly become more marginalized in an expanded European Union, are experiences shared by many Irish young people. The class dimension to the travails of Irish youth is but one factor which exacerbates the problems for some, as does the inherent sexism of a patriarchal Irish society (Gaetz 1992, 1993; N. D. Smith 1998). Although emigration continues to serve a de-pressurizing function in Ireland, in particular for many young people, the traditional receiving countries such as Great Britain, the United States and Australia are instituting measures to block continued Irish immigration. The movement of Irish youth in future may well be to the continent, where they will swell the ranks of unemployed and put pressure on the labour markets of other European nations.

Anthropological research in Ireland serves as an example of how the realities of local social and cultural life often do not match the ideal constructions of national societies as seen from the spectrum of European 'centres', be they national capitals, core regions in states or the key institutions and bodies of the European Union in Brussels and Strasbourg. The 'democratic deficit' which seemingly marks the powerful apparatuses of the EU, where the only elected body, the European Parliament, has relatively little power in comparison to other Union bodies, affects the overall social science of the EU. The anthropology of the European Union is small in scale and influence when compared with the vast literature in political science and economics on the EU and integration, most of which is based on top-down and centre-out perspectives on national trends. Policies determined in metropoles distant from the localities of Ireland often have a variety of effects on Irish everyday life that are both unintended and unnoticed by policy-makers. To many Irish people, for example, national and European Union economic policies provide a variety of changing contexts for local initiatives. As we show in chapter four, this is especially apparent in the informal and black economies, wherein any amount of statistical analysis cannot fail to omit a wide range of productive economic activities which define many local communities' notions of work, wealth and class. For example, Howe (1989a, 1989b, 1990) has documented the different ways in which the Belfast unemployed make a living through a variety of legal and illegal actions. Their 'doing the double' is an apt term for claiming social welfare benefits, sometimes in more than one location, while at the same time working in such occupations as labourers, taxi drivers, thieves, baby-sitters and bouncers.

People in the borderlands between the Republic of Ireland and Northern Ireland have made fortunes through smuggling, especially in agricultural goods, fuel, tobacco, alcohol and consumer durables, and in money laundering (see chapters four and six). The many large bungalows and holiday homes built along the Irish border not only reflect the wealth made by large-scale smugglers, but also indicate the thriving construction trade in the borderlands, where locals collect the dole (unemployment benefits) in both the Republic and the North, while at the same time working a full week off the books at construction. Smuggling and welfare fraud are often difficult for social scientists to document, but they are so essential to local community life that they are elemental to any ethnographic study of a community (for a review of aspects of the commodification of life at the Irish border, see Wilson 1993c). Because of the nature of participant observation, still the mainstay of anthropological research, it is all but impossible for ethnographers to avoid understanding the local informal economy. As such, ethnographers can do much to fill in the gaps in the social science of public policy in Europe, precisely because of their perspective from the 'ground up'.

Other problems in the social fabric of Ireland are also drawing the attention of ethnographers, many of whom wish to apply their research findings in order to alleviate the conditions of the poor and dispossessed, whose ranks are perceived by many Irish people to be on the rise. Ethnographic methods, in particular participant observation, allow anthropologists to describe the experiences of Travelling People (Helleiner 1993, 2000) and homeless men (O'Sullivan 1993) in ways that enable readers to experience, if only vicariously, the everyday pressures to survive, in a society which prides itself on its culture, civilization and charity. And while Irish social environments suffer from a variety of human forces, so too does the physical environment, on an island that is increasingly becoming a tourist haven for continental Europeans precisely because of their expectations of traditional ways and unspoilt countryside. Urban planners, government leaders, industrial developers and environmental lobbies are engaged in what seems to some to be a never-ending debate over the future of the Irish landscape, a battle of wills in which some anthropologists have been active campaigners (Milton 1990, 1993, 1994, 1997; Peace 1993, 1997). These anthropologists, like many of their colleagues, are adding to a scholarly movement which is also a movement of concerned citizens, who want to use their research in ways that matter to the quality of the lives of the people among whom they live and work.

Such aspirations, we maintain, are consistent with anthropology's historic commitment as a humanistic social science dedicated to understanding how people actually live. With its systematic focus on the everyday, and its emphasis on the meanings, values and voices of those with whom it works, anthropology can both complement and offer an alternative to other disciplinary readings of the issues that affect Irish society and culture. In the next chapter we consider how anthropologists have put this approach into practice, in their local ethnographic accounts of the workings of church and state.

–3–

Controlling Bodies

Individuals are the vehicles of power, not its points of application
Michel Foucault (1994: 214)

Among the most valuable contributions of the Irish ethnographic record are the insights it offers into the everyday lives of ordinary people, and the human dimension with which it complements more generalized and abstract accounts of Irish society and culture. We learn about real people as they celebrate the joys and engage the difficulties that combine to make up their lives. It is this systematic and sustained commitment to the human story with its first-hand narratives and thick description of richly observed social and cultural practice that perhaps above all else distinguishes anthropology from the other social sciences researching Ireland. Although other social scientists too, of course, periodically deploy the personal narrative and illustrative case study (e.g. as in the Irish Sociological Chronicles series edited by Corcoran and Peillon 2002; Peillon and Corcoran 2004; Peillon and Slater 1998; Slater and Peillon 2000), it is probably not an exaggeration to say that it is only anthropology – as a collective disciplinary endeavour and not just as the personal orientation of individual practitioners – that privileges and fore-grounds such material above all the other kinds of data that anthropologists collect. This gives to anthropology a distinctive perspective on social life that has been characterized as a view from 'below', one which approaches the understanding of societal structures and institutional forms from the bottom up.

Not surprisingly this has been reflected in how anthropologists of Ireland have understood some of the dominant and most encompassing institutions of Irish life, such as church and state, and in the kinds of topics and issues that they have researched in relation to these bodies. Where other researchers have stressed the relationship between such institutions and wider social, political, economic and historical processes, anthropologists have emphasized what such institutions mean in the everyday lives of ordinary people (although neither of these emphases is, of course, mutually exclusive). And where other researchers have provided general, societal-level accounts of, for example, the church, state health care provision and law and order, anthropologists have been more inclined to offer specific and context-rich analyses of local forms of religious belief and practice, informal welfare and social control in a particular town or village. As a result, anthropologists have perhaps been better than most in exploring how the state and church bodies that have influenced so much of Irish life actually operate and function in specific, local contexts and with specific groups and categories of people. This has enabled them to show how attempts by these bodies to shape and control people's lives and worldviews have been received and variously internalized or questioned.

In this chapter we focus on what anthropologists have said about how people's lives are regulated at the local level by the church, the state and other bodies, and about the different responses to this. Different forms of power are often seen at play in this relationship, from the disciplinary might and ability to coerce of some institutional forms of control, to the more informal and illegal forms of power in the hands of those who resist. Much of this research has emphasized the struggle over the body, which Michel Foucault has encouraged us to see as the site and origin of power. Foucault (1991: 170) argues that it is through the 'exercise of discipline' upon the body that the body politic is ordered; such disciplinary power deploys a range of 'simple instruments', such as 'hierarchical observation, normalizing judgement…and the examination', and becomes so pervasive that every aspect of people's lives is affected, even the apparently most intimate:

> The workshop, the school, the army were subject to a whole micro-penalty of time (lateness, absences, interruptions of tasks), of activity (inattention, negligence, lack of zeal), of behaviour (impoliteness, disobedience), of speech (idle chatter, indolence), of the body ('incorrect' attitudes, irregular gestures, lack of cleanliness), of sexuality (impurity, indecency). At the same time, by way of punishment, a whole series of subtle procedures was used, from light physical punishment to minor deprivations and petty humiliations. It was a question both of making the slightest departures from correct behaviour subject to punishment, and of giving a punitive function to the apparently indifferent elements of the disciplinary apparatus: so that, if necessary, everything might serve to punish the slightest thing; each subject find himself caught in a punishable, punishing universality. (Foucault 1991: 178)

Foucault's analysis of disciplinary regimes, with their elaborate systems of reprimand and retribution, can seem tailor-made for Irish society, which has sometimes been characterized as a repressive, 'no' culture with a tendency to forbid and prohibit. His insights thus frequently resonate with the ethnographic depictions discussed below, even where these do not explicitly draw upon them. We begin by considering two issues about which Foucault had much to say: sex and madness.

Sex, Madness and Sex Madness

> Why did God create orgasms for women? To give them something else to moan about!
> Joke widely told by women in Dublin in the 1990s (Throop 1999: 139)

Anthropologists of Ireland, and many Irish people, including those who were the subject of the study, were shocked when John Messenger (1969, 1971) published his account of Irish sex and sexuality, based on fieldwork that he and his wife had carried out on the pseudonymous isle of Inis Beag in Galway Bay in the 1950s and early 1960s. If Messenger were to be believed, the average Irish islander's knowledge of sex was so woeful and limited that it is difficult to understand how the country could have been populated at all. According to Messenger, the islanders he studied, and by implication much of the rest of Ireland's rural population, were the most sexually ignorant and most puritan in the whole of Europe. Marriageable men in their 'late twenties [were] usually sexually repressed to an unbelievable degree. ... Several bachelors and spinsters almost have married several times in succession, only to find the sexual commitment on each occasion too difficult to make at the last moment' (J. C. Messenger 1969: 68–9). In a curious and culturally unusual reversal of what seems to have long been the preference of many Western men for seeking sex without marriage, the island men of Inis Beag, it seems, would have favoured marriage without sex, for it was chiefly an unwillingness to accept the sexual responsibilities of marital status, Messenger argues, that resulted in late marriage and high rates of celibacy among them. When we recall that Messenger was writing in the midst of the sexual revolution of the 1960s – his monograph was published in the same year that sexual and other forms of liberation were being celebrated at Woodstock – he had indeed appeared to have uncovered a cultural curio as shocking in its sexual abstinence as Margaret Mead's revelations of pre-pubertal and pre-marital Samoan sexual cavortings had been to a sexually conservative America a generation or so earlier.

Messenger (1971: 14–15) anticipated that his account of the islanders' sex lives would offend, alienate and probably be denied, a pretty reasonable expectation to hold for someone who can write with confidence that 'Inis Beag [is] one of the most sexually naïve of the world's societies', even if this assertion should turn out to be verifiable. One can almost hear the islanders mutter 'Feck, feck, feck' as they picked up their copies from the post office. There is certainly a patronizing and paternalistic tone to Messenger's revelation that he and his wife saw themselves as 'counsellors' and the islanders as their 'clients' whose 'distress' they were concerned 'to alleviate' by imparting 'our sexual knowledge', a role the Messengers had performed before 'among primitive Nigerians, and for similar reasons' (J. C. Messenger 1971: 13–14).

Messenger outlines how the Inis Beag islanders were generally coy and embarrassed about their bodies and their sexuality. As far as possible, men and women carried out their activities separately, despatching children for errands rather than risk encountering each other in the shop, and gathering together in single-sex groupings at church and to chat. They did not draw attention to sexual matters in their behaviour or their conversation, avoiding styles of dancing that required bodily contact and refusing to tell what Messenger refers to as 'dirty jokes' (a reticence that is in contrast to the banter among small farmers reported by Arensberg and Kimball 1968: 206–7). He recounts a range of observations and conversations to support his view that 'sexual misconceptions are myriad in Inis Beag' (J. C. Messenger 1971: 16). Few women, he reports, understood the physiological significance of menstruation and menopause, and Betty Messenger had to explain these processes to them. Nudity was associated with sex, and was generally avoided, even in small children and babies. Men preferred to risk drowning while fishing at sea rather than expose their naked bodies in order to learn to swim. Defecation and urination were also shrouded in secrecy because of their sexual overtones. Intercourse was brief and foreplay limited, with 'orgasm, for the man, … achieved quickly, almost immediately after which he falls asleep' (J. C. Messenger 1971: 17).

Jokes aside about the persistence of this practice in Ireland and elsewhere, such activities do not seem to have been isolated. To varying degrees other anthropologists have recorded similar attitudes towards the body and to sex in Ireland. Writing about Tory Island in the 1960s, Fox (1978: 160) notes that 'immediate orgasm is the goal and boast of sophisticates', with 'intercourse clothed and brief', and little time devoted to foreplay. Such views were not confined to the West, and Humphreys (1966: 139) describes how in 1940s Dublin sex was thought to be just as unpleasant, a view largely unchanged some fifty years later when the city's more working-class residents still found sex distasteful and experienced 'anxiety about the body and bodily control' (Throop 1999: 139; but a far cry from the 'normalization of erotica' more recently reported by Sugrue 2002; cf. Inglis 1998b). But perhaps best known because of the controversy it generated is the work of Nancy Scheper-Hughes, who describes how the residents of the County Kerry village of 'Ballybran' (a pseudonym), where she studied in the 1970s, had internalized similar norms about sex and their bodies. Like Messenger, she too was interested in the high incidence of celibacy and late marriage, and in particular in the relationship between these and mental illness, a cultural analysis of Irish psychology that won the Margaret Mead Award in 1981 at the same time as it provoked an outcry among the local residents and heated debate in the Irish national press. Scheper-Hughes (1987: 73) later wrote about how she was surprised by this outcry, though at least one reviewer remarked at the time on the irony of publishing such an intimate portrait of a community that she herself had described as being wary of outsiders and anxious of 'penetration' (Callahan 1979: 311).

Scheper-Hughes used Thematic Apperception Tests (TAT), in which respondents are shown picture cards of people in everyday situations and are asked to make up a story about them and to describe their feelings, in order to uncover the dynamics of family life in Ballybran, and in particular the tensions among siblings and between the ties of blood and marriage. According to Scheper-Hughes, the

TAT responses revealed a lovelessness and lack of warmth in personal relationships and an ambivalence towards intimacy composed of both longing and fear, an
attitude she considers 'quintessentially Irish' in its 'suspiciousness of the flesh and
sexuality' (1979: 118). She notes that sexual repression and personal asceticism
were strong themes throughout her TAT records, irrespective of whether test
respondents were young or old, male or female. As on Inis Beag, men and women
in Ballybran were strictly separated, with a clearly gendered allocation of tasks and
informal associational patterns that stressed single-sex contact in pub, church and
village shop. When members of the opposite sex were present 'body posture is
rigid and conversations distant, often sardonic, and elusive', in contrast to the
warmth, intimacy and personal contact that characterized same-sex gatherings
(1979: 106). Villagers were careful about the boundaries of their body, and were
anxious both about activities (such as dancing) that might bring them into physical
contact with the opposite sex, as well as about what they put into their body and
what came out, a concern with bodily orifices that Scheper-Hughes – following
Mary Douglas (1966) – reminds us is closely associated with sexual purity.
Ballybran bodies were clothed 'defensively', concealing their form, and nudity
was considered an embarrassment to be avoided or quickly covered up.

Each of these ethnographers refers to socio-economic factors like late inheritance, the teachings of the Catholic Church and the deep religiosity of the rural
Irish to explain these conservative and repressive attitudes towards the body and
sexuality, and though others have argued that the Irish obsession with land and
religion, and the particular forms which this took, were a strategic response to the
'asymmetrical power relations' characteristic of the colonial experience (Stahl
1979; cf. Scheper-Hughes 1987: 57), it has generally been on the role of religion
that the wider discussion has fixed. The power of the church was both ideological,
in determining how people viewed the body and its functions, and behavioural, in
so far as it controlled what people actually did (or did not do). John Messenger
suggests that

[p]riests of Jansenist persuasion have had subtle means of repressing the sexual
instincts of the islanders in addition to the more extreme methods of controlling
behavior – 'clerical social control', such as employing informers, allocating indul-
gences, and refusing the sacraments to, and placing curses on, miscreants. Through
sermons and informal classroom talks, the pulpit and the national school have served
as effective vehicles of church discipline. (1971: 28)

Some curates 'suppressed courting, dancing, visiting, and other behavior either
directly or "indirectly" ... sexual in nature' by taking physical action: they policed
the lanes at night to deter young lovers and inhibited dancing by their disapproving
presence (J. C. Messenger 1971: 28). The role of the local curate was reinforced
by the preaching of visiting missions and by what Messenger refers to as 'secular

social control', in which gossip played its part, as well as by the moral influence of the family and mothers in particular (see also Inglis 1998a: chapter 8; Scheper-Hughes 1979: chapter 5; Throop 1999: 94). Scheper-Hughes similarly sees an ascetic Catholic tradition as encouraging anxiety about the body and a lack of sexual vitality. The rural clergy, she notes (1979: 120), 'maintained a firm control over the bodies as well as the souls of their notoriously obedient parishioners' (in some cases literally, as the exposure of sexual abuse by priests subsequently revealed).

These ethnographic accounts of sexuality and the body in different times and places offer an insight into the functioning at the local level of the church hegemony described in more general and institutional terms by Inglis (1998a) and Dillon (1993), and give us an idea of how church control actually operated and what it meant for those who were subject to it. This focus on the everyday practice of sexuality – on how it is 'thought of, enacted and talked about in concrete social situations' – is largely absent from studies of Irish sexuality influenced by Foucault, even though such studies sometimes recognize its importance (see Inglis 1997: 17). Inglis (1991, 1998a) provides a sophisticated account of how church and state struggled for 'control of the Irish body' throughout the nineteenth century in which he argues that the British colonial state's attempts to repress the Irish economically and politically were gradually supplanted by a policy of pacification and control, tasks ultimately conceded to the Roman Catholic Church. Under the church, being civilized, mannerly, well disciplined and respectable quickly 'became associated with a disciplined control of the body', a notion that was 'instilled into the homes and bodies of most Irish Catholics through the organizations and buildings supervised by priests and religious [orders]' (Inglis 1991: 62, 63). The Irish were thereby transformed into a modern civilized people through the 'systematic discipline, surveillance, and sexualization of the body'. It was, says Inglis, a transformation in what people did and said, of lifestyle, customs, and manners, and of 'the body in terms of the mechanisms by which it was controlled', 'from open, passionate bodies to closed, moral bodies' (1991: 64, 65). Only recently has the power of the church as a controlling body in Irish society been challenged – principally by the media, according to Inglis (1997) – and it was long the sole arbiter of right and wrong, defining what it meant to be a decent person and monopolizing moral authority in every walk of life from the most public to the most private and intimate.

However, the ethnographies of Messenger and Scheper-Hughes tell us that it is not only morality that depends on the successful regulation and control of bodies and sexuality. Sanity too depends upon it, and bodies that are sexually repressed or out of control may result in madness. According to Messenger (1971: 30), 'Dysfunctional sociocultural forms, mental aberrations (neuroses, psychoses, and psychosomatic disorders), and exaggerated defense postures abound' on Inis Beag.

He reports how the story told by one old man – about a priest hospitalized for mental illness when his pretty housekeeper 'drove him mad from frustration' – reveals how erotic desire 'is probably the major cause of neuroses and psychoses in Ireland' (J. C. Messenger 1971: 15). Scheper-Hughes similarly identifies a connection between mental illness, sex and celibacy. The oppositions between flesh and spirit, purity and pollution, and guilt and shame that are 'expressed through body image as well as reinforced by folklore' are 'so basic to rural Irish personality modalities', she argues, that they inhibit the free expression of sexuality and make 'celibacy a natural way of life for the great number' (Scheper-Hughes 1979: 125). Sexual repression and anxiety about bodily control thrive within the structures of rural Irish kinship and family patterns, which tend to value the bonds of siblingship over those of marriage and to define the 'family' in terms of consanguineal rather than affinal ties (cf. Fox 1979). This, Scheper-Hughes suggests, contributes to the high rates of celibacy that she sees as clearly associated with mental illness, especially schizophrenia (Scheper-Hughes 1979: 98, 112).

These associations between sex and mental illness, and the allegedly spiralling rates of schizophrenia, have been widely questioned in the literature (Throop 1999: 58n; Kane 1986). They have been challenged methodologically and for flying in the face of the statistical evidence, as well as for accepting as 'fact', and so failing to interrogate, a persistent assumption that mental illness is a cultural attribute of the Irish (Herr 1990: 21; Kane 1979b, 1986). In addition to offending local sensibilities, as mentioned earlier, such claims also tend to be ahistorical, to over-generalize (both within the community studied and from that community to all of Ireland), and to treat the relationship between the individual and the institutional as unproblematic.

Of course, the introduction and construction of asylums across Ireland from the early nineteenth century on, together with the widespread introduction of schools, hospitals and prisons, was part of the colonial state's efforts to pacify, civilize, modernize and discipline the Irish body. The introduction of these institutions, many of which were promptly handed over to the Catholic Church (see Inglis 1991: 58; 1998a: chapter 6), was intended to educate the Irish in civil and respectable ways and to inculcate in them the worldviews and behaviours of the decent, upright, moral citizen modelled on the dominant anglophone colonizing class. But modernizing and disciplining the Irish body was never a simple, straightforward or one-way process. Institutions introduced to bend the Irish body to new ways were sometimes softened, domesticated and appropriated by local cultural forms through which they were imbued with different meanings appended to those originally intended.

With their emphasis on locality and particularity, anthropologists have been able to show that it would be misleading to conceive the modernizing process in Ireland in terms of a hard-edged dichotomy between tradition and modernity (see also chapter five). The transition, instead, was a much more blurred and muddied one, as demonstrated by their detailed ethnographic knowledge with its proximate and rich understanding of local lives. The broad civilizing and controlling institutions such as asylum, hospital and school were always received and reacted to in complex ways that reflected existing values, beliefs and practices, as Jamie Saris (1996, 1997, 1999, 2000) elaborates for a large mental hospital in Sligo in northwest Ireland.

Saris reminds us that in the nineteenth-century colonial view, lunacy was linked to a constellation of related disorders, of space, work and relationships (see also Inglis 1991). State institutions, like the asylum, would institute a 'specific regime – moral therapy – that would redeem the pathological irrationality of the inmates by stressing self-control, the functional organization of space, and the linear periodization of time' (Saris 1999: 701). This regime would broadly replicate the conditions found within the factory, and would thus inculcate within the inmates an economic rationality that would help to integrate rural Ireland, and this peripheral part of it in particular, into the state economy. In short, the Irish body would be transformed by being directed away from a socially backward and economically irrational tradition towards a modern world of market values and commodity logic.

The social, physical and architectural environment of the Sligo hospital both reflected this vision and was designed in such a way as to bring it about. The 'asylum qua physical thing possesses a virtue to transform' and control people's bodies, with its division into wards, treatment rooms, spaces for work, recreation, exercise and rest and named functional units for Admissions, Geriatrics, and so on (Saris 1996: 540). Each inmate learned these divisions and 'labored within them as a major step towards the production of himself or herself as a new person', a transformative potential inherent in the institution that 'meshed surprisingly well with local understandings of transformative places in the narrative memories of country people', such as holy wells and other indigenously recognized sites of occult possibility (Saris 1996: 543, 544). At the same time, inmates and hospital workers operated with a very different mental map and terminology to those that structured the hospital, one with a much more local historical origin and provenance that enabled them to lay claim to the place as their own (Saris 1996, 2000: 27). Hospital units were thereby absorbed into a local spatial logic and nomenclature that referred not to a particular ward or treatment room, but to 'the Hill', 'the Bowery' or the 'Ballroom', parts of the institution so-named because of the history and stories told about them rather than their physical features or function, an appropriation that tempered and reshaped institutional classifications and parameters intended to regulate, organize and restrain. Saris sees resistance of a sort here. For while the asylum's aims and architecture – social as well as physical – are designed to discipline and control the body, these objectives are challenged by being channelled along pre-existing cultural lines that give form to and articulate a local presence. This theme of resistance towards bodies that control is also evident in the other examples considered in this chapter, including that to which we turn next, young people in Ireland.

Keeping Control of 'the Lads'

> The only place ... to be is up on Cloud Nine. It's so boring around here ... there's nothing to do, so you might as well be high. You get high, your body's on the ground, but your mind is way up there [points to the sky] in those clouds, and you're looking down ... You listen to a bit of music ... There's nothing better.
>
> Young joyrider in Cork (cited in Gaetz 1997: 100)

In this section we look at some aspects of the social control of young people's bodies, and at how they comply with or resist efforts to regulate and organize their activities. We also look at who claims the right to exercise such control over young people, and at how this can be contested by different organizations based inside and outside a particular community. In other words, we focus here not just on the relationship between young people and the bodies that try to regulate their behaviour, but also on how different organizations may compete to exert such control.

In Ireland, 'young people causing a nuisance' is an increasingly visible 'problem' (Jarman 2005: 344) that can include everything from hanging around shopping malls in an apparently threatening manner to serious involvement in crime. Such anti-social behaviour may involve activities that are seen as a nuisance to the wider public, like skateboarding and cycling on footpaths, trampling on people's gardens, and general rowdiness. Or it may involve activities more likely to attract the might of the law, such as drug dealing, substance abuse, petty crime, car theft and joyriding, activities which the police, judiciary and social workers are charged by the state with controlling.

Many different state and non-state institutions, then, are concerned with policing the social order in relation to young people. Various state agencies as well as the church and a broad range of community groups monitor and control the activities of the young where these disrupt or are thought to threaten the rights, property and everyday lives of the wider public. In exceptional cases, as in some parts of Northern Ireland, as we shall see later, young people may also find themselves subject to the control of paramilitary organizations, which ironically exert their own illegal forms of power to curtail the activities of others, including those actions by young people that paramilitaries consider 'anti-social': a situation where two 'wrongs' are used to make a 'right'.

As with much of their work, anthropologists have usually approached these issues by concentrating on the voices of young people themselves and trying to account for the linkages between social order 'on the ground' and that at the more institutional level. Indeed, one means of identifying the underlying logic of social control is by observing social order 'on the ground'. Buckley (1983, 1984, 1987), for example, argues that the parent–child relationship provides the paradigm of social control for all complementary relationships in society, including those between men and women, employer and employee, and official and non-official. He describes how in the Northern Irish village where he did his fieldwork, women frequently adopted a 'Parent frame and mode of social control' in relation to their menfolk, who adopted a 'Rebellious' or 'Compliant' Child frame in their reciprocal interactions. In other words, women must keep a check on men's behaviour, since men are like children who 'seem to be primarily regarded as potential tearaways who are in need of control' (Buckley 1984 : 27). Consequently, women regulate men's drinking, fighting, gambling and other excessive, 'rough' and 'unruly' behaviour (cf. Fox 1975: 138). Control and regulation of young people's bodies thus here provide a model as well as a metaphor for social control more generally in Irish society.

Anthropologists have also sought to see young people 'in the round', situating their activities within the context of their lives more generally in order to avoid the pathologizing of young people's behaviour that characterizes some media and even some academic debate. By drawing out the diversity along the lines of social class, gender and ethnicity, such work helps to temper the oversimplified and pedestrian images of young people occasionally found in the literature.

Stephen Gaetz's (1997) study of community action and young people in the pseudonymous parish of Ballinaclasha in Cork, the second largest city in the Irish Republic, illustrates many of these characteristics. Gaetz's principal concern is to understand the fluctuating fortunes of 'community action' in providing youth services in Ballinaclasha, and to show how such forms of community 'empowerment' – where local activists take control and try to exert an influence over the social and economic processes that most affect their lives – can emerge within the 'spaces' left by society's dominant institutions. In the Republic, youth services are largely delivered by the Catholic Church and Irish government, institutions which Gaetz (1997: 79) describes as being characterized by highly authoritarian, centralized and hierarchical forms of organization. At the same time, Ballinaclasha community activists have offered their own youth programmes, which for a long time were highly successful. Gaetz focuses on the tensions between these two levels, using Gramsci's concept of hegemony to understand how 'large' institutions like the church exercise domination at the local level, as well as the forms of resistance to this domination and the manner in which that resistance is contained. For Gramsci, hegemony entails the 'naturalization' and legitimation of elite ideology, whose authority is widely accepted and even taken for granted by subordinate groups because it has become so embedded in the structures of society (Gaetz 1997: 11–15; Gramsci 1971). Subordinated groups thus acquiesce to their own domination, and this is often brought about through provision of social welfare programmes of the kind that Gaetz examines.

Reflecting the Republic's wider demography, a high proportion of the residents of Ballinaclasha in the 1980s were under twenty-five years old, many of them unemployed school-leavers who were marginalized in their own neighbourhood and whose main complaint was 'boredom'. These are the 'lads' of the book's title, who gave rise to the youth 'crisis' much debated in Ballinaclasha at that time, and to which local people responded by developing a series of community-controlled youth projects.

Gaetz suggests that the institutions of Irish society which seek to control the behaviour of young people, such as church and state, tend to operate with the notion that young people are all the same. In fact, the category of 'youth' is largely their construction, and they treat it as more or less homogeneous, providing leisure and sports facilities intended for all (Gaetz 1997: 79). But as Gaetz notes, young people are of course a diverse group, and although the structural differences amongst them have long been recognized by researchers, these insights have been slow to be incorporated into the perspectives of those who design and deliver youth programmes, particularly in Ireland. Youth services in Ballinaclasha are thus generally insensitive to the range of youth who live there, and do not always meet the needs of every category of young person.

Gaetz identifies three types of young person in the parish, based principally on differences of social class, on lifestyle and on where they live, a three-fold classification that reflects how these young people see themselves (1997: 78–95). The 'advantaged youth' are those from private housing estates in the neighbourhood, from 'good' family backgrounds which encourage upward mobility. They are usually still at school and, if not, are likely to be employed. Not only are their opportunities in the labour market much greater than those of other young people in Ballinaclasha, but their wealthier background results in networks of friends and choices of leisure pursuits that are also much broader and often extend beyond the locality. At the other extreme are the 'lads' or 'boys' who hang around street corners, and are most likely to have left school and be unemployed. Their family backgrounds are often ones of unemployment, abuse and alcoholism, and they are very disadvantaged in the labour market and educationally. Their involvement in the youth services is extremely low, and some of them alleviate their self-proclaimed boredom by joyriding and involvement in other forms of crime, activities which simultaneously give them a reputation for being 'hard' and alienate them from the other young people in the area. Somewhere in between these two categories, and sharing some characteristics of each, are the 'mainstream youth', whom Gaetz describes as being the more conservative and respectable members of the working class. Like the advantaged youth, they have aspirations to do better, and even though they suffer from many of the same disadvantages as the lads, such as limited opportunities and less prosperous family backgrounds, they do not respond to these difficulties in the same way. Instead, they express concern about the level of youth provision in the area, and look to these youth services for improved recreational facilities and help with employment.

Teenage girls are a much less visible element of Ballinaclasha's street youth culture and have a much lower participation rate in the youth services than their male counterparts. According to Gaetz (1993), this is because they are socialized very differently to the boys and because of the stronger moral control exerted on them both by their families and by the Catholic Church, which raise them within a largely patriarchal context that limits and directs their opportunities towards becoming wives and mothers. Responsible for domestic chores and minding younger siblings, they have less free time than boys, and are more likely to spend this in a 'private bedroom-oriented female set of behaviours' rather than on the street (Gaetz 1997: 92). Moreover, control of teenage sexual conduct is a major goal of church and parents, and for girls a product of peer group pressure through gossip, mocking and ostracism for inappropriate behaviour, a result of which is less freedom for girls than for boys (Gaetz 1997: 94). In truth, however, as Gaetz indicates, little is known about teenage girls in Ireland, and their lives there remain under-researched (though see Bradby 1994; Jenkins 1983: 47-8, 133; and for Travellers, Helleiner 2000: 191-3; N. D. Smith 1998).

Given the diversity of its young people, it is not surprising that there are many competing perspectives on what 'youth problems' in Ballinaclasha actually are and how they should be addressed, a situation exacerbated by the socio-economic and other differences that characterize and divide this 'community' more generally. In the struggle for local leadership, many different actors – including community activists, the diocesan priest, the local councillors and parliamentary representatives – advance their own definitions and sets of solutions, some of which reflect the national-level organizations to which they belong (such as government and church bodies), and others that have their origin in more local understandings and sympathies. For almost a decade community activists of the Ballinaclasha Community Association were successful in this struggle for control over the provision of local youth services, and they effectively challenged, resisted and provided an alternative to the hegemony enjoyed by church and state in this field.

In Northern Ireland much of the early writing about controlling young people's behaviour was influenced by the 'Troubles', the impact of which came to dominate the social research conducted there after 1969 when conflict erupted. Government bodies, community workers and psychiatrists all worried about the long-term impact that street violence and the breakdown of the rule of law would have on juvenile delinquency and predicted that behaviour learned in the streets – during rioting, stoning the police and in clashes between sectarian gangs – would spill over into other areas of young people's lives too, at home, in school and in their attitudes towards work. Combined with segregated schooling, this all added up to an 'education for aggro' (Fraser 1973). As Desmond Bell (1990: 45) has pointed out, early psychiatric research pathologized Northern Irish young people, constructing them as a 'category at risk', and effectively playing down and undermining the role of their behaviour in the developing political dissent. This legitimated an explicitly 'correctional' approach to youth policy that resulted in 'a major expansion of the interventions of the state in the lives of the adolescents of Northern Ireland via the youth service and Youth Training machinery' (D. Bell 1990: 27). As in Ballinaclasha, such bodies sought to bring youth behaviour 'under control' by managing educational, training and leisure activities. They 'functioned essentially as state-sponsored instruments of social discipline for the marginalized young' (D. Bell 1990: 190).

Bell (1990: 23) argues that, far from being pathological, the activities of the working-class Protestant youth he studied in Derry must be seen as having real political content, one moulded by the sectarian context of their lives and in response to their loyalist parental culture. It is not just class and generation that are important here, as considered by Gaetz for Cork, but also ethnicity, for, as Bell shows, there is considerable continuity between the political views and 'traditions' of these young people and those of their parents. Derry young people actually help to sustain rather than transcend sectarian 'tradition', and in contrast to the 'oppositional' youth subcultures emphasized by the Birmingham Centre for Contemporary Cultural Studies (Hall and Jefferson 1976), they perpetuate their parents' political perspectives rather than challenge them. Indeed, Bell argues, 'subcultural practices can just as easily embrace and resuscitate "traditional" values as undermine or reject them' (1990: 37), as his study of loyalist youth demonstrates.

In his book on Protestant working-class youth in Belfast, Richard Jenkins (1983) too focuses on cultural reproduction, although he emphasizes class and the labour market rather than the reproduction of sectarian division. Many of the factors affecting working-class youth throughout the United Kingdom were also present in Northern Ireland – such as educational inequality, lack of opportunity and a labour market characterized by soaring rates of unemployment – but such factors were often missed by researchers mesmerized by sectarian conflict. For Jenkins's Belfast youth it was not just sectarian division but these other structural, organizational and institutional parameters and contexts of their lives that circumscribed their ambitions and achievements and that resulted in lifestyle differences among them.

Based on their own models, Jenkins outlines three main lifestyle differences among the young people with whom he worked, which to some extent parallel those later used by Gaetz in Cork: the 'lads', who are the 'rougher' element, those more likely to be rebels, to be involved in gangs, and to have a criminal record; the 'citizens', who by contrast are church-going, 'respectable', 'good living' and aspire to be upwardly mobile; and the 'ordinary kids', a category made up of all the other young people whose identity is not as strongly articulated as that of the lads and the citizens (Jenkins 1982: 12–13; 1983: 50). While each of these lifestyles is associated with distinct family patterns, different degrees of involvement in crime, and particular educational experiences, they are not reducible to this set of differences in any straightforward manner. Rather, it is the interaction of young people's everyday practices with the practices of 'significant others' and the 'institutional context within which both sets of practices are located' (such as those of school and the workplace) that explains the production and reproduction of these divisions among them (Jenkins 1983: 130). The reciprocal interconnections among these elements in the end account for the reproduction of the existing systems of subordination and control in these young people's lives, and for the reproduction of a class system that turns out these youth as workers or potential workers within it.

Both Bell and Jenkins focus chiefly on the role of official institutions in the lives of young people, such as schools, state-run youth training schemes, youth clubs and the world of work. Rosellen Roche (2003) is one of few researchers to offer a view of young people's experiences of unofficial and illegal bodies of control such as the paramilitaries. She is also the only researcher to have carried out long-term ethnographic field research among both Catholic and Protestant young people. Roche completed twenty-two months of fieldwork in Derry, primarily with school-leavers, exploring their relationship to authority within a context of urban deprivation and long-term violent conflict. The nature of this violence had changed, however, from the 'high-level' violence of paramilitary attacks that had characterized the periods studied by Bell and Jenkins to the 'low-level' violence characteristic of a 'post-conflict' Northern Ireland transformed by paramilitary cease-fires and political developments such as the Good Friday (Belfast) Agreement of 1998 (see Jarman 2004; Stewart and Strathern 2002: 37–51). She is particularly concerned to understand the nature of violence among these young people, which she contends is different in important ways to the over-dichotomized and oppositional sectarian violence usually reported in the media, and often privileged in academic writing in Northern Ireland (as in Feldman 1991 and Sluka 1989, 1995).

Low-level violence, Roche demonstrates, is a 'normalized' feature of young people's everyday lives, something they expect, anticipate and negotiate as a routine and habitual feature of where and how they live: it is 'just the way it is', rather than something special and unique. Even very young children are routinely accepting of the violence around them, devising strategies to avoid it and playing it down at school (Lanclos 2003: 146–7). Some of this violence is sectarian, and occurs between Protestant and Catholic gangs and individuals. But much of it is not sectarian, and violence takes place 'between and with young people and forms of authority for reasons as varied as detestation, spite, loathing, taunting or display, boredom or for fun' (Roche 2003: 19). It may be no more than a 'recreational aggression' (Buckley and Kenney 1995: 154) or a display of 'braggadocio rather than outright hatred' (Carter 2003b: 263). Roche's young people fight in the streets with their peers from other neighbourhoods, they organize 'riot nights' when police are lured into housing estates with the sole purpose of stoning and petrol bombing them 'for fun', and they may experience the cold metal of a paramilitary gun pressed against their knees. Irrespective of gender and sectarian affiliation, violence is a daily feature of their lives, part of the 'craic' of being a young person in Derry, and the taken-for-granted means of interaction with other young people as well as with state and paramilitary figures of authority. Roche pays particular attention to the relationship between violence and young women, something often ignored in the literature, where 'youth violence' is too readily assumed to equate with violence among young men (Jarman 2005). She vividly illustrates the 'tangled, personalised nature of violent interplay' among these young people (Roche 2003: 4), clearly demonstrating how violence is never just or is not only a consequence of 'sectarian' opposition, however amenable it might be to being represented in these terms.

Growing up in Derry and dealing with the institutions that exercise control over one's life, whether these are state bodies or illegal organizations like the IRA and loyalist paramilitaries, entails learning how to negotiate and enact the kinds and levels of violence considered culturally appropriate for relations in different types of situation and for different kinds of audience. Violence may be appropriate between Catholic and Protestant, or be a form of state and anti-state interaction, but it does not always stem straightforwardly from such dichotomized and oppositional categories. Instead, as Roche (2003: 21) suggests, violence is sometimes sectarian, sometimes 'for fun', and sometimes occurs simply because the young people feel that it is expected of them. Much of the violence is about 'pushing against' individuals or situations, to see how far they can go, to demonstrate bravado and 'hardness', and to negotiate and establish the boundaries of control. For instance, Roche describes how a routine practice among some of the younger people she studied was stoning police and British Army patrols. The response was different in each case:

> The 'Brits' see. If ye hit the cops, the cops would usually chase ye right? But the 'Brits' canny life ye. So if ye hit the 'Brits', the 'Brits' just drive on. Know, they don't do nothing. (Young Derry man quoted in Roche 2003: 233)

So too the paramilitaries were 'pushed against'. Sometimes they would not be taken seriously by the young people (especially if known to them as neighbours or family members), who would follow the 'Provos' to see 'what they are up to', or shoot pellet guns at their windows just to 'test the line', and generate a 'sense of control over what may seem overwhelming odds against such authority' (Roche 2003: 203, 225–7).

Roche's analysis opens up a much more dynamic and flexible understanding of the relationships between young people and the bodies that control them, and she communicates a real feel for the fluidity of young people's everyday lives as they deal with their peers and with youth workers, teachers, the police and the paramilitaries. In a very real sense it is through their physical bodies that they mediate the lines of control between themselves and these organizations, and it is their bodies that are on the line as they probe how far they can go. Paramilitary punishments for 'anti-social behaviour' (such as being a general nuisance, underage drinking, joyriding, theft or drug dealing) almost always focused explicitly and directly on the young person's body (although occasionally punishment could involve enforced exile from Northern Ireland), with the severity of the punishment varying according to the perceived scale of the offence and including physical beatings of different degrees of brutality (and focusing on different parts of the body according to the crime), tarring and feathering of a person's head and torso (a punishment often considered appropriate for women judged guilty of sexual transgression), kneecappings and killings. While not everyone approves of violent physical and bodily attack, many agree that it 'has proved useful in controlling things that went on within our community, simply because taking them to court doesn't work' (testimony in Knox 2001: 92, cited in Roche 2003: 42).

Young people's bodies are also at the forefront of their relationships and interactions with the organs of state control – the police and British Army – and it is there that their compliance or resistance is ultimately etched. Throughout the 1980s and 1990s, state security in Northern Ireland became increasingly hi-tech, with the installation of sophisticated surveillance equipment, cameras and listening devices. There was allegedly nothing that this equipment could not see or hear. As the young woman telling her story to Roche remarked: 'ye can do fuck all about it':

See that Rosemount barracks? The tower I was on about earlier. There was this girl … and she was getting ready for school wan morning, had her blinds open, didn't realise that your man was looking in at her from the tower. Aye. She took off her pyjamas, and then put on her … changed her underwear and whatever. She comes back in te the bedroom te put on her uniform. She was comin' home, she went te school anyway and came back. On her way home the 'Brits' stopped her, and says ah, 'Them pink knickers you were wearin' this morning were lovely', and all. And she thought oh dear Jesus! They were fuckin' standin' watchin' her. Through the fuckin' window. '*Them pink knickers ye were wearin*' this morning was beautiful'. She was fuckin' mortified. (Young Derry woman, quoted in Roche 2003: 139–40, emphasis in original)

But if hi-tech surveillance can be an invasion of privacy and a form of bodily control, the body can turn the camera to its advantage, as Roche goes on to illustrate in another case where a police camera observed two young women apparently smoking marijuana. Although there was little the police could do about this – 'if they were to come up here I could just say: "Well, what are you doing invading my privacy, looking in my fucking window?" – they drove up and down the road all night beeping their horn:

> [S]o Christine goes to me, 'Emer, I dare you the next time that camera looks in the window to flash'. I was all for a bit of craic, 'Will ye? 'Cause they can't do fuck all anyway'. So me and Christine stood up and we seen the camera slowly but surely coming around, and me and Christine just swiped up the tops. I just stood in there in fucking shock. I couldn't believe we done it! 'Ah, nah, put your fucking top down!' And we ran away from the window. The camera just stayed there for half an hour looking in my window. I think they were in shock too. (Young Derry woman, quoted in Roche 2003: 140)

In the next section we develop this theme of the body as a weapon of resistance towards the powers that seek to control it.

Resisting Bodies

> From the moment we entered the H-Blocks we had used our bodies as a protest weapon. It came from the understanding that the Brits were using our bodies to break us.
>
> Male Provisional IRA prisoner (cited in Feldman 1991: 232)

> They literally had to pull the clothes off you. That was embarrassing because you were kicking and struggling and they were ripping the clothes completely off you and you feel … I cannot describe the way I used to feel. You felt as if you were nothing, you feel degraded. It's like a rape of some kind. They are ripping the bra and panties off you [sigh] you felt like crying, you felt like rolling back in a ball and getting into the corner and never coming out of there again!
>
> Female Provisional IRA prisoner (cited in Aretxaga 2001a: 15–16)

One area in which Irish ethnography has been at the forefront of contemporary post-structural theorizing is that of political subjectivity and control over the body. Drawing on the work of Foucault and René Girard, Feldman (1991) offers a sustained and systematic analysis of how the perpetrators and victims of violence in the Northern Ireland conflict represent and deploy the body in their narratives of political terror. He shows how the body may be 'othered' as target for sectarian attack, broken and subdued in state interrogation centres, or become the subject of different kinds of self-directed violence as a form of political protest. In each case, the body is considered a text from which can be read the various forms and formations of violence that construct, deform and reform the body as object and agent in a field characterized by bombings, murder and political instability. Feldman's work on Northern Ireland has been controversial, not least among ethnographers who have lived or worked in Ireland, and it has been criticized for relying on largely de-contextualized interviews, for mystifying rather than clarifying the Northern Irish conflict through its rarefied analytical style, and for its occasional flights of 'elitist' theoretical fancy (see, for instance, Jenkins 1992a, 1992b; Sluka 1992c; and for a response to some of this criticism, Feldman 1992). The theoretical language of his account is challenging, the text dense and heavy with abstract reference and allusion; ironically, as one reviewer wryly remarked, Feldman's own language would have benefited from a glossary in addition to the one provided to explain Belfast paramilitary slang (Taylor 1993b: 154).

For Feldman, political subjectivity comes into being by being performed across a range of 'surfaces', which includes the urban landscape of West Belfast, the state interrogation centres and the prison cell. These constitute the terrain on which the military and symbolic campaign for hearts and minds and bodies has been fought. They provide the locus for a performative dynamics in which the central actors are locked into a dialectic through which the power of all involved arises out of violent enactments on the body, sometimes on one's own, more often on that of others (cf. Malkki 1995: 88–9). Both the state and the paramilitaries who seek to overthrow the state demonstrate, legitimize, claim and create their power by their actions on the body, which becomes the 'bearer of seminal political messages', an 'embodied transcript' and 'political text' to be decoded (Feldman 1991: 8). The centrality of the body in narratives of political violence and its primacy in the production and confirmation of power becomes especially clear in Feldman's discussion of the prison protests undertaken by republican paramilitaries in the late 1970s and early 1980s.

From the work of Goffman (1961) and of Foucault (1991) we know well the dehumanizing and depersonalizing affect of 'total institutions' like the asylum and the prison, where inmates are stripped of an individuated identity by being numbered, uniformed and subjected to the same disciplinary routine. As with the Sligo hospital mentioned earlier, the objective of these institutional regulatory regimes is the production of docile, passive bodies, which are acquiescent to the demands of the controlling body concerned. In this sense, prisons are not just about punishing the body, they are also about disciplining it. As ethnic and anti-state conflict intensified in Northern Ireland from 1969, so the British state's prison policy was modified in accordance with its prevailing strategic objectives and shifting counter-insurgency tactics. In the early 1970s, as 'civil disobedience' gave way to frequent bombings and assassinations, the British government responded by rounding up and imprisoning without trial those they suspected of active involvement in political violence. At first internees were incarcerated in a disused Second World War air force camp in Long Kesh, just outside Belfast, and later in a purpose-built prison on the same site, the Maze, which was later to become notorious as the H-Blocks (so-called because of its layout). Prisoners initially had 'Special Category' status, which essentially identified them as political prisoners, who were permitted to associate freely with one another, wear their own clothes, and receive food parcels in a prison regime that moderated the total institutional conditions sketched above and that distinguished them from the ODCs or 'Ordinary Decent Criminals' convicted of burglary or theft. But by the late 1970s British government policy had shifted, and a new policy of 'normalizing' the Northern Ireland conflict was introduced. On the city streets this meant more policemen from the Royal Ulster Constabulary (RUC) on the beat alongside the British soldiers who for the previous three or four years had dominated security; while in the prisons it meant a policy of 'criminalization' and the removal after March 1976 of Special Category status from those hitherto treated as political prisoners. In other words, state strategy was aimed at weakening political resistance by classifying those engaged in political violence as 'ordinary criminals' and subjecting them to the same prison regime.

In response to 'criminalization', republican paramilitary prisoners in the Maze prison began a campaign to restore their political status, a campaign that was as much or more about achieving recognition of the legitimacy of their war as it was about demanding the right to wear their own clothes and of free association. At first this resistance took the form of a refusal to wear prison uniform and subsequently of a refusal to wash. Prisoners refused to subject their bodies to the order demanded by the prison regime by rejecting the 'monkey suit', the prison uniform that would subject them to the hierarchy of the prison structure and incorporate them within the ordinary prisoner population. As Feldman points out, to clothe one's body in the prison suit would have been a form of depoliticization for these prisoners, a destruction of their political identity, and an outward confirmation of their conformity to the prison regime. Left naked but for a prison blanket draped around their body, these 'Blanketmen', as they became known, thereby subverted use of the uniform as a central tactic in the prison's 'optics of domination', the means by which the prison controlled the body's visibility and transformed its meaning (Feldman 1991: 156). They were later to transform the political power of the uniform again, when they decided to wear it only in order to receive prison visits, which were their only opportunity to smuggle messages and other items in and out of the prison. They thus began to 'use the uniform as a political tool rather than be used by it', a 'countertextualization' and interpretive reversal that, according to Feldman (1991: 160), was to come to characterize the prison resistance as a whole and the ways in which prisoners deployed their bodies within it.

As the prison failed 'to imprint the bodies of the Blanketmen with the disciplines of the prison uniform and the prison number ... [it] extended the logic of compulsory visibility from the surface to the interior of the prisoner's body' in a process that Feldman (1991: 173) calls the 'colon-ization' of inmates' digestive and elimination tracts. Strip searches became common. These involved the intimate probing of the prisoner's body, as one H-Block inmate graphically describes:

> In the showers the screw [prison warder] would put a mirror on the floor and tell you to stand over the mirror ...We wouldn't do it. So right then and there you got a fucking digging [beating] ... 'Squat'. We didn't squat; they kicked the back of your legs to make you go down. That meant you were squatting over the mirror. They parted the cheeks of the arse and looked up them and all the rest. You always got the screw who struck [sic] his finger up your arse and hooked about, and they said to ye, 'Open your mouth', to see if anything was there. And the screw used the same finger into your mouth, this same shitty finger searched your nose, your ears, and searched your beard. All with the same finger. Some of them went to the extreme, and this is true as fuck, to search below the foreskin. They were bastards of the first order ... It was all just to fuck guys about, trying to break them. (Member of the Irish National Liberation Army, quoted by Feldman 1991: 167)

Symbolic reversal and the textual transformation of the body became particularly striking with the initiation in March 1978 of the 'Dirty Protest', when in response to the strip searches and frequent beatings that accompanied their visits to the bathroom, prisoners refused to wash and slop out. With the Dirty Protest, prisoner resistance was immediately visible on their bodies and in their cells. Refusing now to use the bathrooms, prisoners smeared their faeces on the walls of their cells, and pushed their urine out under the cell door. Unwashed, unshaven and with long matted hair, prisoners reclothed 'their naked bodies with a new and repellent surface of resistance' (Feldman 1991: 175), making their cells into an extension of their bodies. Like the clown or shaman empowered by the consumption of polluting substances, this transformed their bodily waste into 'power-laden medicine', and symbolically turned the tables on the prison authorities by wresting back that which the regime had sought to control: their own bodily interior. As Feldman remarks, 'Through the mirror searches, the prison regime had turned the prisoners' bodies inside out. So the Blanketmen reciprocated by imprinting this defiled interior of their bodies onto their cell walls' (1991: 181), in a recodification of faeces that restored the prisoners' political potency. The bodily violation intended to intensify their vulnerability was reversed and turned back on the prison. The prison warders who had sought to subjugate the bodies of the prisoners now went home as the 'inadvertent emissar[ies] of the Blanketmen', their own bodies stinking with the polluting and contagious stench of the prison cells (Feldman 1991: 195). Indeed, to the extent that the prisoners now determined the working conditions of the warders, it was they who 'were in control' (O'Malley 1990: 22).

Life in prison revealed to prisoners the political potentiality of their own bodies, as one Provisional IRA inmate recalled: 'The H-Blocks broke all your inhibitions about your body. It made you more aware of your body. You never thought you had so much fucking space up there' (cited in Feldman 1991: 201). All of the body's orifices were used as hiding places: the nose, navel, ears, mouth, rectum and foreskin were used to smuggle messages, writing paper, pens and tobacco in and out of prison. Like the cell, they 'became protective and sheltering recesses that repulsed the optical penetrations of the prison regime' (Feldman 1991: 199). In the end, then, it was the prisoners' willingness to explore and deploy the body's subversive potentiality as a diverse modality of resistance, and their readiness to deprive themselves and their own bodies that 'undermined the authority of the regime to do so' (O'Malley 1990: 23). This culminated in self-starvation as the ultimate act in the fight for political status.

When the Dirty Protest looked like continuing indefinitely, the prisoners resolved to escalate their resistance by embarking on a hunger strike, the first in 1980, which ended without fatalities, and again in 1981, when the strike resulted in the deaths of ten men. Much was made in the media at the time, and in subsequent journalistic and scholarly accounts, of the historical reverberations of this strike, and of the Christ-like image the bodies of these dying men evoked, with their long beards, unshorn hair, staring eyes and wasted frames (Clarke 1987; O'Malley 1990; Sweeney 1993a, 1993b). Feldman suggests, however, that despite the 'multiplicity of meanings' and representations of the strike outside the prison (including evocations of the Irish famine), and despite the political benefits derived by the republican movement from such images, the inmates themselves were insistent on a secular interpretation of their protest (though see O'Malley 1990: 64). For them the strike was not a religiously purificatory or pacifist action, as some have contended, but a military campaign and a 'modality of insurrectionary violence in which they deployed their bodies as weapons' (Feldman 1991: 220). Inmates conceived their hunger strike as equivalent and complementary to the violent military campaign that was being waged by the Provisional IRA on the outside. Feldman identifies the symbolic homology between the two. Violence on the outside, he suggests, may be other-directed, perpetrated on the bodies of others, while violence on the inside, in the form of the self-starvation of the hunger strike, is directed at oneself. Both forms of violence, however, result in dead bodies, and dead bodies, Feldman argues, have long been the 'elemental communicative unit of political performance' in the Northern Ireland conflict (Feldman 1991: 232, 233). The hunger strike that resulted in death and a succession of corpses carried from prison was a logical extension of the bodily and biological subversion of the state-imposed prison order that had begun with smearing faeces on the prison cells, and, like that protest, was a means of using one's body to recodify and appropriate state power to oneself (Feldman 1991: 225, 237). While Feldman writes at great length about the role of the body in republican resistance to the British state, he writes entirely about male paramilitaries incarcerated in the Maze, and makes only passing reference to the Dirty Protest initiated in 1980 by thirty-two IRA women in Armagh women's prison (Feldman 1991: 174). In this emphasis on men's resistance, Feldman is little different to the IRA leadership, which at best was ambivalent to and at worst condemned the way in which their female recruits deployed their bodies against the state. But the gendering of political subjectivity and prison resistance has been a crucial if largely unremarked dimension of the nationalist struggle in Northern Ireland, according to Begoña Aretxaga (1997), and it made a critical difference to the nature of Armagh women's Dirty Protest. Like the men in the H-Blocks, the women prisoners in Armagh were subject to the state policy of criminalization which denied them political status. Unlike the men, however, they were allowed to wear their own clothes, and from these they would improvise parts of the IRA uniform to symbolize the political identity that was denied them. It was in an effort to find these bits of clothing that male warders in Armagh prison launched a violent search of the prisoners' cells in early 1980, an assault that Aretxaga (1997: 125) argues was not just about state subjugation of prisoners, but also about male subjugation of women. Why else, she asks, were male officers brought in other than to inflict a 'gendered form of punishment'? Technologies of power are often 'supported by a fantasy of sexual violence' (Aretxaga 2001a: 8), and the words of one inmate suggest the gendered and sexual connotations of this search:

> I was suddenly pinned to the bed by a shield and the weight of a male screw on top of me. Then my shoes were dragged off my feet. I was bodily assaulted, thumped, trailed and kicked. I was then trailed out of my cell, and during the course of my being dragged and hauled from the wing both my breasts were exposed to the jeering and mocking eyes of all the screws, there must have been about twenty of them. While being carried, I was also abused with punches to the back of my head and my stomach. I was eventually carried into the governor; my breasts were still exposed. While I was held by the screws the governor carried out the adjudication, and I was then trailed back and thrown into a cell. (Inmate's testimony recorded by Women Against Imperialism 1980, cited in Aretxaga 1997: 124)

While there were obviously many similarities between the men's and women's protests, and while the gender specificity of the women's campaign was widely minimized by commentators of all political persuasions, there is, Aretxaga suggests, an 'inextricable connection' between the significance of the Armagh women's Dirty Protest and 'the play of gender and sexual difference in the production and deployment of power' (1997: 126–7).

This play of power around the gendering of the women's protest also focused on the culturally transgressive nature of their actions, and on the visibility given to their sexuality. As we saw earlier, the Catholic Church in Ireland has long promoted sexual modesty and sexual abstinence among young women like those imprisoned in Armagh jail, and has done much to discourage public and explicit discussion of sexual issues, contributing to a wider cultural squeamishness about women's bodies, and in particular about their bodily functions. Like the men in the Maze, the Armagh women refused to slop out, accumulating their bodily waste in their cells and spreading their excrement on the walls. As young women, these bodily wastes included their menstrual blood, and it is this that Aretxaga sees as the most powerful instrument and symbol of their resistance, its transgressive potential arising from 'an excess of signification that threatens the boundaries that constitute the social order' (1997: 127). She sees menstrual blood as a 'primordial symbol', highly elaborated in every culture, condensing multiple strands of meaning, and tapping into a broad range of different experiences (Aretxaga 1995: 125-6). Following Kristeva's (1982) analysis of 'excremental' and 'menstrual' pollution, Aretxaga (1997: 142) maintains that, as the symbol of sexual identity, menstrual blood can potentially endanger the cultural construction of gender difference and threaten the boundaries between men and women. Ironically, then, as Aretxaga notes, although the Armagh women had embarked on their protest in an attempt to have their political contribution to republican resistance recognized as equal to the men's, the image of their menstrual blood smeared on the walls of their cells only helped to underscore their sexual difference.

Aretxaga interprets the assault of the male prison warders on the bodies of the female inmates in Armagh and Maghaberry prisons within a wider context of institutional and militarized sexual harassment that characterized the Northern Ireland of the time, and that included demeaning body searches and sexual abuse during interrogation that one inmate described in detail:

They start asking you whatever [it] is that you were arrested for, and then they would mention the name of a man and say, 'Did you fuck him?' and continue, 'You Catholic girls just fuck anybody, you sluts. You know we can rape you right here, and nobody is going to believe you, because you are all fucking taigs.' The abuse is filthy, continuous sexual abuse. I had big breasts when young that always embarrassed me. And they said 'Who gropes them? Everybody in the IRA has gotten their hands on them at some point … We know all about you: you all have your legs permanently opened for the cause and for Ireland.' You just want to disappear. This is a man the age of your father, and he is talking like this to you. You just want the floor to open and swallow you. Then they go back to the initial question and then back again to the sexual abuse. You are sitting there pretending it is not upsetting you – but it's really upsetting you. You are seventeen and these men are older and they come in relays. It is very disturbing. (Cited in Aretxaga 1997: 133)

Aretxaga sees strip searches in particular as a gendered form of political domination through which political and gender identities are 'reinscribed with the power of a state acting as a male body politic' (2001a: 1), something of which we have already caught a glimpse in our discussion of the military gaze on the young woman's body mentioned above. Such practices, in Aretxaga's (2001b) view, entail the sexualization of state forms of control.

Institutional control of women's bodies in the Armagh prison thus evoked wider issues of male dominance and sexual abuse that resonated with the embryonic Irish feminist movement at the time, even if Protestant women continued to maintain that the protest was a 'sectarian' rather than a 'feminist' issue (Clarke 1987: 113; Loughran 1986; McCafferty 1984). Moreover, the actions of these Armagh women in making visible that which should be culturally hidden – their menstrual blood – challenged the preconceptions about gender and the female body held by the republican movement, which was embarrassed by the women's Dirty Protest and did its best to dissuade them from it. For Aretxaga, then, events in Armagh were not just about institutional discipline and punishment, nor just about resistance to it, but were also an assertion of male dominance over the bodies of women. 'Another kind of shit had surfaced', she suggests (Aretxaga 1997: 145), and as 'the stinking reality of male violence against women' became more visible, 'it deconstructed both Catholic models of gender and the nationalist heroic epic'.

Powerful Bodies

In the republican prison protests of the late 1970s and early 1980s the body's potential centrality and force as the focus for the reception and enactment of power is very clear. It is at once both the site of domination and discipline, and the means of resistance to it. Recalling the symbolic inversions of the Bakhtinian carnivalesque, the actions of the prison inmates overturned everyday cultural norms and formalized, bureaucratic forms of power, in a subversive reversal through which the grotesque is generated out of the ordinary and everyday – young men's and women's bodily functions – performed in the context of the extraordinary and exceptional setting of incarceration (see Bakhtin 1984). Moreover, the agency of women that we saw earlier as implicitly denied by John Messenger's (1971: 16) claims about Irish islanders' lack of knowledge about the physiological processes of menstruation and menopause on Inis Beag is here in the hunger strike recovered and reclaimed. At one extreme, on Inis Beag, knowledge of these processes and the processes themselves are downplayed, concealed and controlled, and women are no more than their ignorant and passive instrument. At the other extreme, in Armagh jail, the processes are made public as highly visible symbols of resistance and alternative forms of power by female activists intent on overthrowing the state. In each case, in a process that Feldman (1991: 178) refers to as the 'mimesis of alterity', the body is the locus of power as well as the place where that power can be reversed and redirected, a kind of mirror in which can be reflected back the savagery of a power that seeks to dominate (cf. Aretxaga 1995: 137). As Foucault suggests, the sexual body is 'an especially dense transfer point for relations of power ... one of those endowed with the greatest instrumentality ... and capable of serving ... the most varied strategies' (1981: 103).

In this chapter we have seen the interplay and operation of different forms of power: the moral power of the Catholic Church hierarchy; formal, state-sanctioned legal power; and illegal, illicit and subversive forms of power in the hands of those who resist, invert and transform official forms of power for their own ends. Anthropologists have not always focused equally on all of these forms of power, and have not always given equal voice to each. Nor have they always noted how they can be mediated by gender. Feldman's book, for instance, cites prisoners extensively but rarely prison warders or other state agents, and it cites men, rarely women. Yet each one of these may perform power differently, and thereby alter the direction of the 'play' (cf. Taylor 1993b: 152). In chapter five we focus explicitly on this potential diversity and difference, not just in relation to how power can be performed differently, but with regard to how 'Irishness' itself can be variously performed, claimed and represented. These identification processes rely on important, often compelling, notions of selves and others, where Irish culture moulds bodies as surely as it frames its expression in music, dance, poetry and parades. Before we turn to the performance and representation of identity and power in Ireland, we look at how anthropologists have revealed the alternative, informal and the hidden in the 'other(ing)' of Ireland's economies.

–4–

Ireland's 'Other(ing)' Economies

the second economy … may not only evade civil obligations but also express resistance
to the state.

Janet MacGaffey (1991: 10)

Ireland is now widely known for its 'Celtic Tiger economy', an evocative charac-
terization that suggests, on the model of East and Southeast Asia, aggressive economic growth, with cutting-edge development in information and communication
technologies and highly successful participation in global markets, combined with
a spirituality, mysticism and easy warmth and hospitality of a people on the
periphery of Europe. Many people on the island have readily identified with this
apparent oxymoron, and see themselves as rational, sophisticated modern entrepreneurs who have retained their connection with their romantic, mythic past, as
able to clinch a deal in the executive boardroom as to sink a pint of Guinness and
sing their party piece. For many of them the image of a Celtic Tiger is a welcome
and long overdue deliverance from an earlier stereotype as backward peasant
farmers (see chapter two), or the 'wild Irish' in some historical British narratives,
and it has been quickly embraced as a new identification by Irish people both at
home and abroad. Popular and academic commentary on the Celtic Tiger has
understandably focused largely on its material outcomes and benefits, and on some
of its more detrimental impacts, such as sprawling suburbanization, with the
spread of Dublin across the landscape and increasing criminal and racist violence
there and in other cities.

Yet at the same time as the Celtic Tiger has had an economic impact, it has also
been an integral part of over a decade of cultural production as an idea and image,
which, together with *Riverdance*, the renovation of Dublin's Temple Bar area and
the export of Irish themed pubs, has made 'being Irish' and 'acting Irish' a much
sought after cultural identity by those with the slightest claim to it, and even by
those with no obvious national or cultural link to Irishness (as witnessed by
O'Carroll 2005 in Irish pubs in Germany). National pride, if such could be meas-
ured, has soared as a result of this rebranding of Ireland, mirroring the negative
and positive results of such national branding elsewhere, as in Scotland
(McCrone, Morris and Kiely 1995). While the Celtic Tiger has increased the
money in many people's pockets, it has also offered a positive identity that has

boosted the confidence and esteem of those who see themselves as part of it. Yet as we shall see below, there are many who do not see themselves as part of it, and who are excluded from, or do not buy into, the Celtic Tiger experience, either as an economic miracle or as the basis of a new Irish personality.

This chapter explores in the Irish context something that has long interested anthropologists more generally, namely, the relationship between people's economic practices and their sense of who they and others are. This linking of economics and culture and society is not as common in contemporary social science as it once was, where even less is said about the relationship between economy and identity. However, the anthropological literature is full of examples of how claims to identity and cultural distinctiveness are rooted not just in differences in dress, language and food, but in what people do for a living, and how their work practices and ideologies are represented both by themselves and by others. Anthropologists have shown, for instance, how some economic activities may have far greater significance as claims to identity than as ways of making a living. The Shetland crofters studied by Anthony Cohen (1979) persist in tilling their small plots of land, cutting peat and tending their sheep principally because of the symbolic value these activities have in marking out the limits of their community (on the relationship between notions of community and those of personal identity, see A. P. Cohen 1994). The activities themselves may not be profitable, and may in fact be downright 'uneconomical' in that they swallow up capital, time and labour, but they are critical in defining the Shetland crofting community. They distinguish people involved in other kinds of economic activity as 'them', as different and 'other' because they do not practise crofting. Such economic acts may seem irrational, at least when viewed from the perspective of classic Western economic theory, which emphasizes maximizing profit, but they enable Shetlanders to construct symbolically the boundaries of their community and sense of self. In this regard, crofting can be seen as symbolic rather than (or as well as) economic labour. As we shall see, all of the examples in this chapter stress this close connection between identity and economy.

With some notable exceptions, anthropologists researching Ireland have had little to say about the state economies of the two parts of the island, and have rarely included them in their analyses as any more than a backdrop. There have been some works of historical anthropology that have traced the island's economic development, such as the emergence of the linen industry and manufacturing sector in the north (M. Cohen 1993; Jenkins 1984) and the growth of a market town in the south (Gulliver and Silverman 1995; Silverman 1993), linking these to ethnic polarization, socio-economic class and political hegemony (see especially Silverman 2001). And other work has focused on the provision and impact of start-up capital for small businesses (Dilley 1989), on equal opportunities legislation, labour supply and fair employment (Ingram 1997; McLaughlin

1989), on community development and economic change (Curtin and Varley 1989; Shutes 1989), and on the impact of multinational corporations on local work practices and traditional livelihoods, especially among farmers and fishermen (Eipper 1986, 1989; Ruane 1989). Of course, in one sense, given the discipline's historical holistic approach, all of Irish ethnography has been concerned with economic activities, and with how these are embedded in Ireland's diverse social, cultural and political milieu. In almost everything that has been written by anthropologists about Ireland we find at least some reference to economic issues. What we consider to be 'economic', and how we separate it out analytically from other social and cultural phenomena, depends of course on what we mean by the term and how we define it. In its broadest sense, we think of the economy in terms of the activities, objects, relationships and institutions that are important in the processes of production, distribution and exchange of objects, ideas and images. The economy 'is the portion of the world where human beings are tied to each other through their relationships with things they have created' (Wilk 1996: 32).

Nevertheless, some of the more sustained explorations of Irish economic life have focused on the small-scale, the irregular and the unofficial. It is these aspects of the economy that have been explored to great effect in an anthropology of Ireland that, rightly or wrongly, has largely left the wider formal economy of big business, large-scale manufacturing and banking to the other social sciences. Accordingly, we emphasize such work on the informal economy here, focusing particularly on three main examples – the Irish Travellers, the long-term unemployed and cross-border consumers – all of whose economic activities have been viewed as 'other' in different ways. (These examples emphasize informal economic activity in urban areas. But we should not forget the informal cooperative exchanges that often characterize, or once characterized, the rural economy, and which have been widely documented by anthropologists; for overviews, see J. Bell 1978, 2005: chapter 5; Donnan and McFarlane 1983; Kockel 2002: 44–55; Wilson 1984.)

Like the notion of 'alternative economic spaces', the concept of 'other economies' is 'highly unstable and relational', and can vary through both time and space (Leyshon and Lee 2003: 17–18). But though particular economies that count as 'other' need not always and everywhere remain so, they share certain central characteristics. Some sectors of contemporary Irish economic life, we suggest, can be seen as 'other' in several respects. First, and in an obvious sense, there are those economies associated with particular groups that might be said to occupy an economic niche on the basis of their ethnicity. The Irish Travellers on whom we focus in this chapter are one such group (cf. Okely 1983: chapter 4). Occupying a distinctive niche at the edges of the wider economy, they perform a multiplicity of jobs to survive, and with which they are now stereotypically associated, such as children's work and 'child begging' (Helleiner 2003). Just as early in the last century the Tinkers emerged as an 'othered' economic group (G. Gmelch 1977: 10), and were described in images that sometimes reflected in extreme form those 'othered' images of the Irish in general (Ní Shúinéar n.d.), so too Irish Travellers continue to be othered and occasionally criminalized for the economic activities they pursue today. Although not examined here, it is worth remembering that other minorities in Ireland might similarly be seen as occupying a distinctive economic niche on the basis of their ethnic identity, such as the Chinese (Marger 1989).

The idea of the 'other' economy might also be applied to those who are excluded or exclude themselves from mainstream economic practice and paid employment, and who survive on the margins of Irish economic life. Many of these may earn a living by being involved in the informal, black, hidden, second, shadow or alternative economies, terms which, though they differentiate different kinds of relationship to the formal, 'state' economy (such as legal or illegal), all emphasize the embeddedness of the economic in the social and the cultural. One thing anthropology has been rather good at has been recognizing and researching activities that do not appear to be 'economic' in formal economic terms, or which do not appear at first sight to make an economic contribution. The literature offers many examples of how a broad and diverse range of legal and illegal small-scale informal economic activities are organized and operate, from pilfering at work to prostitution, and from baby-sitting networks to doing 'homers'(i.e. doing odd jobs for personal gain using the resources of one's salaried employment). (For a typology based on the legal status of different activities, see Henry [1981]. Jenkins and Harding [1986] provide an overview of informal economic activity in Northern Ireland under the following headings: self-employment, the household, the community, homework and outwork, between work and employment, informality on the job, corruption and crime.) Participation in formal and informal economies need not be mutually exclusive, and individuals may move between one and the other, or operate simultaneously in both. These 'other' economies do not exist independently of the formal economic sector, but depend upon and contribute to it in a variety of ways, some of which we consider below.

Ireland's other economies might be seen as 'other' in yet a further sense. There are those who are othered by the nature of their economic practice, and who are constructed as culturally different by those who earn their living by other means. In this case, the character of one's economic pursuits is used symbolically to draw a boundary between 'us' and 'them', as with the Shetland crofters. Sometimes all of these senses of economic 'othering' operate simultaneously, and ethnicity, exclusion and economic practice coincide, as with the case of the Travellers considered below.

We have already mentioned that anthropologists have been rather good at researching the economically less obvious, the unfamiliar and the marginal, and have tended to focus on just such aspects of the Irish economy. In a very basic sense, then, by '*other* economies' we mean, simply, those dimensions of economic life that other disciplines have been more inclined to leave out, but which figure prominently in Irish ethnography.

The Irish Travellers

The Travellers – or Travelling People, Tinkers and Gypsies, as they have been variously called – have long caught the imagination of scholars working in Ireland, and are among the more widely studied populations on the island. Much of the discussion has focused on the question of origins, and on the distinctiveness or otherwise of Traveller culture and way of life, and of their language (referred to as Cant, Gammon or Shelta; see Kirk and Ó Baoill 2002). At issue here is not just an arcane interest in where these people might have come from (and there is a range of opinion on this, from the most eccentric to the well-reasoned; see Ní Shúinéar 1994 for an overview), but a concern with informing and formulating public policy in a manner appropriate to the needs, demands and rights of the Traveller population. More recently, this debate has been framed in terms of ethnicity, and has specifically asked whether or not Travellers can be considered a minority 'ethnic' group. This question has become more pressing as anti-Traveller racism has steadily increased (or at least has become more widely reported; we address this racism more fully in chapter seven), and raises a number of associated issues, from Traveller education and children's schooling to health care, sedentarization and the provision of permanent sites or hardstands where mobile Travellers can legally camp and access services and facilities.

To varying degrees anthropology has engaged almost all of these debates. If anthropologists in Ireland have sometimes been slow to enter public policy discussion in other contexts, this has not been true of their work on Travellers, much of which has had a direct or indirect bearing on the practical concerns of Traveller life. Some of this work has been specifically commissioned as policy-related research (e.g. Butler 1985), or has sought to bring the lives and history of Irish Travellers to the attention of a general readership (see S. B. Gmelch 1986), while yet other work with more academic origins has had clear policy implications. Settlement policies and provision of hardstands (Butler 1985; S. B. Gmelch and Gmelch 1976; Helleiner 1993), culture, ethnicity and language (S. B. Gmelch and Gmelch 1976; Ní Shúinéar 1994), and social exclusion and racism (Helleiner 2000; Helleiner and Szuchewycz 1997) have all been of concern to anthropologists working with Irish Travellers, and also to the discipline's professional body on the island – the Anthropological Association of Ireland – which organized a two-day conference in Dublin in 1991 that resulted in an edited collection addressing these issues (see McCann, Ó Síocháin and Ruane 1994).

Almost all of these issues have been seen as tied in one way or another to the Traveller economy, which has been presented by many commentators as radically different in certain key respects from the formal, waged labour economy of the wider society. Among the features often emphasized as distinctive of Traveller work are its adaptability and seasonality, and the necessity of geographical mobility. These features were especially prominent historically, and were characteristic of a 'traditional' economy (G. Gmelch 1977: chapter 2) in which Travellers traversed Ireland offering a variety of services to the island's farming population. These could range from the provision of casual labour at times of particularly intense activity in the agricultural cycle, such as harvest, weeding and turnip cutting, to more specialized services that have become stereotypically associated with Irish Travellers, such as tinsmithing. Travellers made and repaired an assortment of tin articles for both domestic and agricultural use, including mugs, buckets, cooking pots and kettles, and sometimes supplemented this practice by sharpening knives, shears and scythes. But tinsmithing was rarely the only task that Travellers performed, however much this came to characterize them in the popular and scholarly imagination. The rural economy was such that surviving by tinsmithing alone was not a viable option, and Travellers had to be adept at a range of other activities that might include scavenging, peddling, telling fortunes and begging as well as the seasonal farm labouring already mentioned. Peddlers played a crucial role, for example, in distributing goods in rural areas where the local farming population could not easily visit towns on shopping trips (G. Gmelch 1977: 18). Multi-occupationality thus also tended to characterize Traveller economic activities as much as their ability to move and adapt according to seasonal demands (Helleiner 2000: 132), and this again contributed to the sense of an 'other' economy, one distinct from the largely occupationally specialized and sedentary economic activities of most of the wider population.

In a pioneering and influential monograph, George Gmelch (1977, 1985) set out to examine how this 'traditional' Traveller economy had changed as Ireland modernized and urbanized. After the Second World War, many of the goods and services offered historically by Travellers were no longer required: mass consumption of cheap and durable domestic and agricultural artefacts replaced the products of the tinsmith, while agricultural mechanization reduced the demand for casual labour. Many predicted the demise of Irish itinerant society and culture as Travellers increasingly migrated to the cities and set up camp on the edge of town or on more central 'waste' ground. However, on the basis of fieldwork carried out with Sharon Bohn Gmelch in the Traveller camp of Holylands on the outskirts of Dublin, Gmelch argues that Travellers quickly adapted to city life by developing strategies to exploit the resources and opportunities offered by their new environment.

Many of the economic activities they had pursued in the past were still to be found, such as scavenging, begging and doing odd jobs. But the city also offered possibilities unavailable or less easy to realize with a nomadic, rural lifestyle. Scrap metal was easier to collect, sort and sell in Dublin than was the case in the countryside, and recycling metals soon became a major source of income for many urban-based Travellers. Gmelch (1977: 63–9) describes how Travellers would systematically work neighbourhoods, going from door to door soliciting broken pots and pans, bicycles and car batteries, as well as collecting old cars and obsolete machinery from businesses and construction sites. These were taken back to the camp site to be sorted, stripped and cleaned before being sold to the scrap dealer. At the time of Gmelch's fieldwork, horse and cart were still used to collect and transport scrap metal, and though gradually replaced by vans and lorries, these still gave to the Traveller an exotic otherness in the eyes of many Dubliners. It was also easier to claim welfare and unemployment benefits, or the 'dole', while based in the city, since benefits had to be collected in person each week at the same labour exchange, and this was problematic while travelling the country (see G. Gmelch 1977: 46–7). As a result, more Travellers became sedentary, or at least began to travel less, or travelled for shorter periods of time and over shorter routes.

In these urban economic adaptations, to use Gmelch's term, we once again see how Travellers earned their living by taking on the tasks that most other people did not want to do, or by finding or creating a niche in the economy that they could exploit to advantage because of their mobility, adaptability and use of family labour. Although the economic activities of Gmelch's Dublin Travellers were poorly regarded and easily represented as 'other', their contribution was crucial for supplying raw materials to dealers at competitive rates. It was crucial in other ways too, as Gmelch notes:

> The Travellers' scavenging serves a valuable economic and ecological function in Irish society. Tons of steel, iron, copper, lead, and other metals would be wasted if not reclaimed in this way; the Travellers also recycle used clothing, appliances, and furniture from the middle class to the poor. Dublin metal merchants estimate that Tinkers account for about half of all the scrap metal collected outside of industry. Significantly, they gather the odd bits and pieces – the broken toasters, worn-out washing machines, and rusted drain pipes – that large-scale settled dealers do not bother with. Travellers also save the city of Dublin considerable expense each year by clearing away the hundreds of abandoned or dumped autos. (1977: 70)

While Gmelch's urban Travellers might thus seem to be surviving on the edges of the wider economy, or even outside it altogether, they were nevertheless a part of it, and subject to its fluctuations. When the price of scrap metal fell, Travellers compensated by intensifying the activities of unpaid family labour, as Helleiner (2000: 137) has pointed out. Their economic survival in Dublin depended on such flexibility and the informal deployment of family labour across a range of 'marginal occupations' (G. Gmelch 1977: 25) according to demand, just as it had in the days when they travelled the countryside.

In both rural and urban settings, then, Travellers have managed to earn a living in the interstices of the wider economy and have developed and sustained a lifestyle that has enabled them to exploit economic opportunities that require mobility, flexibility and multi-tasking. Often these activities were seen as disreputable, dirty and demeaning by the settled population. Sometimes they were considered to be a nuisance, and even to verge on the criminal. And sometimes they barely seemed to settled people to be economic activities at all, since they alternated with long periods of apparent inactivity, and mixed the social, domestic and familial with the economic, an approach that drew no hard and fast boundaries between work and leisure, unlike the sharply dichotomized world in which most working Dubliners lived (see G. Gmelch 1977: 34–9). Such characteristics, especially when added to the high rate of Traveller endogamy and the use of a Traveller argot, made the Travellers seem very exotic. For their part, Travellers viewed the sedentary lifestyle and wage labouring of the settled population in similarly negative terms. One young man, who found a well-paid job as a window cleaner, kept it for only three weeks:

There is also a strong levelling tendency within Traveller society which can result in the application of negative sanctions against an individual who takes a job and thus appears to be rising above his proper station in life. Even men who do not themselves desire jobs do not like to see others obtain them. During the three weeks Michael worked for the cleaning firm, he was the target of much abusive gossip. His peers, envious of the money he was able to spend on drink and movies, ridiculed him for having to get up at eight o'clock in the morning and for struggling back to camp exhausted in the evening. Some derisively called him 'buffer' and 'margarine eater' – pejorative labels Holylanders used for settled people. (G. Gmelch 1977: 84–5).

The only way for the young window cleaner to have kept his job would have been to change identity; to drop his claims to be a Traveller and to become absorbed into the settled population. His continued existence as a Traveller was dependent on his continuing to behave as a Traveller, since it was according to their values that he was judged, and these did not include a positive evaluation of wage labouring for anything other than the length of time it took to accumulate sufficient cash to meet a particular need. In this sense, Michael's identity as a Traveller was irrevocably bound up with some kinds of economic activity rather than others, and it was his involvement in this 'Traveller economy' that marked him out as 'other' as far as the surrounding Dublin population was concerned. Traveller reluctance to wage labour can thus be seen in part as stemming from a self-definition that expresses identity according to a rather different set of economic values and practices. To wage labour would be to cease to be a Traveller.

Gmelch suggests that the negative sanctioning of the young Traveller's window cleaning activities acts as a kind of levelling mechanism, a view that would support a widely held perception of nomadic peoples as egalitarian. However, there is some evidence today to suggest that Travellers have changed and are more stratified than this view of 1970s Dublin might imply. Helleiner has recently argued that 'class-based divisions among Travellers are created and simultaneously obscured and legitimated by constructions of Traveller cultural identity that emphasize economic self-sufficiency' (2000: 132). Indeed, she continues, 'Travellers' social relations of work and exchange' produce and reproduce not only the social inequalities of class, but also those of gender and generation. Many of the accounts of the Traveller economy found in the literature are male accounts, and these privilege the involvement and role of men by emphasizing their entrepreneurial ingenuity and perspicacity and by playing down the unpaid contributions of women and children (see Helleiner 2000: chapters 6 and 7). In this sense, the economic contributions of Traveller women are doubly 'hidden', as an 'other' economy within an 'othered' economy, much, in fact, as women's domestic labour and other economic roles have been under-emphasized in the wider society.

The Traveller economy also sometimes entailed the exploitation of other Travellers. Those Travellers who owned transport were in a position to lend money, and some who had a knack for securing a disproportionate share of funds and other benefits targeted at Travellers prospered at the expense of others. Yet, Travellers were forced to maintain the 'elaborated ideology and practice of self-sufficiency and economic agency' as a way of 'challenging racism through the valorizing of male work as central to an ethnicized Traveller identity' (Helleiner 2000: 160). In other words, while Traveller celebration of men's entrepreneurial skills reflected to some extent the realities of Traveller economic life and offered them a means of responding to 'the reality of a racist exclusion from the formal economy', it also tended to obscure, legitimate and reproduce the internal inequalities of their group: those of gender, generation and class.

Unemployment and the Othering of Class

Helleiner's analysis of class-based inequalities among Travellers is to be welcomed for its nuanced and sensitive understanding of the Traveller economy, especially since some of the earlier ethnographic research among Travellers had flattened out the socio-economic differences among them, presenting them as a uniformly economically impoverished group. Walsh (1971), for instance, drew on Oscar Lewis's research in Latin America to present Irish Travellers in terms of a 'culture of poverty'. According to Lewis (1966), populations characterized by a culture of poverty display a constellation of characteristics, which include matrifocal families, a high incidence of lone parenthood, low self-esteem and an orientation to the present and associated inability to defer gratification. Such traits are passed from generation to generation, both reflecting and contributing to a vicious cycle of perpetual impoverishment. Here poverty is seen primarily as a result of cultural values and dispositions, rather than as the result of any inequalities in the social system. This model seemed to some observers to fit the Irish Traveller case. It is difficult to say to what extent such social scientific views actually informed and affected public policy at the time, but they certainly resonated with the prevailing mood of the 1960s and 1970s, when the dominant policy orientation towards Travellers was integrationist and assimilationist, emphasizing education and the incorporation into 'mainstream' society of what was depicted and (mis)understood as a subculture of poverty.

As Helleiner (2000: 12) points out, the work of Sharon and George Gmelch too is sometimes ironically reminiscent of the culture of poverty thesis, even though they explicitly set out to reject it (see S. B. Gmelch 1989), and it also chimed with the policy direction dominant at the time they were carrying out their fieldwork (in the 1970s). Thus they often seemed to support – even if unintentionally – the settlement of Travellers as a solution to what they identified as some of their potentially more dysfunctional adaptations to urban society. Low self-esteem, excessive drinking, withdrawal from social interaction, marital conflict and boredom all seemed to threaten the breakdown of an otherwise adaptive and resilient urban Traveller culture, according to George Gmelch (1977: 160-2), a somewhat pessimistic prognosis that in many ways also recalls the dominant anthropological paradigm of the period that we discussed earlier: that of the dying and pathological peasant community (more usually associated with the rural west but here apparently characteristic of the urban east as well).

Ethnographers and others increasingly recognized, however, that analyses of structural inequalities like race and class, rather than the cultural traits emphasized by the culture of poverty thesis, shed more light on Irish Travellers (cf. MacLaughlin 1995). Some twenty years after the original study had been carried out, the author of the report advocating the application of a culture of poverty model to the Travellers retracted her position (McCarthy 1994), much to the appreciation of Travellers themselves (see, for example, Collins 1994). And while traces of the model periodically resurface, particularly in popular accounts of other chronically poor people such as the long-term unemployed and other socially excluded groups, anthropological analyses are now more likely to view the identity and culture of such groups within a context of socio-economic and structural inequality rather than as the 'cause' or 'explanation' for their position.

A team of ethnographers from the National University of Ireland in Maynooth has done much to understand life in a housing estate on the outskirts of Dublin in terms of just such structural inequalities. Cherry Orchard is a 'neighbourhood in trouble', marginalized socially and economically even though it is only a few miles from the city centre glitz of the Celtic Tiger: it is an area of high crime, high rates of heroin use and high unemployment, particularly among young, unskilled men. Many of the residents are dependent on welfare payments or on what they can earn on 'the side', and have all the characteristics of an 'underclass' who feel themselves largely forgotten by the state and the Dublin Corporation, which they say have dumped them into the 'skip' of Cherry Orchard as 'the last stop on the line before final eviction from the system' (Saris and Bartley 2002: 15). And yet, Saris and Bartley imply, Cherry Orchard is as much a part of the Celtic Tiger as the prosperity and opulence to be found in Dublin's upmarket suburbs. It is just that Cherry Orchard is the price to be paid for other people's affluence, kept as far as possible out of sight 'just beneath the surface of everyday life' (Saris and Bartley 2002: 19), and its residents othered as the hidden cost of other people's economic success.

Cherry Orchard's relationship to the wider economy can be read off the graffiti and murals found throughout the neighbourhood. One piece of graffiti is particularly revealing. It is a childlike drawing of a figure with arms and legs outstretched, the arms scarred from intravenous drug use and the legs inscribed with 'USA'. On the chest is emblazoned 'Nike' underlined by the tick that is this company's trademark. In one hand the figure holds a syringe, about a quarter full. While it would be easy to overinterpret a drawing so symbolically loaded in the context of Cherry Orchard, Saris and Bartley offer a persuasive reading of this grotesque cartoon that ties the Cherry Orchard economy to the economy beyond:

> The instrument that does the scarring, the hypodermic needle and syringe, is both the privileged channel between the inside and outside of the body and an important means of drawing the life blood of the global economy, money, into local worlds from the outside environment. Robberies at syringe-point became a daily occurrence in Dublin's city centre in the 1990s, and they continue at present. Such crimes do not only threaten, materially and symbolically, the injection of dirt and contagion into the respectable body politic; they also draw into local markets the money that sustains and reproduces a local dystopia. (Saris and Bartley 2002: 19)

As Saris and Bartley explain, the writing on the figure indicates just how closely Cherry Orchard's residents are tied into external economic markets. The USA is the centre of the global market, while Nike is one of the world's most successful international traders. Expensive Nike sportswear is the preferred clothing of the local Cherry Orchard drug dealers because of its association with success (as it and other sports strip are elsewhere). At the same time it is an index of the suffering and exploitation of the workers in the Southeast Asian sweatshops that produced it. Just like the Celtic Tiger metaphor, then, the Nike logo indexes a 'wider world of capital and commodities that elevates some to opulence while ruthlessly confining others to misery' (Saris and Bartley 2002: 19). This is an 'other' side of suburban Dublin (cf. Bartley and Saris 1999), one with an 'other' economy that is the dark side of the Republic's recent economic boom. Integrally bound together, each economy risks contamination by the other in different ways. And yet, they are mutually sustaining, an interdependency which in the case of Cherry Orchard results in the reproduction of its 'underclass', as the quotation above suggests.

In these circumstances, local residents struggle to make ends meet and to generate a positive image of their lives and community. Some achieve this through horse ownership, which in this urban neighbourhood has become a strikingly visible badge of identity and, as the city authorities have tried to curtail the number of horses kept in the area, a symbol of resistance to the state. Conflict over these urban horses is related to class division in Irish society and to the way in which the socially excluded and urban poor have become increasingly ghettoized and segregated in particular neighbourhoods that function like 'national parks' in which people can be herded and controlled. Horse ownership in such areas is seen by those outside them as an irrational and useless pursuit, an exotic and 'other' activity that only further hampers the effective and productive involvement of local residents in the market economy (Saris et al. 2000: 127–9).

Anthropologists have perhaps been at the forefront of social scientists in analysing the everyday economic life of such excluded and disadvantaged populations in Ireland. They have sought to probe behind the survey headlines of rising unemployment rates, increased poverty and economic breakdown to ask how people manage to get by and survive in such economically depressed circumstances. If they have made a singular contribution to the understanding of Irish economic life, it has been to these less formal and potentially less accessible (to the researcher) aspects of it. Only long-term, 'community'-focused fieldwork and ethnographic methods have enabled the sensitivity needed to develop and sustain the relationships of trust through which such understanding can be acquired. Leo Howe's research on the informal economy among the long-term unemployed in two working-class Belfast housing estates is exemplary in this regard.

Hidden Work

Howe's fieldwork focused on the two neighbourhoods of Mallon Park and Eastlough, the former a Catholic area in the west of the city and the latter a Protestant district in the east. Both neighbourhoods had high rates of unemployment at the time Howe carried out his research in the mid-1980s – over fifty per cent in the former and about half of that in Eastlough – and the residents of both relied heavily on welfare benefits, which all found insufficient to meet their needs. The areas differed substantially, however, in their strategies for supplementing their income. As in Dublin's Cherry Orchard, one option was to work in paid employment while claiming benefits, but Howe (1989a, 1989b, 1990) found that attitudes towards 'doing the double' in this way (called 'nixers' in the south;

Kierans and McCormack 2002: 118), and the actual incidence with which it was practised, varied significantly between the two Belfast estates. The unemployed men in Eastlough had largely been made redundant just a few years before Howe began his research, and had been previously employed in the manufacturing sector, particularly shipbuilding and aeronautical engineering, which dominated the local labour market. Such men remained very optimistic about finding future employment in this sector once 'things picked up' and when these industries emerged from the economic recession that characterized the period. Consequently, their job-seeking strategies were extremely focused, submitting applications to the firms in which they had been previously employed, and emphasizing their skills and experience. Informal channels of information via kin, friends and former workmates were kept open as sources of news about possible work, rather than seeking jobs through state agencies such as the Job Market, which was felt to be full of inappropriate and poorly paid positions (despite the potential for distortion of information channelled through informal networks; see Blacking, Byrne and Ingram 1989). Very few of the unemployed Eastlough men interviewed by Howe had engaged in doing the double in any substantial or profitable way, or had done it for any length of time. Because the area was characterized by large firms, and to some extent because of a fear of being caught, there were few realistic options for engaging in undeclared economic activity, and few saw it as anything more than a short-term prospect, a mere 'interruption' rather than a viable replacement for formal, waged employment (Howe 1989a, 1990: 51–8), the absence of which was attributed to either structural or individual factors, depending on context (Howe 1994).

In these respects Mallon Park could not be more different, and Howe's account of doing the double there, with its case histories of an array of imaginative, undeclared money-making ventures, is in striking contrast to Eastlough, where 'there is little point in detailing the double jobs … as they are … rather trivial' (Howe 1990: 79). Long-term and widespread unemployment is not new to Mallon Park, where the formal economy has virtually collapsed, and where all the area's former manufacturing industries have long since disappeared with no apparent hope of recovery. In these circumstances a mix of earning strategies is the only option, and doing the double the only thing keeping the neighbourhood economy afloat. The presence of many small enterprises, the absence of a dominant firm or firms, the greater acceptance of doing the double as a 'way of life', and the unlikely chance of being caught all facilitate involvement in undeclared economic pursuits in Mallon Park. As one man put it: 'the double is the only way to make a living. The way I look at it, it would take me to be coming home with over £100 and there's no jobs like that now' (in Howe 1990: 64). Mallon Park men engage in a range of occupations, from periodic work in the construction industry, to taxi driving, work in shops and scavenging for scrap metal. Most of this work is part-time and irregular, so that it is only in exceptional cases that it becomes a realistic alternative to claiming benefits. Howe (1989b: 166–7) records only one such instance; all other paid work carried out while claiming benefits is either a short-term, one-off job, short-spell jobs at infrequent intervals, work which an individual makes for him- or herself (such as gardening or repairing cars), or more permanent part-time jobs. In most cases, then, doing the double is no more than a supplement to the dole, and cannot replace it. Nor is the double just a way of filling in until the economy improves. Since there are no other local options for making a living, it can never constitute an '*alternative* economy'. Claiming benefits and doing the double are both necessary to survive in an economy that offers few other opportunities.

Howe argues that these different strategies for coping with unemployment in Mallon Park and Eastlough are a consequence not so much of contrasting Catholic and Protestant orientations to work, as of the nature of the labour market in the two neighbourhoods. It is the relationship between the formal availability of jobs and the possibilities of engaging in informal economic activities that generates such different strategies, and where Mallon Park has more informal than formal opportunities for employment, the reverse is true in Eastlough (Howe 1989b). Catholic and Protestant may thus apparently have different ways of being unemployed, but it is their economic situation that accounts for this rather than divergent cultural preconceptions *per se*. Nevertheless, these local differences in the labour market do generate two contrasting sets of stereotypes, which for each side of the sectarian divide function to reproduce the ethnic 'other'. In contrast to what they see as their own reliability and industriousness, the Protestant unemployed of Eastlough characterize their Catholic counterparts as lazy, feckless scroungers adept at milking welfare benefits for all they can get. They regard Catholics as exploiting the system and threatening the state by doing the double and so avoiding tax. For their part, Catholics see Protestants as bigoted, narrow-minded and money-centred, which they contrast with their own 'tolerance, openness and interest in culture' (Donnan and McFarlane 1986a: 386). 'Doing the double has … become part of the [Protestant] stereotypical representation of Catholics. In a sense, Protestants who do the double reduce the cultural distance between themselves and Catholics' (Howe 1990: 55). A willingness to embrace participation in the informal economy has thus become a part of the othering process in a society divided along ethnopolitical lines.

At the same time, however, the residents of Mallon Park and Eastlough share much in common as members of a working class subject to the fluctuations of national and international markets, and even though historically culture and sectarian division at the level of the local neighbourhood have mediated the effects of such instability to the relative advantage of Protestants (see Howe 1990: 68–76; Jenkins 1984), in neither case has unemployment been averted altogether. In responding to their situation – whether by submitting multiple applications to their former employer or by finding some other less formal way of gaining a livelihood – the unemployed of both neighbourhoods have their position in the region's socioeconomic system confirmed. Whether Catholic or Protestant, the unemployed in Mallon Park and Eastlough are othered in the class system by virtue of their lack of access to power and wealth.

Howe's analysis has little to say about gender and unemployment, though this has been the focus of other ethnographic research. Eithne McLaughlin (1991, 1997), for instance, shows how unemployed men are often inflexible in their job seeking, refusing to apply for jobs that are casual or part-time, not so much because these jobs are usually classed as 'women's work', as out of a belief that because they are seen in this way, employers are unlikely to employ a man. Such jobs are also thought to be low-paid. McLaughlin (1989) also explores the popular image of the 'female breadwinner' in Derry City, where it is believed that women assume more power within the household when they enter paid employment following a partner's redundancy. However, despite this notion being widely held across the city, McLaughlin (1989: 59) argues that it is something of a myth, and that gender roles in Derry are little different from those elsewhere in Northern Ireland. Widely influential in the policy field, McLaughlin has been something of a lone voice in the ethnography of women's unemployment, which in many respects has been just as 'hidden' as the other practices considered here.

'Doing the double' and its relationship to economy and identity are not just features of Ireland's cities. In the Northern Ireland borderlands, at the land border between the Republic and Northern Ireland (see chapter six), it has been common practice in some circles to do the double on both sides. This has been especially true among nationalists on the northern side, many of whom can claim unemployment benefits in both constituencies, and even work off the books on both sides of the border. This 'doing the quadruple' (Wilson 1998c) depends on supportive and sympathetic social networks, and in contrast to the case presented by Howe, where the Belfast economy is segregated into friendly and hostile zones (Howe 1990: 72), the borderlands of the Republic are viewed consistently by Northern Ireland Catholics as welcoming. It is to the 'othering' economics of that borderland to which we now turn.

Bargain Hunters and Boycott Busters

So far we have noted some of the ways in which economic activities can be used to express identity and mark out ethnic and class boundaries in different parts of Ireland. Boundaries of another kind are marked out by informal economic activities that cross from one part of Ireland to another, as the activities of the smugglers and cross-border shoppers considered in this section exemplify. When consumers and entrepreneurs cross state borders, they move from one economic space to another, from 'our' economy to 'their' economy, often in the hope of capitalizing on the opportunities and transformations of value that such border-crossing entails (cf. Donnan and Wilson 1999: 107–8). These opportunities may be economic, but such crossings may also raise questions of identity, and of just whose economy it is in which one is participating. Where state boundaries intersect and cross-cut those of ethnicity, as is the case at the Irish border, the notion of what is 'our' economy may shift and blur: in one context it may be taken to correspond to the economy of the state in which one lives, in another – as we shall see below – it may be held to encompass those who live on the other side of the border with whom one shares the same identity. And as the parameters of 'our' economy vary, so too obviously do the boundaries of the 'other' economy. In the case of shoppers, such identifications may determine where and how they spend their money.

Many commentators have remarked on the strikingly different development of the economy in Northern Ireland and the Irish Republic. The former was characterized historically by the dramatic growth of the manufacturing industry (in linen and shipbuilding in particular) and by early urbanization, while the latter remained a primarily rural society and economy until comparatively recently. Divergent stereotypical representations paralleled these two trajectories. In a set of stereotypes that recall and historically underpin the contrasting stereotypes of the Catholic and Protestant unemployed mentioned in the previous section, the Republic characterized Northern Ireland economic life as cut-throat, impersonal and money grabbing, while the north viewed the Republic as economically backward, moribund and handicapped by an irrational system of patronage. As recently as the 1960s and 1970s, travelling from the north to the south was seen by northerners as a journey into the pre-industrial past, with its donkey carts, turf cutters and absent infrastructure. In the eyes of southerners, in contrast, to travel north was to experience the coldness of capitalism with its hard-driven sales pitch and ruthless business deal (for changes in Catholic and Protestant constructions of the Northern Ireland economy over the last thirty years, see Kelleher 2003: 145–7). Irrespective of on which side one stood, the view across the border was thus of a distinctly 'other' economy.

When the Irish border was first established in the early 1920s, economic contact across it was facilitated by a range of factors: the absence of export tariffs on goods exported from the Republic to the United Kingdom; the use of the same monetary system on both sides; and the fact that no identification was needed to cross it. Yet by the 1990s each side of the border looked largely to its own metropolitan core as the centre of activity and patronage, a situation aggravated by the poor infrastructure in the borderlands and by the closure for security reasons of many cross-border roads following the outbreak of sectarian violence in the 1960s. Trade between north and south was limited, with Northern Ireland exporting only 6 per cent of its manufactured goods to the Republic, and the Republic sending just

3 per cent of its output to Northern Ireland (D'Arcy and Dickson 1995: xv). Cross-border economic cooperation and contact was limited in what had become for all intents and purposes a 'back-to-back' economy. Officially recognized as 'amongst the least economically and socially developed [areas] in Europe' (European Economic and Social Committee, cited in Robb 1995: 133), and economically marginal to the two states which it separates, the Irish border has been the focus of successive policies aimed at economic and social regeneration. It nevertheless remains an area of high underemployment, high emigration and sectarian polarization. Anthropologists have focused particularly on how sectarian loyalties play a substantial role in shaping everyday local economic practice there, and have suggested that two economies exist, a Catholic and a Protestant one, each of which sees its counterpart as the 'other', reflecting the back-to-back relationship of north and south outlined above. These parallel economies are highly visible in relation to the provision of goods and services.

Rosemary Harris (1972) has described how in one border town in the early 1950s sectarian loyalties were responsible for limiting competition between shops, so that though the town was small, it could still support a relatively large number of businesses. Townsfolk mainly patronized their co-religionists, and a shopkeeper could only hope to attract customers of the other religion by offering services unavailable anywhere else (cf. Donnan and McFarlane 1983: 130–1). More recent ethnography has confirmed the continued resilience of this pattern of segregated shopping where the religion of the trader rather than the price of goods determines where people shop (Murtagh 1996, 1998). Anthropologists have built on these accounts of segregated shopping by researching consumer relations across the border. They have identified two types of cross-border shopper, referred to here as bargain hunters and boycott busters, to show how the nature and meaning of cross-border consumption reflects and is transformed by wider economic and political developments.

Cross-border shopping, which shades into smuggling where tax is avoided, has a long if limited history in relations between Northern Ireland and the Republic. The border divided villages, and in some cases people's homes and fields, giving rise to numerous colourful accounts of how goods were sometimes 'smuggled' by being brought in through the back door and out of the front, or of pipes laid across fields to pump fuel from one jurisdiction to another depending on where it was cheaper. The Second World War saw an informal cross-border trade in commodities only available on one side or the other. Travellers were sometimes allegedly the source of such goods (see G. Gmelch 1977: 17, 71). By the 1950s and into the 1960s, shoppers travelled north mainly for 'condoms, hats, [and] cheap butter' (O'Faolain 1996: 64). But as Wilson has shown (1993c, 1995; Donnan and Wilson 1999: 120–2), it was not until the 1980s that cross-border shopping dramatically increased following the Republic's entry into the European Monetary System and the consequent fluctuation of its currency values in relation to the pound sterling. Cheaper prices and greater availability of some goods had always been the attraction, particularly for those in the Republic who did their shopping in the north, but by the 1980s the possibilities of obtaining a bargain had become so great that even those normally deterred by the threat of violence were prepared to take the risk. In October 1987 consumer prices in the Republic were running at approximately 15 per cent above those in Northern Ireland, so the savings could be considerable. In 1986, for example, there was a 30 per cent difference in the cost of alcohol, with similar savings on the cost of petrol and tobacco, making these the most frequent purchases of the southern shoppers in addition to the television sets and VCRs on which hundreds of pounds could be saved (Wilson 1993c: 296). Given such savings, it was not uncommon for coachloads of consumers to travel from the other end of Ireland for a bout of frenzied shopping before the long journey home. As a result, business boomed in border town economies long marginalized by violence and isolation, and new commercial premises and consumer outlets were hastily constructed to meet the demand.

As far as the southern exchequer was concerned, however, this 'other' economy just over the border and beyond its control was a drain on state coffers that had to be stopped. By the mid-1980s cross-border shopping accounted for almost 10 per cent of the total expenditure of households in border areas (Fitzgerald et al. 1988: xiv). Long-distance southern bargain hunters spent even more in the north, with one estimate putting the figure as high as IR£300 million in 1986 alone (Fitzgerald et al. 1988: 78). Systematic demands began to be made to stop the shopping, and to stem the massive loss of revenue for the Irish government. Disgruntled shopkeepers just south of the border, pointing to the marked decline in their profits, added their voice to the protest. This loss of revenue, both to the government and to local shopkeepers in the south, became so critical that the Republic risked the wrath of the European Union to stop it by ruling that only those outside its jurisdiction for more than forty-eight hours would be legally entitled to a tax-free allowance on imported goods from the north. The European Union eventually compelled the Irish government to modify this measure, though the Republic's policies continued to be more restrictive than other member states.

Large-scale cross-border shopping now declined rapidly as the Republic began to enforce the new rule, stopping travellers at border checkpoints, and imposing value added tax and excise duties on those who could not demonstrate that they had been out of the country for longer than the period required. At around this time many a law-abiding citizen was turned smuggler almost overnight. These developments were enormously damaging to the economies of those northern commercial centres which had come to depend on this trade. Sales dropped dramatically, and while shoppers still travelled north, they did so much less frequently. By 1989 the cross-border trade in electrical appliances had all but ceased.

Wilson (1993c) suggests that this disruption to the local cross-border economy must be seen in a wider context, in terms of policies enacted by the state and by the European Union. It is, in part, through the Single European Market and the promotion of free trade that the European Union hopes better to integrate its member states. However, Wilson argues, comparability of prices is likely to rupture emergent socio-cultural relations at the Irish border, so that the process of European Union integration may ironically end up by strengthening 'the symbolic boundaries between Border towns, creating less of a common culture and more of an international divide' (1993c: 298). While careful not to over-emphasize the positive effects of consumer relations, given their relatively fleeting and impersonal nature, Wilson suggests that cross-border shopping has had a beneficial impact on cross-border relations, 'transcend[ing] ethnic, national, and sectarian barriers' and fostering 'ties in the face of ethnic and national prejudices, values, and war' (1995: 240, 253). However, in the mid-1990s cross-border shopping took a more sinister turn, as a strategy to isolate those who did not share one's religious and political allegiance. Widespread civil unrest surrounded a bitter dispute over the 'right' of the Protestant Orange Order to march through a Catholic neighbourhood in Portadown, a town Orangemen regarded as 'Protestant' (see chapter five and Fig. 2.3). Militant nationalists expressed their frustration and anger by erecting roadblocks, and by boycotting Protestant businesses on both sides of the border, even if owned by their neighbours and fellow villagers. Protestants promptly responded by calling for a boycott of Catholic businesses, and by demanding that in future Protestants should only buy Protestant goods, extending the existing practice of segregated shopping by systematically organizing it rather than leaving it to the will of individual consumers (Donnan 1999). Once again busloads of shoppers could be observed heading purposefully up and down and across the border, but this time their goal was not the pursuit of the cross-border bargain. Protestant businessmen operated 'boycott-busters' at weekends and evenings when coachloads of consumers were bussed to towns and villages where Protestant businesses were felt to be under threat, even though the shoppers involved often had to pay higher prices for the privilege.

In one case, then, it was the possibility of a bargain that stimulated cross-border shopping in Ireland. In another case, cross-border shopping was encouraged by elevating ethnic loyalties above economic gain. In both cases, though, these grassroots economic activities lie outside and beyond the reach of the formal economy, which has to enact special legislation or introduce unique measures to bring them under its control. In this sense, they are truly 'other' economies, set apart from the official and regulated economy of so much of everyday life. Though not in themselves illicit or illegal, they are resistant and even subversive – unruly economies that allow the revenue of the nation to leak out beyond the boundaries of the state, and apparently defy the rules of formal economics that advocate pursuit of profit.

Economies of Subversion and Resistance

In this chapter we have examined what anthropologists working in Ireland have had to say about economic relationships and activities on the island, and have suggested that by concentrating on the informal and unofficial, much of such work has emphasized and brought to light those aspects of economic life that many other disciplines regard as economically marginal. While they may lack the loud roar of the Tiger, such 'other' economic pursuits not only provide a living for large sections of the population, but they also function as a means by which to express and sustain a sense of identity that distinguishes those who practise them from others in their midst. And where economists and other social scientists have been good at sighting tigers, anthropologists, with their willingness to stick around, have perhaps been better able to target more elusive game. In this respect anthropologists of Ireland have followed the lead of anthropologists in general by focusing on informal and hidden economies and on the social and cultural embeddedness and implications of economic activities, where the practices of 'other' economies are simultaneously the practices of the 'othering' of class, ethnic and national identities.

Although by no means a defining characteristic, one of the striking features of the 'other' economies outlined in this chapter is their ambivalent and at times strained and conflictual relationship to the state. In some cases the reasons for this are obvious. It is because the economic activity in question is illegal. This is certainly true of doing the double. As Howe elaborates, the British government stamped down hard on those who sought to claim welfare benefits while in paid employment. Neighbourhood surveillance of claimants' movements, doorstep questioning of family members, and rigorous checking and monitoring of claims by social security staff were measures introduced to prevent and limit benefit fraud, often at a cost that far outweighed the money saved. Everyday practice in social security offices reproduced a commonsensical and widely held distinction between what were seen as the 'deserving' and 'undeserving' unemployed, and those classified as 'undeserving' found themselves in a vicious spiral whereby the more assertively and confidently they tried to claim their entitlements, the more difficult and less likely it became that they would receive them (see Donnan and McFarlane 1997d; Howe 1985). Such tensions between social security counter staff and benefit claimants could only strain an already asymmetrical, disempowering and hierarchical relationship.

In their everyday economic pursuits, Travellers and the residents of Cherry Orchard also frequently grate up against the agents of the state, and both have experienced problematic relationships with the police, council officials, government bureaucrats, health workers and school staff. Travellers, for instance, have been subject to surveillance, control and harassment by the police, particularly over the location of their roadside campsites (Helleiner 1993, 2000: 74), and had an especially strained relationship with the Irish state during the 1960s and 1970s when the Republic's Traveller settlement policy threatened their mobility and thus their means of livelihood. Traveller children's periodic and repeated absence from school because they have been helping with the family business has frequently brought them and their parents into conflict with teachers and officials, as too in Cherry Orchard, where about one third of children skip school in order to participate in the 'thriving heroin and cannabis trade' (Kierans and McCormack 2002: 116). In Cherry Orchard, the public housing authority in Dublin evicted those they saw as the most troublesome tenants in an attempt to control drug dealing, while the Gardaí (police), who were recruited mainly from middle-class or rural backgrounds, began to lump all activity on the estate into 'street culture' and 'criminality', thereby justifying what Saris and Bartley (2002: 15) refer to as a 'warfare model of policing' that could do little other than exacerbate the already tense relations with residents.

While some of the 'other' economic activities we have described may border on the criminal, others verge on the subversive, and sometimes seem to be adopted solely as a strategy of resistance to the state. Some welfare officers and some Protestant unemployed, for example, believed that many Catholic unemployed worked the double and exploited the benefit system as 'tactics to sabotage the Northern Ireland state' (Howe 1990: 55, 1998; see also Jenkins and Harding 1986: 31). And despite their declared loyalty to this same state, Northern Ireland Protestants themselves were not averse to occasional acts of non-compliance and defiance. The 'boycott busters' in the 1990s, for instance, may have been responding to threats to the businesses of their fellow Protestants, but they were also signalling their grave dissatisfaction with what they regarded as a tendency for the state to support the Catholic position. Indeed, Protestant actions in shopping across the border and outside the state, with the loss of revenue involved, were all the more powerful for the fact that the state outside of which they shopped was the very one to which they otherwise professed allegiance. In Cherry Orchard, residents resisted what they saw as police oppression and state neglect through a culture and economy of running horses (Saris et al. 2000), and by blockading government attempts to construct further public housing in the area (Kierans and McCormack 2002). Alongside these visible and open conflicts with the state are sometimes more muted forms of resistance, such as footdragging, feigned ignorance and mock compliance, strategies adopted particularly when dealing with bureaucrats (and, if detected or suspected, feeding in to the distinction between the 'deserving' and the 'undeserving' mentioned above). Some aspects of Ireland's other economies thereby bear comparison to Scott's (1990) 'hidden transcripts' in so far as they act as ciphers which contain a shared repertoire of strategies for expressing discontent towards the state and its agents in ways that strengthen a group by symbolically establishing its boundaries (cf. Kierans and McCormack 2002: 122). Nevertheless, we must be careful not to exaggerate the power exercised through informal economic activities, and not to over-emphasize the role of resistance (Howe 1998; Kockel 2002: 99).

The economies we have been considering here, then, remain 'other' in so far as they evade and even actively resist the efforts of the state to classify, monitor and control and even eradicate them altogether. By standing outside the state and its formal economic structures at the same time as they engage with them, such economies cannot easily be counted, regulated and managed. Despite state attempts to tax, integrate and 'normalize' them, such other economies continue to survive and thrive and so also do the diverse identifications that spring from them. Questions of identity, resistance and support for the state and its legal structures inevitably lead anthropologists to consider other cultural dimensions to the creation and wielding of social and political power. In the next chapter we consider the part played by cultural performance in the construction and representation of contemporary Irish society.

–5–

Re-presenting 'Irishness'

Ideas or systems of ideas do not … float about in incorporeal space; they acquire substance through communication in discourse and performance.

Eric Wolf (1999: 6)

Many commentators have remarked on how recent transformations in Ireland have
resulted in an explosion of new forms and ways of being 'Irish'. Globalization,
Europeanization, the Celtic Tiger, the peace process and secularization are among
the factors usually listed as having stimulated a more liberal, cosmopolitan and
diverse society, a society more open to a multiplicity of identities that is a far cry
from an Ireland that appeared to be stalled in a dominant Catholic and rural past.
Some have characterized this new Ireland as post-national (Kearney 1997). Others
have argued that a diversity and plurality of ways of being Irish always underlay
historic nation-building narratives of homogeneity (cf. B. Graham 1997b *passim*).
And yet others maintain that the old ways of being Irish with their oppositional
nationalisms are still never far below the surface, forever threatening to bubble up
at any moment (Ruane 1994; Shirlow 2003a). As we have argued above, the reinvention of Irish identities depends to a great extent on past notions of local and
national identity, but which notions, and to what extent, are matters of ethnographic and other forms of empirical inquiry. Whatever stance is taken, however,
all seem agreed that an identity as 'Irish' has recently been undergoing a dramatic
transformation, in changes that raise the sometimes divisive issues of authenticity
and tradition, wherein one is often called upon to take sides in the continuing
culture wars of Ireland, North and South. As one wag remarked on the introduction of the smoking ban to public houses in the Republic of Ireland in 2004 – an
issue referred to as 'the most calamitous cultural change in the country since the
Great Famine of 1847' (cited in *The Guardian*, 27 March 2004) – 'soon the only
real Irish pub will be in Brussels!'

In this chapter we consider some of the different ways of representing and
demonstrating Irishness, and explore how it has been variously performed, achieved
and imagined in a range of contexts that have been the subject of ethnographic
study. Communal acts of remembering and celebration offer one kind of opportunity for the 'creation' and 're-creation' of Ireland and Irishness both at home and
abroad, especially in the heritage and tourist industries. In the mid-1990s, for

instance, the 150th anniversary of the Famine was marked by several years of commemorative events, including the opening of a 200-acre Famine Theme Park in Limerick and a memorial in New York, events quickly followed by the commemorations of the 1798 rising (Foster 2001: 23-36; McLean 1999, 2004). Other kinds of public spectacle have also offered a chance to present and re-present particular versions of Irishness, internationally as well as domestically, such as sporting events, street festivals and other forms of urban cultural display.

Anthropologists have written extensively about such public events, and generally recognize their importance as 'dense concentrations of symbols and their associations that are of relevance to a particular people' (Handelman 1998: 9), even when they disagree about whether to emphasize their structure or practice, design or enactment. Much of this work has focused on the experiential aspects of public events, arguing that the emotions and passions that are evident there can be best understood through a performative approach like that proposed by Victor Turner (1988; see also Schechner 1995). Turner (1988: 22) was interested in the relationship between the everyday socio-cultural processes of a particular society and what he called, following Milton Singer (1972), their 'dominant genres of "cultural performance"'. This relationship, he argued, is reciprocal rather than unidirectional: a cultural performance does not simply 'reflect' or 'express' the social and cultural relationships in society, but may also be directly or indirectly critical of them, as an 'evaluation ... of the way society handles history' (Turner 1988: 22; 1982: 100–1). In contrast to 'traditional rituals', modern performance genres like the 'spectacle' have the ability 'to subvert the system and formulate alternatives' (Manning 1992: 294). Cultural performances are consequently full of tensions and contradictions, and often operate as contests over different understandings of what they are thought to represent. In this sense, cultural performances are about the exercise of power, as people assert, challenge, undermine or lay claim to one understanding or another. The sporting events, street parades and Eurovision-inspired dance extravaganzas outlined in this chapter have all the elements of theatre and spectacle that the dramaturgical metaphors of performance evoke, and are at the core of transforming national identities.

Troupes and Tropes in Dancing Ireland

In the mid-1990s at the height of the Celtic Tiger boom, the debate about contemporary Irishness and how it should be represented was engendered literally overnight due to a startling and show-stopping performance by a company of Irish 'traditional' dancers that was aired on the international stage of Europe-wide television. This high-octane seven-minute performance, which brought its live audience to their feet and which seemingly transfixed the millions of viewers of the 1994 Eurovision Song Contest, was the first unveiling of *Riverdance*. This performance was no usual display of Irish dancing skill, but a sophisticated combination of elements of glitz, glamour and showbiz excitement that engaged and has sustained the popular imagination ever since. Performances of the shows that derived from that initial television outing continue globally today, despite some indications of growing '*Riverdance* fatigue' (Wulff in press), a result of how *Riverdance* and its stage spin-offs like *Lord of the Dance* have saturated their markets at home and abroad. One thing is clear, though. The short original performance of *Riverdance* was immensely successful, quickly developing into a two-hour stage show that has toured worldwide, and resulted in best-selling videos, DVDs and CDs.

Unlike some other fields of social science, where the subject was neglected until recently, the study of dance has a long history in anthropology, even if it tended to be pushed to the margins of the discipline (see, for instance, Kaeppler 1978, 1992; Mitchell 1956; Spencer 1985; Williams 2003). Nor was dance much studied in Irish ethnography until John Blacking's (1987–8) six-part television series, *Dancing*. Now, however, dance is widely seen as a contemporary cultural product like any other which, far from being dismissed as a pursuit of passing significance, is an activity understood to shape and be shaped by local, national and global forces of modernity (cf. Thomas 1995, 2003). Ethnographers have thus been drawn to *Riverdance* as an event and symbol of changing notions of national and global identities, documenting how it has come to be understood as representing 'Irishness', and disentangling the elements of which it is composed. In so doing, anthropologists have used their approaches to *Riverdance* to contribute to theorizations of the body and of the senses, for as Wulff (2003a, 2003c, in press) shows, dancing has the ability to move people, literally and figuratively, to action and to emotional heights.

One of the remarkable features of *Riverdance: The Show* has been its widespread global appeal and popularity. It has filled stadiums in Europe, America and Australia with audiences drawn from diverse backgrounds, and not just with those interested in dance or with nostalgic memories of a half-remembered homeland. It has spawned new dance companies in Ireland and elsewhere that perform a similar repertoire (in some cases with dancers who broke away from the original show), as well as smaller, localized dance troupes that offer a scaled down and abridged routine in *Riverdance* style for local weddings and corporate entertainment. And it has encouraged many fans to identify with Ireland and the Irish, even where their connections to Ireland are tenuous or non-existent. For many fans and commentators alike, the show quickly came to be seen as a celebration of Irishness, and a symbol of a new-found confidence in Irish identity on the global stage, generating much popular and scholarly debate about its 'authenticity', its relationship to 'traditional' Irish dance, and about what all of this meant for how Irish identity could or should be imagined and 'performed'.

One view in the social science literature has understood the *Riverdance* 'phenomenon' in terms of the commodification of culture, as the packaging and representing of cultural identities and artefacts for commercial gain. This reflects theories about the 'consumption' of Ireland, Irishness and the Irish countryside more generally (see Casey 2003; Milton 1997), some of which see the show as an inherently unequal practice through which to 'maintain and reinforce colonial relations of power' (Negra 2001: 78). *Riverdance* may have helped to generate a new and more self-assured sense of cultural identity, but its principal objective was to make money, which for some critics is a motive, and a capitalistic pattern, at the heart of the new 'Tiger' Irishness. Joyce Sherlock (1999) has suggested that though audiences may respond to sentimental notions of homeland, they are also being manipulated for profit, by a show whose representations and evocations of harmony and community cohesion sit uncomfortably with and sometimes contradict the realities of modern life in Ireland and the Irish diaspora. Much is left out or misrepresented. The female dancers, for example, embody the waif-like figure and the slim, toned bodies of the catwalks, an image that reflects the values and desires of a globalized consumer culture rather than Irish history and society (except perhaps, ironically, by recalling the emaciated bodies of the Famine). Heterosexuality and the nuclear family also feature prominently in the performance, reflecting the wider values of church and capitalist ideology, while the reality of Irish domestic life is often one of family dispersal and a growing population of single people. And the show is also filled with harmonious images of community solidarity, yet through much of the 1990s violent conflict continued to rage in Northern Ireland, and interpersonal and local community violence has risen steadily in the Republic over the same period.

However uplifting the show might be, it is at times a 'distortion' and a 'romantic opiate' that constructs a particular version of Irishness and dulls us to the ways in which consumer capitalism determines how we feel and think. At the same time *Riverdance* is empowering, by offering the promise of 'belonging' to a cultural identity that is sure of itself and to which the audience might aspire, one capable of offering breathtaking skill, choreographic precision and a 'disciplined co-operation' that 'contradicts prejudicial stereotypes of the lazy, "boozy", inefficient, disorganized, spontaneous, fun-loving Irishman' (Sherlock 1999: 209). Going to see the show, Sherlock continues, can take on all the aspects of a 'pilgrimage', where people are rededicated and revitalized as 'Irish', or as 'Irish-American'. In the end, though, she warns us to 'be sceptical of ...nostalgic diversions from the real struggles in consumer capitalism' (Sherlock 1999: 217).

Riverdance thus presents a particular view of Irishness by selecting and performing only certain aspects of 'tradition' that are fashioned according to the demands of the global market, a theme developed by Barbara O'Connor (1998) in her consideration of the 'spectacularization' of Irish dance. O'Connor reminds us that Irish dance has always been selectively presented and shaped by wider political concerns, beginning in the nineteenth century with the Gaelic League's creation of an 'authentic' national canon of dance styles and dance steps as Ireland struggled to become a nation-state (cf. F. Hall 1996: 263). Indeed, she argues, Irish dance might be regarded as having progressed along a three-tier historical trajectory as its geographical range expanded: from the local rural context, where dance was an integral element of domestic and community life; to the national arena, within which it was standardized as an essential component (along with sports and language, as we shall see later) of nineteenth- and twentieth-century Irish cultural nationalism; to its current point, as the 'international' dance style of *Riverdance*. What has characterized this development, she suggests, has been an increasing emphasis on the visual, which initially focused on the costumes and hair styles of young female dancers, with their elaborately Celtic-motifed dresses and 'bouncing curls', and ultimately resulted in the profusion of colour, sound and variety of dance styles that constitute *Riverdance*.

As O'Connor documents, this internationalization and transformation of an 'Irish' dance style into Riverdance has entailed the incorporation of other dance repertoires into the show, such as Spanish flamenco, as well as modifications to the Irish dance form. Increasing emphasis is put on combining high leaps and jumps and extravagant horizontal movements across the stage – movements not typical of Irish dance but incorporated from dance styles (such as ballet) familiar to the audience from elsewhere – with more traditional and exotic elements of Irish dance such as the immobility of the arms against a rigid upper body (see F. Hall 1996). Similarly, the costumes in *Riverdance* are more visual and glitzy and have tended to sexualize the female body in particular, resulting in a dramatic fusion of movement, sound and colour, and in an expression of female sexuality that recalls and intensifies the flirtatious 'sexual grazing' of Dublin set-dancing classes (B. O'Connor 1997: 159). The representation of Irishness which results, then, is a hybrid form, though it is not one which challenges or subverts received and dominant understandings of Irish identity, but is rather one that takes these up and reshapes them for global consumption.

Instead of seeing *Riverdance* as some simple and radical departure or break with tradition, therefore, we should view it in terms of an internationalized Irishness, an identity forged between the 'local' and the 'global' that reverberates with both past and contemporary dance forms. Helena Wulff (2002, 2003a, 2003b, 2003c, in press) develops this theoretical argument in a series of articles that provides some of the richest analyses of *Riverdance*. She emphasizes just such cultural continuities and shows how dance has long been a focus for the working through of different defining elements of Irishness. Locating *Riverdance* in a historical and comparative context, she demonstrates how dance was a feature of nation-building in Ireland and elsewhere, and explains how the show has both drawn on and helped to sustain and even reinvigorate Irish dancing classes across the island and beyond. A form of movement in itself, dance also moves across geographical space when the dancers tour, as well as across the space of the imagination (Wulff 2005). Yet there remains a distinctive and discernible 'Irish' storyline in 'Irish' dance, evident not only in the narrative and thematic content but also in the nature of its 'theatricality' and the posture of the dancers (Wulff 2003b: 73–4; as well as in the stories told about it, see F. Hall 1999). These have clearly been transformed and reworked in *Riverdance*, but they are identifiable and are danced and experienced as 'authentically' Irish by the dancers themselves (Wulff 2002: 127), a conclusion also reached by Barbara O'Connor (2003) in her study of Irish pub dance shows in Dublin's Temple Bar, and evident too among young Irish musicians, who increasingly draw on a range of transnational musical styles (Basegmez 2005).

Observers are thus agreed that *Riverdance* constitutes a transformative moment in representations of Irishness and Irish dance. Standing at the intersection of the local and the global, the present and the past, and of tradition and modernity, it is a powerful illustration of how notions of Irishness are truly at a crossroads. Wulff deploys this metaphor of the crossroads to explore the changing notions of Irishness reflected in Irish dance, and in particular how it has been a focal point for the many convergences between national identity, morality and sexuality. Crossroads is a particularly apt and evocative metaphor in this context, as Wulff notes (and uses as the title of her book), for it recalls not only the crossroads' dances that famously epitomize the Irish dancing of the past, but also a speech in 1943 by Eamon de Valera, in which he is fondly remembered as referring to 'comely maidens dancing at the crossroads' (erroneously, according to Wulff 2003a: 192). Irish dance has thus long been a cultural form where identity and morality meet and intertwine, and where they have been negotiated, contested or established. As Wulff (2003a) shows, in the early twentieth century dance became a focus of moral concern for the Catholic Church because of the potentially licentiousness behaviour it was believed to facilitate and encourage. In chapter three we saw how the Catholic Church sought to impose bodily discipline on Irish men and women, regulating their activities through strict behavioural regimes and limiting opportunities for physical contact. According to Wulff, the rigid upper body posture may have been introduced as part of the package of civilizing the Irish and training them in manners (cf. F. Hall 1996).

Helen Brennan (1999: 123–4) offers a vivid account of the form taken by this disciplining of the dancing body, and describes how in the 1920s Catholic priests sometimes set fire to the wooden platforms used for dancing, or bulldozed them with the parochial car. One colourful tale tells of a Donegal priest who grabbed the shawls from women as they danced so that when they came to the parochial house to reclaim them, he could identify the women and impose a penance, a punishment sometimes subverted by this shawl-snatcher's housekeeper, who secretly returned the garments via the back door. Private dance halls in particular were subject to condemnation, and in 1925 the church issued a statement on the 'evils of dancing' which advocated strict supervision for such 'occasions of sin', a debate that ultimately led to the Public Dance Hall Act of 1935, which required the licensing of dance halls and a tax on the admission price, a development which the church quickly capitalized on by building parochial halls everywhere in which dancing could be legally held (Brennan 1999: 125, 126). As Fintan O'Toole pithily remarked, 'An unsupervised dance was not an Irish Dance', for all Irish dancing was 'a homage to the holy trinity of Catholicism, Irish nationalism and sexual continence' (1997a: 147).

The political and moral control of dance thus became one means for those cultural nationalists wishing to impose their particular view of Irishness, and, as we noted earlier, the Gaelic League introduced dancing classes and competitions in an effort to impose a uniformity and standardization of style, one that would clearly distinguish Irish dancing from foreign forms of dance, especially those of the English. Irish dancing thus came to be one way in which 'to embody the history of Ireland', a process of nation-building 'the latest brick ... [of which] ... is *Riverdance*' (Wulff 2003a: 186–7). And while there may be different, contested and even resistant versions of Irishness performed through dance, as Wulff is careful to point out, especially in her discussion of contemporary dance forms, she concludes that Irish dancing and *Riverdance* 'have represented and created different versions of Irish national identity and ... played some role in the building of an Irish nation, first as part of the Gaelic cultural nationalist revival and now as a part of Ireland as a modern European nation' (Wulff 2003a: 190; 2002: 133).

Wulff argues that developments in technology have been central to these transformations. Television, for instance, was responsible for first exposing *Riverdance* to the millions of viewers internationally watching the Eurovision Song Contest, and has subsequently screened the many trailers, documentaries and feature programmes about *Riverdance* and Irish dancing that extended the show's popularity and were usually broadcast in advance of a local performance. Similarly, the video of the show and the CD of the soundtrack were bestsellers. Above all, however, it was the technological innovations employed in the staging of the performance itself that played a central and significant part in its overall success. In particular, Wulff suggests, it was the insertion of small microphones in the dancing shoes of the lead dancers that was particularly ingenious, for it was this that enabled audiences in huge stadiums to hear the dancers' hard shoe taps and 'clicks', and so to 'listen to the dance' as well as to see it. Moreover, the large, fast-paced and repetitive dancing lines that are often taken as the defining feature of *Riverdance* – and whose prominent percussive step beat recalls for Wulff (2003a: 187) the annual sectarian marches in Northern Ireland examined below – with rows of dancers moving and tapping in unison, were achieved not just through the skill and dexterity of the dancers but by what Wulff refers to as 'sonorous manipulation', namely by broadcasting an accompanying soundtrack that helped to mask any errors the dancers might make. By technologizing the body in this way (B. O'Connor 1998: 59; Wulff 2003c: 198), these features contributed to *Riverdance*'s spectacular and dazzling impact on the audience, and made it such a breathtaking piece of theatre and compelling contemporaneous display of 'Irishness'. We will see in the next section how such 'spectacularization' has also become a feature amplifying the identifications evident in sport, for here too the global, televised public event frames very personal notions of local, regional and national identity.

Patriot Games[1]

Like dance, sport has only recently begun to be taken seriously by social scientists as a feature of popular culture worthy of investigation. In Ireland it is only in the last decade or so that social researchers have begun systematically to study and understand sport as an activity that shapes and is shaped by local, national and global forces of modernity. This is slightly surprising, since sport has long been a prominent feature of the island's political and cultural identifications, and Ireland has been widely recognized as an almost paradigmatic case of sport both integrating and dividing along ethnic and national lines (see MacClancy 1996: 11).

In a systematic analysis of the integrative and divisive role of sport in Ireland, Sugden and Bairner (1993) argue that, while not inherently political, sport is especially susceptible to political manipulation and can offer an effective means of fashioning identifications with a particular social formation. The oppositional dualities of team sports like football seem especially well suited for mapping on to the oppositional form of contemporary nationalism, and can act as a focus either for active national affiliations or as evocative metaphors and analogies for them (cf. Buckley and Kenney 1995: 195; Nic Craith 2003: 141–2). Sugden and Bairner (1993) note this special affinity between sport and nationalism and trace this connection in relation to Ireland, devoting separate chapters of their book to the relationship between Gaelic games and Irish politics; to British sports and Irish identity; and to sports with no particular cultural or political identifications. Gaelic games (such as hurling and Gaelic football)[2] are played almost exclusively in Ireland, and as a minority sport among the Irish diaspora in some parts of the USA, Australia and Canada. These games were revived and developed by the Gaelic Athletic Association (GAA), in a parallel to the revival of Irish dancing by the Gaelic League, as part of an explicit strategy to resist what Irish nationalists saw as the spread of foreign, British sports such as cricket and rugby. Playing and supporting Gaelic games thus became a way of demonstrating Irishness and part of the wider struggle for a national identity against imperial domination by a British colonizing power. The link between sport and nationality in Ireland was epitomized for many by the Gaelic Athletic Association's Rule 21, which prevented members of the Royal Irish Constabulary and the British Army from joining the organization (a prohibition that following partition remained relevant in Northern Ireland, though not in the Republic), as well as by Rule 42, which prohibited the playing of soccer and rugby at GAA grounds (Hassan 2005: 129–31). As Sugden and Bairner (1993: 37) explain, in Northern Ireland especially Gaelic sport was never just a game, but came to be regarded by all sides 'as a reservoir of Irish identity'.

Rugby and cricket, by contrast, were, as noted, seen as British sports, introduced to Ireland by an imperial and colonizing power, and played only by those whose identifications and identities were British and Protestant. They were consequently resisted by the GAA, and despite cricket's initial spread throughout the island, it was played from the early twentieth century on mainly in the North or those areas of the Republic of Ireland, such as Dublin, 'where anglophile sympathies were sufficiently strong to withstand the nationalist onslaught' (Sugden and Bairner 1993: 50). So too with rugby, the response to which in Ireland was heavily influenced by the fact that the game was introduced by the British. Despite the fact, then, that both rugby and cricket are organized and their teams selected on an all-Ireland basis, they remain closely associated with Britain. This generates certain ambivalences about the identifications of those who play them.

Writing more recently, Bairner (2005b) now considers his earlier analysis of 'British games' and 'Irish games' a little too mechanical and over-dichotomized. While it remains the case that participation in Gaelic sports implies an identification with Irishness – since it is largely only those who self-identify and are recognized as 'Irish' who play them, despite the lifting of the exclusionary Rule 21 in 2001 – the situation is less clear-cut in some of the other sports. Even within Gaelic sports the greater opposition in Northern Ireland to the removal of Rule 21 suggests that there may be 'very real differences' in nationalist representations of Irishness between the two parts of Ireland (Bairner 2003: 202). Moreover, the Irishness performed on the Gaelic football pitch may not be quite the same as that which celebrates a victory for the Irish rugby team. Jason Tuck (2005: 114) has drawn attention to what he refers to as the 'complex duality of Irishness' within rugby. Irish rugby union is central to notions of Irishness, he suggests, but its organization on an all-Ireland basis has created some ambivalences and anomalies. Players from North and South may be selected to play for the Irish team, which may also include both Protestants and Catholics. This throws up various paradoxes: of northerners and southerners playing side by side as representatives of 'Ireland' at the home of Irish rugby in Dublin's Lansdowne Road; of northern unionists representing a thirty-two county Ireland that they would not wish to see become a political reality; of southern 'Irish' playing a 'British' game; and even of members of the Irish team being selected to play for the 'British Lions'.[3] The

Irishness (Irishness*es* might be more accurate, as multiple identities come into *play* here) that is performed when the Irish rugby team takes the field, therefore, is nuanced, complex and potentially transcendent, incorporating or subduing otherwise apparently competing nationalisms and political identifications. It demonstrates clearly the complexities, ambivalences and shifting nature of national identifications such as Irish, and muddies a view that would see such identifications in sport (or elsewhere) in rigidly fixed terms. The result is a 'Celtic antisyzygy' or 'yoking of opposites' (Bairner 2005b: 171), whereby some southern (and northern) Catholics perform their Irishness through the British game of rugby, while their northern Protestant teammates combine an enduring sense of Britishness with participation in a national team that indicates their Irishness. Nevertheless, the 'question of the various forms of Protestant commitment to Irish identity' remains (Foster 1989: 13), and continues to be worked through in sport in a range of ways (Bairner 2001: chapter 2).

All of this suggests that there exists 'a multiplicity of ways in which people … articulate their Irishness in sporting … contexts' (Bairner 2005a: 3). Moreover, as we saw with Irish dance, the Irishness presented in Irish sport is beginning to be transformed and questioned in other ways too, as the forces of globalization impact every aspect of sport, from its organization, financial arrangements, mode of presentation and pace of play to those who play it and are selected for the national teams. Rugby union again serves as an instructive example, as the sport becomes increasingly professionalized and as global capital and market interests penetrate ever more deeply into what was a principally amateur and local concern. Eamonn Slater (1998) has argued that the money flooding Irish rugby is primarily media capital, which by its nature expects a particular kind of return (and so too with Irish soccer, see O'Brien 2004). As with *Riverdance*, the result has been a spectacularization of local rugby forms into globally marketable commodities: 'local events like the England/Ireland match at Lansdowne Road … become global events when they are transformed into visual commodities in transnational broadcasting' (Slater 1998: 65; for the impact of televised aesthetics on golf, see Slater 2000a). As we watch a match, the global brands are inescapable on the logos of the players' shirts, on the hoardings that surround the ground, and less visibly in the structure of the game. Once again, as we saw with Irish dance, we find Irish sport squeezed between the local and the global, the past and the present, with the forces of tradition apparently pitted against those of modernity as Ireland strives to reinvent itself. And culture and identity are branded as quickly and as often as any other commodity in a global capitalist system (see Hazelkorn and Murphy 2002).

Issues too are raised about who the Irish are, and about who is qualified to participate in performances of Irishness. Many of the dancers in *Riverdance* are Irish-American, including the original stars, yet at the world championships in Irish traditional dancing – the 'Worlds', as they are known – there remains a lingering suspicion among the many Irish-American and other overseas Irish competitors that only someone born in Ireland really has a chance of winning, thus generating a tension between the Irish from Ireland and those of the diaspora (see Wulff in press). Irish rugby players express a similar view, as two former English-born members of the Irish World Cup squad indicated (both cited in Tuck 2005: 117, 118):

> I consider myself very Irish. The only thing is that I was born in England. ... If you go up to an Irish person ... [having been] born in England, having an English accent and having been educated in England ... and say I'm Irish, they'd probably laugh at me.

> It's very easy for people to knock (especially with this [English] accent) and ... ask how Irish can he be?

There is a sense here, then, that while sport may be a prime context within which to present an identification of Irishness, the Irishness presented is fundamentally transformed, perhaps extended or 'diluted', depending on one's view, by the incorporation into national sides of those born outside Ireland and by the large numbers of non-native professionals now playing in and coaching teams (see Carter 2003a: 20; Sugden and Bairner 1993: 42-43; Tuck 2005: 106). Hence the old joke about how the initials of the Football Association of Ireland (FAI), soccer's governing body in the Republic, actually stand for 'Find Another Irishman!' (Sugden and Bairner 1993: 75).

Even at the level of local teams, the participation of increasing numbers of professional migrant athletes is beginning to alter what are sometimes represented as national styles of play in some sports, and may be squeezing 'locals' out (Carter, Donnan and Wardle 2003: 36). Thus the classically 'Irish' Garryowen style of rugby may be modified or supplemented by other 'national' forms of play with the recruitment of team mates from other parts of Europe or elsewhere, a transformation that has become particularly evident in soccer (cf. Tuck 2005: 110). And in cricket, competing national understandings of acceptable styles and strategies of play have sometimes led to conflict, transforming notions of the sense of national identity that the game is thought to represent (Carter 2003a; Carter, Donnan and Wardle 2003: 50-52). In this regard the 'Irishness' of both the player and the style of play are beginning to be questioned (Tuck 2005: 119–21). Just as we saw earlier with dance, so it is with sport: professionalization, spectacularization and commodification of a popular cultural form would once again seem to raise the issue of authenticity under threat from global forces.

However, we should not be too quick to conclude that globalization has led to uniformity and homogeneity, or that the function of sport as a vehicle for the expression and representation of national and ethnic belonging has been eroded. Striking evidence to the contrary has been provided by Bairner and Shirlow

(1998), whose analysis of national and ethnic affiliations in Irish soccer (which, unlike rugby, is not organized on an all-Ireland basis) demonstrates how a particular football team and the stadium in which they play have become highly symbolic representations of identity in a Belfast rigidly divided along ethno-political lines. Linfield Football Club and their Windsor Park stadium are widely associated with working-class Protestants and with a loyalist political stance that is stridently supportive of continuing constitutional union with Britain. The anti-Catholic graffiti on the stadium walls, the location of the stadium in an exclusively Protestant neighbourhood, and the chanting of overtly sectarian songs at matches ensure that attendance at games is largely limited to one side rather than the other, despite the fact that in recent years Linfield has recruited a few Catholic players. Northern Ireland Catholics consequently feel excluded and threatened, and generally stay away, even though Windsor Park is also home to the Northern Ireland 'national' team, which plays its home matches there (Bairner 1997: 99-100; cf. Hassan 2005: 138).[4] As a result, the national footballing loyalties of Northern Irish Catholics seem largely to have been transferred to the Irish Republic, whose team they 'imagine' as representing the entire island, and through support for which they can construct an Irish identity that transcends the border. This too entailed symbolic struggle, in this case over which side – Northern Ireland or the Republic – had the right to use the term 'Ireland' to describe the national soccer team, and only in the late 1970s was 'Ireland' dropped by the northern side in favour of the current 'Northern Ireland', a situation characterized by Fulton as 'not so much *playing for*' Ireland as '*playing with* ... Irish identities' (2005: 146, emphases in original).

Bairner and Shirlow (1998: 169) suggest that the attempt by Protestants to maintain control over Northern Ireland soccer is one way in which they can emphasize the existence of Northern Ireland 'as a separate place', especially in a context like sport where, as we noted above, many sports are organized on an all-Ireland basis. Windsor Park provides a metaphor for the whole of Northern Ireland, whose territorial and political integrity Northern Ireland Protestants see themselves as defending against the perceived threat of Irish re-unification. By dominating the stadium, and keeping control of the game, Protestants symbolically assert its Britishness and their own special role in upholding the Union. When the Northern Ireland 'national' team takes the field, the identity it represents seems clear, at least as far as its supporters are concerned:

> Supporting ... the Northern Ireland team provides ... a context for the celebration of a wider culture. ... Wearing the colours and singing the songs, young men avail themselves of the opportunity to exhibit their sense of what it means to be Ulster Protestants. (Bairner and Shirlow 1998: 173)

In this context, therefore, a substantial proportion of the population expresses a very different understanding of what it means to them to live on the island of

Ireland when compared to the understandings we looked at earlier. In the following section we consider how various forms of Irishness are similarly stamped on territory as different identities symbolically claim and reclaim space by marching through the streets.

Identity Parades[5]

If sport can sometimes encompass the 'complex duality' of what it means to be Irish, the public parades explored in this section tend to draw out the separate strands of Irishness, leaving less room for ambivalence and different understandings, at least when viewed externally.[6] Throughout the 1990s, one of the most frequent media images of violent sectarian confrontation in Northern Ireland was of large processions of men in dark suits, bowler hats and orange collarettes parading through the streets to the accompaniment of flute and pipe bands and carrying colourful banners depicting biblical scenes. 'Tradition' figures large in these public displays, both in the minds of those who march and who see their procession as the contemporary manifestation of an activity undertaken by their forebears for generations, and in the opinions of those who oppose or comment critically on the marches and who see them, at best, as an anachronistic and outmoded representation of a past that has disappeared and at worst as an offensive and provocative affront. Either way, the marching bodies recall a past that has become sedimented in the body itself, as Connerton (1989: 72) might put it. Or, more prosaically, as in the old joke about these parades: Why did the Orange chicken cross the road? Because its feathers and forefeathers did.

Dominic Bryan (1998, 1999, 2000, 2003) and Neil Jarman (1997, 1998a, 1999, 2000) have separately and jointly provided what stands as the most extensive and comprehensive ethnographic record of these Orange parades, contributing not only to our academic understanding of them, but also to public policy discussion about how best they might be managed (Bryan and Jarman 1997; Jarman and Bryan 1996, 1998, 2000b; Jarman, Bryan et al. 1998). Both argue that we will fail to understand the role these rituals play in politics if we accept their apparent continuity of form and content at face value. On the contrary, they demonstrate that the processions are not static and fixed, but are responsive to changing political circumstance, envisioning, creating and re-creating the past for purposes in the present (Silverman and Gulliver 1992b: 19). Drawing on the classic work of Abner Cohen (1980) on the Notting Hill Carnival in London, which shows how old symbols can be rearranged to serve new political ends, and on the insights of David Kertzer (1988) on symbol and ritual, Bryan (2000; Bryan, Fraser and Dunn 1995) shows how ritualized public spectacles are capable of incorporating diverse ideological and sectoral interests in a public performance that communicates cohesiveness and consensus. The power of such events lies in their ability to encompass multiple interpretations, allowing participants to attribute 'quite different meanings' to their actions while engaging in a common practice (Jarman 1999: 172). In the case of Orange marches, denominational and class interests are subsumed under a collective demonstration of commitment to a shared past and common cause of continued union with Britain so that to outsiders, and even to insiders themselves, the diversity and tendency to fragmentation that characterize Ulster Protestants are at least momentarily and publicly transcended. The ability of this public performance to draw together the divergent political and economic interests of Ulster Protestantism may have varied historically, but its centrality as an emotive reference point that commemorates a defining moment of ethnic origin and sense of belonging seems never to have wavered. More than one interpretation of events may co-exist, but through negotiation of different interests dominant meanings do emerge, and the 'parades clearly provide a sense of belonging and identity' (Bryan 2000: 178) to large numbers of participants

> from a wide range of social backgrounds, including people from diverse Protestant Churches and many non-church attendees, abstainers and heavy drinkers, young teenage girls dressed in the latest fashion and old men in dark suits and bowler hats, supporters of at least half a dozen different political parties, young men carrying paramilitary emblems and religious ministers carrying Bibles, politicians and party-goers. (Bryan 2000: 17)

It would certainly be misleading to view these Orange processions as an enduring tradition that has persisted unaltered through the ages, even if this is the way in which their participants present them, and even though the aesthetic content of the parades themselves – the banners, the instruments played, the dress of the marchers, the symbols – look superficially as they always did (on the history of banners and uniforms, see Jarman 1998a; on symbols generally in Northern Ireland, see L. Bryson and McCartney 1994; Buckley 1998). Indeed, as Bryan and Jarman both demonstrate, herein lies the efficacy of ritual: to present in apparently consistent and unmodified form the verities of the ages. Orange processions have been fairly successful at this, even as their right to march has been increasingly questioned and their centrality to state power steadily eroded. Moreover, their superficial similarity belies the fact that every Orange procession is unique, and permits a certain degree of creative licence among the participants, as Bryan (2000: 137–54) outlines in his description of a 'generalized' parade on the Twelfth of July. Despite their militaristic and regimented appearance, therefore, such creative licence generates a dynamic tension within Orange parades, and a varied style of procession that reflects and reproduces the internal differentiations of class and power mentioned earlier. Not only do such occasions provide an opportunity to enact an identity as Protestants, but the creativity inherent in the cultural performance allows other identities of class, age and gender to emerge as well (cf.

Buckley and Kenney 1995: 204–6), just as such creative potential permits the display of other identities in the 'terrorist chic' of the personalized and sexualized dress of some republican parades (Herr 2004).

At one level there is what Bryan refers to as the 'respectable' Orangeism of the clergy, politicians and community leaders who lead the Orange Order[7] and are its public and formal political voice. These figures march at the front of the parade on the Twelfth of July and deliver speeches from the platform as the marchers take refreshment and relax in the 'field' between their outward and return processions through the city or the countryside. Historically this elite has tied the Orange Order and its members closely to the Northern Irish state, and has been deployed by them as both a source and a demonstration of their power. At another level, however, there is what this elite regards as a less respectable side to Orange processions – the drinking, the sectarian goading, the display of paramilitary loyalties and sentiments, and the generally unruly and sporadically anti-social behaviour – and which the Orange leadership is inclined to dismiss as the activities of hangers-on, the actions of outsiders and louts rather than of 'true' Orangemen who uphold the Order's principles of decency, righteousness and faith. Bryan questions this interpretation, and suggests instead that this level of the carnivalesque is an integral element of Orange processions and, in fact, preoccupies a large percentage of their participants. Thus, for instance, only a handful of – mainly journalists and researchers – pay any attention to the speeches from the platform in the 'field', while the vast majority of bandsmen and marchers picnic, chat up the young women and relax prior to the march home. Orange demonstrations, Bryan suggests, are for many of their participants 'as much about drinking ... as about Protestant temperance and as much about teenage sexuality as ... about loyalty to the throne' (2000: 153).

These carnivalesque-like activities often take place back stage, at the 'field', at the 'eleventh night' bonfires which precede the march on the Twelfth itself, and at the re-enactment of the Battle of the Boyne on 13 July commemorating the defeat of James II by William of Orange and the succession of a Protestant as British monarch. In this sense, only fellow Protestants are likely to witness them. Yet there is also slippage into the public procession itself, especially on the marchers' return journey, when carnivalesque elements become apparent, with some band members donning face masks, wigs and different costumes, swaggering ever more extravagantly, and increasingly strident in their sectarian chant. Buckley and Kenney have suggested that 'actions that would ordinarily defy norms are reframed and redefined' by the carnival-like nature of the disorder that sometimes accompanies parades, and they argue that 'as in the theater, [those who engage in such activities] act out for their approving audience scenes that reflect a broader rhetorical truth about social and political realities' (1995: 153, 173). But at least some members of the 'audience' may be more ambivalent about such actions than

Buckley and Kenney imply. The increase in 'Blood and Thunder' and 'Kick the Pope' bands alongside the more sedate and respectable military-style bands (D. Bell 1990; Cecil 1993: 158–9; Jarman 2000), and the consequent rise in overt sectarian provocation, have made internal tensions in the Order more visible in public (tensions also reflected in 'traditional' and 'rebellious' styles of Protestant wall murals, see Jarman 1992, 1997, 1998b; Rolston 1991; for what happens to murals when tensions diminish, see McCormick and Jarman 2005). Such rowdy behaviour and the tensions it has created within the institution have not been allowed to dominate or subvert the Order's public performances, where the overriding sense is of a shared Protestant identity. Stewards regulate the marchers on the parade, ensuring that their actions do not get wholly out of hand, and discreetly escort away those who do. Even the media engage in this 'spin', and are complicit in sustaining the idea of a 'respectable', depoliticized Orangeism by ignoring contemporary changes and failing to report the political speeches, the drinking, the sectarianism and the conflict, and much else besides (Bryan 1998, 2000: 168; Taaffe 2001: 17, 2003). The front stage is thereby carefully managed and controlled in favour of stressing 'tradition' and 'community heritage' as the dominant messages in a public performance that is a ritual expression of Protestant historical integrity, one that 'invokes and celebrates a perceived common Protestant past and a perceived common Protestant identity' (Bryan 2000: 163) which the forces of modernity seem barely to have touched. Legitimation for Orange parades is thereby sought in the language of 'tradition', which seeks to establish the ability to march as a 'civil right' (cf. Cairns 2001).

To some extent the audiences for these performances have remained the same, even as the political functions of the rituals have shifted depending on fluctuating class interests. Using Bernstein's notion of 'restricted code', Larsen (1982b) has argued that the Twelfth should be understood as 'communicating' at different levels and as aimed at at least three different kinds of audience. For the 'performers' themselves, who participate in the restricted code, understanding and predictability of messages are high, so that despite internal tensions the procession offers a clear demonstration and legitimation of collective identity, of solidarity and of 'common' Protestant values. For those outside the restricted code, however, the procession has a very different significance. As far as the nationalist and republican Catholic population of Northern Ireland is concerned, the annual processions are a demonstration of Protestant identity, supremacy and control of territory and thus a reminder that Northern Ireland is Protestant, British and part of the United Kingdom.

The frequent controversies over Orange marches and increasing resistance to their passage through Catholic and nationalist neighbourhoods, which intensified dramatically in the mid-1990s and resulted in the conflict at Drumcree in Portadown (Fig. 2.3; see Bryan 1999, 2003; Ryder and Kearney 2001; Taaffe 2001), offer clear evidence of the cultural and political centrality of these processions to Protestant symbolic claims to the streets and highways of Northern Ireland (Anderson and Shuttleworth 1998; Larsen 1982b: 289). They constitute symbolic territorial claims, just as we saw earlier in the case of the Windsor Park stadium (as urban borders that reflect the frontiers considered in chapter six). For Catholics, then, the Twelfth is a blatant demonstration of Protestant power. The British public too, Larsen (1982b: 286–7) suggests, constitute an 'audience' for these processions, one that has become more important following political developments since the 1970s, although it is the relationship of Orange parades to the British state, as Bryan (2000: 7) observes, that has been really crucial in determining the fluctuating fortunes of the Order. The British state was not only audience to the parades but at different historical moments used them for its own ends, allowing Orange parades to dominate public space while confining nationalist processions to their own neighbourhoods (Jarman 1993, 2003: 94). Only as state power began to be challenged by a well-organized armed republican movement did the state shift its position, and the intimate relationship between Orange Order and the state begin to sour and the role of the Orange parades as 'state rituals' begin to wane (Bryan 2000: 60–77).

It is the absence of this intimate relationship with the state that goes a long way to explaining why a tradition of parading has been much less central to the public performance of Catholic identity in Northern Ireland (nationalist parades number only one-tenth of the annual total of Orange parades; cf. Bryan 2000: 182; Jarman and Bryan 1998: 41–58). Nevertheless, given the pervasive dualities of Northern Ireland, it is no surprise to find that Orange processions are often also regarded as having their Catholic mirror image. In both cases, parades help to define and map competing ethnic identities (Jarman 2003). The Ancient Order of Hibernians (AOH), for instance, is often considered the Catholic equivalent of the Orange Order – as the 'Green Orangemen' – and its annual parade on 15 August is seen as broadly comparable to, if less elaborate and on a smaller scale than, the Twelfth of July (Buckley and Kenney 1995: 173; Cecil 1993; de Rosa 1998; Jarman and Bryan 2000a; Santino 1999: 526). Cecil (1993) provides an account of one AOH march, and identifies many superficial similarities with Orange processions: the marching bands, the uniforms, the banners, the military precision and the speeches, all with their 'readily recognizable aesthetic' (Herr 2004: 2). She argues, however, that such similarities of form belie their radical differences (see also Jarman 1999: 189–90), for where the Orange procession is a demonstration of dominance and an affirmation of loyalty to the state, the AOH parade which she observed, with its accompanying paramilitary displays, was a clear expression of rebellion and resistance (on the contrasting iconography of republican wall murals, see Kenney 1998; Sluka 1995).

Others have similarly reported how AOH parades have been a catalyst and opportunity for more open and even violent resistance to the state and its agents.

Sometimes this violence takes the form of what Anthony Buckley and Mary Kenney (1995: 83) refer to as 'recreational rioting', the 'playful' and ritualized stoning of opponents in a cycle of attacking their territory and defending one's own. At other times the violence can escalate and intensify, resulting in exchange of gunfire, serious injury and even death, as Buckley and Kenney (1995: 82–8) describe for the Belfast neighbourhood of Ardoyne, where the AOH procession was shifted from 15 August (the Feast of the Assumption) to 9 August so that it would coincide with the anniversary of the republican prisoners interned in 1971. According to Cecil (1993: 164), it is this contrast between the anti-state position of the AOH parades and the pro-state position of Orange processions that suggests that the meanings underlying them were 'totally different'. Yet while this may have been true of the parades Cecil observed, it was not always and everywhere the case, and Buckley and Kenney (1995: 156–62) describe how Orange processions were also a focus for widespread civil unrest and anti-state demonstrations in opposition to the Anglo-Irish Agreement of 1985, whose greater rapprochement between Irish and British governments many Protestants felt was a betrayal. Subsequent political developments in Northern Ireland in the 1990s have further transformed the ways in which Orangemen and -women understand the 'traditional' Twelfth. What was once seen as 'an expression of loyalty to the state, now provides an opportunity to express … opposition to the present form of the state' (Bryan 2000: 172). If the Twelfth is 'traditional', therefore, this in no way suggests that it has been static or fixed. Rather, as we saw with Irish dance and sport, it too is a 'tradition' that continues to shape and be shaped by the forces of modernity with which it co-exists.

Similar tensions are evident in a colourful cultural pageant long taken to be the quintessential representation of Irishness, particularly among the diasporic Irish: St Patrick's Day parades, when, as the axiom proclaims, 'everyone is Irish'. However, like many of the other events we have examined, this is a prime occasion not just for the expression of ethnicity and national belonging but also for its contestation and potential fragmentation and even violence (see Buckley and Kenney 1995: 156, 162–3). A web-based survey conducted by the Institute of Irish Studies at Queen's University Belfast in 2004 found that St Patrick's Day is 'a "hot-spot" of identity contestation, in which multiple interpretative claims compete to assert the essential meaning of [the] celebrations' (Nagle 2005a: 5). Like the London St Patrick's Day parade described by Nagle (2005b: 571), the parades reported in the survey were often 'politically ambiguous', a lack of definition and focus that their 'remit of inclusivity' tended to encourage. As with Orange processions, different interests seek to be represented on St Patrick's Day and to use the event to perform their particular view of Irishness. It is consequently as often characterized by a struggle for control and a conflict over meaning as it is by consensus on what it represents.

From the mid-nineteenth to the early twentieth century, for example, the struggle over the politics of the parades in New York was between the Orange Order and nationalist Catholics, who remained closely aligned to Irish nationalism and the move to rid Ireland of the British (Cronin and Adair 2002: 65–6). More recently in the US, the parades have assumed a somewhat different meaning, one associated with the 'unethnic Americanness' of all immigrants rather than with Ireland and 'Irishness', to which, Reginald Byron (1999) argues, it is now only superficially related. After all, Byron concludes, 'nothing could be more American than to be a little "Irish" especially on St Patrick's Day' (1999: 267).

In Ireland itself, a liberal, multicultural trend has worked to enhance the parades' cross-community, non-sectarian potential. Yet in spite of efforts at inclusivity, and despite claims that St Patrick's Day does not 'appear particularly tribal' (Cronin and Adair 2002: xv), the Queen's University survey concluded that, far from being 'a benign, cosmopolitan, uncontested and inclusive celebration of community, the day is characterised by profound intra-community cleavage' (Nagle 2005a: 21). As one Protestant remarked: 'as it stands at the minute, St Patrick's Day in Belfast is nothing more than a republican festival', while another suggested that if fewer Tricolours were flown 'it might help Protestants realize they are Irish too!' (cited in Nagle 2005a: 21). In Los Angeles, an Irish-American respondent replied: 'Many of the parades (at least in Los Angeles) have very little in them that I would consider to be truly Irish' (Nagle 2005a: 15). Elsewhere, a letter to *The Irish Times* (16 March 2002) lamented the invitation to 'bounce around' at a 'monster *céilí*' on St Patrick's Day in Dublin on the grounds that 'bouncing around' is not how *céilí* dancers dance, adding that with the increasing carnivalization of the event 'anything that smacked of Irishness was abandoned'. Yet not all participants are so critical, and there are many in the Republic of Ireland who have welcomed the parades' new emphasis on multiculturalism, responding positively to recent attempts at an inclusive Irishness that incorporates 'Catholics, Protestants, Irish, English, blacks and whites' (Basegmez 2005: 253). According to Basegmez, some parades have been particularly effective as 'a way of bringing people together', and she shows how the Galway parade in 1998 successfully reflected 'the mix and complexity of contemporary Ireland' (2005: 251–61). Nevertheless, it was the Dublin parade that remained the focal point for all others, and the city was relentlessly marketed as 'the right place to be in Europe on St Patrick's Day' (Basegmez 2005: 254).

One of the largest and most famous annual St Patrick's Day parades, with invited dignitaries from across the US and from Ireland, is held in New York City, where it is organized by the Ancient Order of Hibernians. Apart from the various ways in which this New York parade is interpreted by different groups in Ireland itself – where to many Protestants it is seen as an affirmation of a Catholic, nationalist diasporic Irishness from which they feel excluded – so too in New York it has generated conflict between the mainly middle-class and elderly AOH organizers and some minority interest groups who wish to participate. According to Sallie Marston (2002), the chief line of fracture since 1990 has been the pressure exerted on the organizers by the Irish Lesbian and Gay Organization (ILGO), which is not permitted to participate or display its banners as a group, although individual members can parade. Jack Santino (1999) analyses a similar conflict between Irish gays and St Patrick's Day parade organizers in Boston, and argues that though both have very different views on by whom and how Irishness should be publicly displayed, they each use the public parade as a means of asserting their claim to identity, a popular style of demonstration that he compares to the kind of oppositional forms of parading in Northern Ireland that we have just considered above. Marston contends that what is at issue in these St Patrick's Day conflicts is not the Irishness or absence of Irishness of ILGO members, but the public affirmation of their sexual identity (see Conrad 2001, who considers why homosexuality is here excluded from what constitutes Irishness). The ILGO membership is diverse and wide-ranging, drawn from mainly young Irish immigrants (both Catholic and Protestant, and North and South), from American-born Irish, and from ILGO supporters with no Irish connections, but this diversity does not seem to generate the concern that we saw earlier it created for national sport. Rather, for those who seek to construct and control representations of Irishness on St Patrick's Day, it is sexuality that matters, and the event has become a highly politicized public arena in which contemporary notions of Irishness are hotly contested along this axis. Marston cites one of her informants to illustrate the kind of abuse ILGO members experience:

> We were chanting 'the AOH is anti-gay and you don't have to be that way, the AOH is anti-gay but please don't raise your kids that way', and this woman with her two kids by their hands, she's like, 'you're sick, you're sick' screaming at us. (2002: 388)

Marston argues that we must see the 'New York Irish' in context of a city shaped by the changing forces of globalization, one in which 'Irish and Irish-Americans do not automatically share a consistent and coherent sense of what it means to be a member of the Irish national community' (2002: 378). Identifications as Irish have fragmented in New York, less on the basis of from what part of Ireland people come, or because of age, gender or even class – although each of these can be important too, as Marston shows – as on the basis of sexuality. It is conflicting narrations of sexual identity that appear to have constructed 'boundaries between people perceived to share a common cultural history' (Marston 2002: 374). This contest over meaning and the representation of what Irishness can be permitted publicly and officially to encompass and express is simultaneously a contest over the ability to control the parade that constructs a particular hierarchy of power in which the ILGO's subversive and resistant protests question the AOH's dominant account of Irishness as the only authentic one. St Patrick's Day is thereby not just about identity, but about power, and about who has the right to represent Irishness, whatever that is constructed to mean. It is about 'the political crisis of representation that erupts when the borders between competing and overlapping identities and narratives are unstable' (Conrad 2001: 134). And there are many parties to this crisis, not least the state and the role it plays in permitting or facilitating particular performances of identity by allowing or encouraging parades to go ahead, and in regulating 'the use of space in the constitution of cultural performance' (Marston 2002: 390), something that has also been a major factor in shaping the changing understandings of Orange processions, as we noted earlier.

The Irishness presented on St Patrick's Day is thus an apparently consensual cultural display that in practice is full of contradictions. With their love of paradox, anthropologists have been quick to fix on one celebration of St Patrick's Day that seems particularly exotic in this regard: the St Patrick's Day activities on the Caribbean island of Montserrat. Here 'the presumed incommensurability of Irish culture with black skin colour' (Skinner 2004: 189) was probably responsible for catching at least one ethnographer's eye (though in contemporary Ireland being Black and Irish is increasingly common). Following his research on Inis Beag (see chapter three), John Messenger carried out fieldwork on Montserrat, where the islanders have celebrated St Patrick's Day annually since 1970. According to Messenger, approximately one thousand 'Black Irish' inhabit the island, the 'descendants of marriages between Irish [landowners] and slaves' (1994: 13), who have retained the surnames, customs, music, motor habits and even facial features of their Irish colonial ancestry. Their celebration of St Patrick's Day, Messenger claims, is a kind of nativist revitalization movement, its form the result of 'an indelible ... cultural imprint' (1967: 31) left by Irish colonists on their former slaves.

More recent research has found little evidence for Messenger's claims, and argues for a rather different view, one that sees Messenger's interpretation of the Montserrat St Patrick's Day as just one view among many local and non-local understandings of the week of activities that constitute the occasion. Local people, the Montserrat Tourist Board, the Montserrat Government, island historians, journalists and anthropologists and other academics all have 'an agenda for ... the "Irishness" debate on Montserrat' (Skinner 2004: 163, 164), with each 'different interest group (casual, political, academic, economic) [having] a different historical reality and understanding (personal, national, anthropological, financial)' of it. For some, it is a commemoration of an eighteenth-century slave uprising, for others a celebration of the Irish connection, and for yet others an opportunity to 'jump up' or party (Skinner 2004: 155). Amidst this range of representations, it is the Montserrat Tourist Board's understanding that currently dominates, for they have recognized the power of invoking a sense of Irishness for drawing the tourists in. The result has been an increasing commodification of the celebration, as Skinner (2004: 183–4; 2006) argues, with a proliferation of Irish symbols and souvenirs. While this has undermined other understandings of the event, it has reinvigorated for the tourist gaze the sense that what St Patrick's Day is about is performing Irishness.

Multi-sided and -sited Irishness

In this chapter we have looked at three kinds of public event, each illustrative in its different way of how the forces of tradition and modernity, the global and the local, and the authentic and the commodified have impacted and been reflected in contemporary Irish cultural performance. We have emphasized how identifications of Irishness are never fixed, but are negotiated, questioned and affirmed according to the situation, as the creation of particular social, historical and political contexts. As Brian Graham has argued, national identity is 'a situated, socially constructed narrative capable both of being read in conflicting ways at any one time and of being transformed through time' (1997a: 7). In fact, the historical discontinuities of notions of 'Irishness' are striking, and reflect 'the fragile and contingent nature of the political and cultural identities that different groups have created for themselves' (Connolly 1997: 44). Like all identifications, Irishness is shifting and relational, and what can count as Irishness may be ambivalent and context-dependent, as when a national soccer side is seen as 'Irish' only because it is 'more Irish' than the opposition (Sugden and Bairner 1993: 19). Moreover, we have seen from the three case studies that there are many ways in which people express and understand their Irishness, and so many more than the 'two Irelands' of north and south. Irishness is variously performed, claimed and represented, and each may come with its own competing claim to authenticity.

At the same time as these cultural performances are negotiations of identity, they are also negotiations of power. In some cases this involves the power of big business, which can commodify Irishness, and shape it to the demands of the market. This may mean Irish themed bars in Berlin or Barcelona, with names like Murphy's, pictures of Yeats and Michael Collins on the walls, and a menu written in a euro-Celtic script; or it may mean the ability to purchase the television rights of major sporting occasions and their transformation into global media events, as in the contract between the Football Association of Ireland and British Sky Broadcasting for the right to broadcast the Republic of Ireland's home internationals (on theme bars see McGovern 2003; Slater 2000b). In other cases, it involves the power of competing political interests, all of which seek to assert their own particular sense and version of Irishness. This may mean the fluctuating fortunes of Orange processions in symbolically claiming the territory of Ulster for their own, or the efforts of the liberal, integrating, multiculturalists who strive to convert St Patrick's Day into a 'day of fun for the whole community'. Or it may mean the resistant, subversive power of those who seek to question, challenge or transform the forms of Irishness that prevail, and who defy attempts to commodify them (Kneafsey 2003).

As we implied at the beginning of this chapter, these different deployments of the cultural material of Irishness in dance, sport and public processions have generated widespread popular and academic debate about the contemporary forms that Irishness might or might not take, as well as a series of questions about authenticity and representation. What is tradition? What is modern? Is Ireland traditional or modern? Or post-modern? Phrased like this, however, such questions may be misleading. Arjun Appadurai (1996) has suggested that the break with the past lies not in the historically precipitous shift from 'tradition' to 'modern' that is enshrined in the classics of social science, and that has become encapsulated in the dichotomies of modernization theory like that between 'traditional' and 'modern societies', but rather in the transformative impact of new electronic media and migration on 'the work of the imagination'. It is this, he argues, that is a 'constitutive feature of modern subjectivity', because migration and mass mediation offer 'new resources and new disciplines for the construction of imagined selves and imagined worlds' (Appadurai 1996: 3). Changing media are thus likely to facilitate new forms of 'authenticity' rather than being a threat to it (C. Graham 2001: 70).

These ideas are especially helpful in understanding cultural performances of the kind examined in this chapter such as *Riverdance*, for, as we saw earlier, the imaginings of Irishness are here forged in the mass-mediated space between the Irish of Ireland and those of the diaspora. Perhaps we should see *Riverdance* not as a denial or radical break with tradition, but as a 'rupture of modernity', whose reimagining of Irishness has been made possible by contemporary forms of media and migration. Wulff (in press) develops this point in interesting ways in relation to *Riverdance*, arguing against a straightforward linear progression from tradition to modernity. From the perspective of *Riverdance*, she suggests, competitive Irish dancing and dance schools represent the 'traditional', while these same dance schools and competitions are regarded by set-dancers at *céilís* as 'modern' (Wulff in press). Each might thus be seen as different worlds that are simultaneously present. In this sense, the traditional is always somewhere else: for those in Ireland it is 'hiding abroad', while for those abroad, it is to be found in Ireland, as Wulff (in press) insightfully shows. So too with Orange parades and some forms of sport, where what is 'modernity' for one person may be 'tradition' for somebody else, each instance of classification to be argued over, agreed or denied in the politics of identification that accompany the kinds of public spectacle examined here. Cultural forms considered characteristic of tradition or modernity, and consequently constituted as 'mutually incommensurable', are actually 'irreducibly contemporaneous with one another' (Lloyd 2001: 22).

Throughout this chapter we have touched on notions of diaspora and displacement, and explored how notions of Irishness have been stretched, contested and transformed in and between and beyond the Irish abroad and those located on the island of Ireland itself. In the following chapter, we return to the significance of place to show the ways in which it too has come to be constructed in a world that is increasingly diasporic and transnational.

–6–

Frontier Tales and the Politics of Emplacement

... the main partitions observed ... [by] ... men are not those in the topography or in the vegetation, but those that are in the minds of men.

Jean Gottman (1951: 164)

In the rush to theorize the processes of deterritorialization that seemingly are the hallmark of the present era of late modernity, many anthropologists have been quick to lose sight of the significance of place to most people, in most configurations of identity, and particularly in those that relate to the public and civic spheres of life. While in the face of this type of theorizing the abiding importance of a 'sense of place' has not been lost to all anthropologists, reminders are still needed (as found in Feld and Basso 1996). Some observers of ethnography and anthropology today suggest that in former types of anthropology, in those that mirrored a modernist sensibility, the importance of 'place' in the social structure, political organization and moral orders of anthropological subjects and informants was always clear. We dispute this notion. Place as a marker and arena of identity creation and cultural reproduction is a relatively recent invention in ethnographic approaches, one that has succeeded (or (re)placed) past emphases on 'the land', 'the village', the street and other geophysical referents for local culture and community.

Regardless of the relative interest in place before, during and after the heyday of modernist ethnographic practice, the significance of locality and place has never been a strong theme in the anthropology of Ireland, in which, according to Peace, 'relations of place and identity have scarcely been touched upon' (2001: 4). Anthropologists worldwide, including those who do research in Ireland, have been distracted from examining the politics of place because of the insistence that we can no longer study communities. These notions are misplaced; the politics of identity, a principal theme in anthropology today, are also the politics of community, and both are about the politics of place.

In line with evolving ideas of ethnography, ethnographic writing and professional research and publishing that are especially prevalent in the United States, no ethnographer does community studies in Ireland any more. But most anthropologists in Ireland study people in particular places and spaces, in socially meaningful localities in which our hosts and respondents often have clear notions of community, or perhaps even the multiple communities in which they reside, work and play. 'Community' as an organizing principle continues to be a salient factor of social, economic and political life in Ireland today, as it is in other places in South Asia, Europe and North America where we have done research. As such, 'community' must continue to be considered in any ethnographic analysis of culture and society, wherever anthropologists do research, including Ireland.

While it has long since been shown that a community was never as neatly bounded and isolated as some anthropologists today assert was once roundly believed by ethnographers,[1] it has also been demonstrated that symbolic boundaries mark the geographical and spatial limits of communities, and the related ideas of community, that are at the core of many notions of identity (as Anthony Cohen has shown in terms of in-depth local studies in the Shetlands and in major comparative studies; see A. P. Cohen 1982, 1985, 1986, 1987, 2000).

In this chapter we examine ways in which the notions of work, residence and social interaction still structure various forms of community in Ireland, as do convergent, divergent and parallel ideas of identity and history. Local identity relies a great deal on identification with people, ideas and forces beyond the locality, in regions, nations, states, 'Europe' and perhaps even 'the globe'. As anthropologists have increasingly shied away from community studies, they have also had to desist from constructing similar precise notions of culture and culture contact, and from a model that approximates one long used by international relations specialists in regard to nations, that of billiard balls colliding and reacting according to predictable forces of physics. It is rare indeed to come upon an anthropologist today who discusses culture contact and acculturation, at least in terms of discrete cultures meeting and mixing.[2]

One metaphor that many scholars have adopted, in place of more constraining terms that continue to suggest the finite and bounded nature of community, culture and identity, has been that of the *frontier*, or *borderland*. In various ways 'frontier' implies an expanse that is not predictable, ordered and contained, where rules are disputed and authority is confronted, where anything might happen. This space, a zone of heightened liminality, is one of social diversity and dynamism, of cultural mix and match, where the patches (with apologies to Lowie 1920) never seem to comprise a whole garment. In this zone of personal and group cultural flows, of common and contested cultures and communities, there are often as many links to territory and place as there are to the social 'landscape' of memory and history, where the politics of emplacement intertwine.

Locality and place are socially meaningful for people in various spots in Ireland, where they are constitutive of wider notions of community and culture, and where the politics of identity are often inseparable from social space and political territory. Through an examination of identities, and the ways in which people 'tell' each other apart, in what might be viewed as hierarchies of identification, we use the metaphors of frontier and border to explicate the diversity and sameness in the politics of place in Ireland. The expectation of interstitiality that is explicit in the frontier metaphor is often found in its clearest terms in the actual borderlands between nations and states, and it is not surprising that the Northern Ireland borderlands have figured prominently in comparative and theoretical treatments of culture, identity and borders in Europe (see, for example, O'Dowd and Wilson 1996). Much of the growing anthropology of borders and borderlands, in Europe and elsewhere, has called for a reconsideration not only of place, space and locality, but also of the role of territory in the politics of identity, nation and state (see, for example, Donnan and Wilson 2003; Wilson and Donnan 2005a, 2005b). How all of these levels of socio-cultural integration, of locality, region, nation, state and 'Europe', connect, in the ordinary lives of ordinary people in what to them are ordinary places, is one of the key concerns of today's anthropology of Ireland, where there are many ways in which social difference and distinction are encoded.

Senses of Difference

Inveresk is the pseudonym for a small community in the West of Ireland with a population not greater than 450 people. According to Adrian Peace, the ethnographer who lived there for a total of three years at different times in the 1980s and 1990s, it is a considerably more diverse and complex community than its size would suggest, and than are its neighbouring communities, which depend almost exclusively on agriculture. Inveresk's diversity, and its regional reputation of being a 'different place altogether', sometimes even a 'queer place altogether', derives as much from its people's sense of being different as it does from its clear differences in business, work, leisure and sociability. As Peace (2001: 1) notes, the residents of Inveresk have a sense of community based in large part on their 'sense of distinction', of 'being a special place in the world' (Inveresk is referred to as 'Clontarf' in earlier work; see Peace 1986, 1992).

There are many reasons for this shared sense of distinction in Inveresk, and for the less laudable ways in which the community members are perceived by some outsiders, who are more likely to view Inveresk as a queer place. Unlike the farming communities that surround it in the West of Ireland, Inveresk has three distinct zones or fields of economic production and work, three areas within the loosely defined geographical limits of the community. Each of these domains has a different character, the sum of which helps to define what Inveresk is as a total community. These three domains, those of the country, the pier and the village, each have their own symbolic boundaries, encompassing spaces where people work, reside and are at their leisure, but none of which are in themselves of the same order as Inveresk taken as a whole. Said differently, there are three communities in one, but the principal loyalty or identification is not to the component domain of work and play, but to 'the one' of Inveresk, the overarching community as a whole.

This provides a surprising turn to those who have followed the ethnography of community in Ireland, where small nucleated settlements and the presumed homogeneity of traditional peasant life led many ethnographers to conclude that rural communities are relatively simple, at least in social structural terms. Inveresk presents a clear challenge to that perspective, showing the layers of meaning that are attached to the practices of work, of residence, of social interaction and of play and leisure between domains. And in the midst of all of this interaction and identification, within the place and among the people of Inveresk, there is also a clear sense of internal difference and distinction.

For while it is often said that the one community, Inveresk, is superordinate in the lives of its people, in that they all identify themselves as being from, and being of, Inveresk, the people of each domain also recognize that they do not share everything, maybe not even very much, with people from outside of their own area of village, pier and country. But they know they share enough, are different enough, together, to have a pride in the distinction of being a resident of Inveresk. Part of that pride is their own recognition of internal differences, and their success in mastering the social tensions that their own diversity causes: 'So when the collective identity of Inveresk is presented (more or less) distinct and enduring to the world at large, this is always against a background of local members having themselves surmounted social differences and political divisions of considerable moment' (Peace 2001: 3).

Notions of identity in the separate domains of pier, village and farm have precise connections to notions of place, where people were born, raised, live and work, and both are articulated in particular 'practices of emplacement'. These practices constitute the politics of action and discourse in Inveresk, and are at the heart of the forces of integration and disintegration that are in continual play there, creating the conditions of continuity and discontinuity between domains and between Inveresk and its neighbours. And it is this complexity of structure and action that draws the ethnographer's gaze towards it: 'To an anthropologist then, what is ultimately most intriguing about the everyday politics of Inveresk is the continuous tension between those relations which express the heterogeneity of the community's parts and those which celebrate the ethos of the whole' (Peace 2001: 3). Thus, while Inveresk is a coherent community, its sense of itself, and the senses of self displayed by the people of Inveresk, are anchored by the forces of difference and discord.

Inveresk as a place is made up of many significant places, each with its own boundaries, and each with its own practices, styles, character and discourses. Within and between these domains, which is Peace's term for the linked but separate social fields of farming, fishing and small business, 'quite contrasting codes of interpersonal conduct and, indeed, of personal morality emerge' (Peace 2001: 1–2). Yet every day the members of each domain cross the frontiers between domains, and those crossings are the lifeblood of Inveresk as a community. To understand this diversity and interaction of which Inveresk people are so proud, one has to understand how each domain is structured and relates to its others, and how all relate to communities and peoples outside of Inveresk, in a modernized and rapidly changing global Ireland. This again brings us back to the politics of emplacement and identity.

The three domains of village, farm and pier are demarcated by clear cultural differences that set off what to locals are distinct physical and social spaces in the 'community's' landscape. These domains are the arenas of personal and familial identification, for creating social distinctions within the community, and between their community and the outside world. The domain that really sets Inveresk apart from other locations in the region is that of fishing, centred at its pier. While less than half a mile from the village, the pier and its people seem much more distant socially from the other residents of Inveresk. This distance is marked by many social differences that are linked to productive enterprise, residence and fun, all within the most circumscribed space of all in Inveresk. As one member of the pier proudly proclaimed, 'We're different all right, the pier's a different place entirely to everywhere else 'round here. We're a real community, nothing like those jumped-up fuckers in the village, we really look after one another – all of the time' (Peace 2001: 23).

What makes these people of the pier so particular? Peace suggests that it has a great deal to do with the necessities of fishing life, which in Inveresk entails intense cooperation between neighbours, within families, and between skippers and crew. Fishing life also entails competition between boats for the depleted stocks of fish, and with the foreign fleets who also fish the Atlantic off the Irish coasts. But the pier is also distinguished by other things, related to fishing and the sea of course, and to other dynamic social relations in the area around the pier. Many residents do not depend directly on fishing. Some are on the dole (unemployment benefits), some have shops, others own bars, while still others provide the household and public services to keep this pier community active. The result of this proximity and local interdependence is a high degree of sociability *within* the pier community. This is best seen on Fridays, pay day, at the pub, when whole families attend, the publican lays on live music, and boat and business owners socialize with their workers, their competitors and their assembled families and friends. However, such festive occasions should not obscure the tensions between many pier residents, especially between skippers whose boats compete for the dwindling catches, or the differences that separate this fishing community from the farmers and the villagers.

The village is the social hub of Inveresk, the crossroads where the two land access routes to the outside world converge. It is the site of Inveresk's main shops, pubs, hotels, butcher, garage, hairdressers, haulage company and fish traders. Like the skippers and publicans of the pier, and the farmers of the country, these businesses are all family-owned, and many of these entrepreneurs reside in their commercial premises. Like the pier, and unlike the country, many of these owners are in direct competition with each other within the small, local market, in what can only be seen as sometimes intense, sometimes disturbing, rivalry for custom: at one point the butcher was fined for 'leaving deposits of excrement on his rival's doorstep' (Peace 2001: 20). And within the village, and in the wider Inveresk, while these entrepreneurs are valued for their economic and social roles, wherein their businesses provide venues for sociability and the transmission of information as surely as they offer commercial services – 'one no more goes into a shop simply to buy a newspaper than one goes into a bar merely to have a drink' (Peace 2001: 20) – they are not seen as some sort of local elite. On the contrary, they are often derided for their avarice and mean spirit, particularly by the residents of pier and country, who take pride in the cooperative and reciprocal (often idealized) relations of their own domain's community. It is clear that these tensions are due to the nature of money-based commerce and services in the village, but other tensions result from the presumed slighting of the long-term unemployed and of the wage-earners who must travel outside of Inveresk for work. Both groups resent the arrogance of the 'business folk'.

The politics of business, sociability and place are complicated in the village due to its centrality to the social life of Inveresk, and as the site not just of its main commercial activities, but also of the church, primary school and community hall. The people of all three domains move in and out of the village on a daily basis, and in so doing generate and regenerate the flows of capital and information that are the lifeblood of Inveresk as a community. The village is also the domain with the highest profile in Inveresk, where business, and secrets, are made most public, and where gossip thrives, for it is not only the community's physical and social centre, but its font of local knowledge. This means that 'symbolic violence is widespread in the village' due to its higher levels of malicious gossip, but it is also where farmer folk go nonetheless to enter into 'the flow of local knowledge about parochial matters', including information about and from the pier, 'the one place which truly respectable farm families avoid contact with altogether' (Peace 2001: 23).

Dairy and tillage are the most common types of farming in Inveresk's country community, where twenty-five farms are located, most of which are family-run. Each of the farms is worked by its owners and kin in a collective venture; where farms are owned by bachelors or by groups of siblings, then the commercial nature of the farm usually reflects the relative lack of labour (thereby necessitating tillage rather than dairying, for example). Spouses and children are pressed into daily and seasonal work. Intra-familial cooperation is necessary; inter-familial cooperation also occurs, but in exceptional circumstances, since most farmers are involved in the same or similar activities at the same times according to the demands of their agricultural strategies and the limits of the environment. As a result of these practices, there is a 'cultural ethos' in the country that sees the family as the natural unit to get the most from the land (Peace 2001: 17).

But this relative farm and family autonomy has other results, in what is seen as 'the country way of doing things':

> Consistent with this is the expectation that the individual will be cautious about being drawn into a wider field of social and political relations. One does not socialise for its own sake but because it might serve some tangible purpose, and when that purpose has been realised, it is appropriate to withdraw once again to the guarded privacy of the farm. (Peace 2001: 17)

Most social relations are with the extended families, and since farms are passed down to males, and farm daughters generally leave Inveresk to marry or work, then most of the mothers' and wives' relations are outside the area. Thus, the farm folk of Inveresk only have limited, if regular, contact with their fellow community members, in the shops, school, community hall and church in the village, and these connections, while important and meaningful, are rather formal and instrumental. These relationships are not about 'sharing confidences', but about dependable social and economic relations, which to the country people are better left brief.

These farmers are clearly involved in quite complex notions of local culture and class, in ways that have been studied elsewhere in Ireland by anthropologists (for example, in the richer farm areas of County Meath; see Wilson 1988, 1989a), but these notions are no more complex than those of their neighbours in village and pier. Overall, however, the impression that lingers from these capsule portraits of the three domains is how little they have in common with each other. Peace was struck by the barriers to community across domain boundaries as much as he was with the overall, real and strong sense of community that sets Inveresk off from other places. Yet how would one account for the obvious commitment all the members of Inveresk have to the community as a whole, given the clear 'pattern of differentiation, division and dispute' (Peace 2001: 67) that is at work there?

The solution to this apparent problem seems to depend on the ways in which and the reasons why the people of each domain cross the boundaries which separate them, to enter into what we are calling the frontiers of their community political life. As Peace concludes (2001: 67–85), the boundaries between domains are permeable, and are crossed often and with intensity, in many ways, not least through economic exchanges and in cooperative ventures. Moreover, there are many exceptions to the general work and residence patterns, further integrating people in Inveresk-wide relations. The high incidence of wage-earners and dole recipients also enhances the general flow of people and information across the domains, as also occurs in the often overlooked but decidedly important roles of children and teenagers, in and after school.

In fact, to Peace, the secret to Inveresk community seems to be in its generalized creation and flow of knowledge, within and between domains, giving all Inveresk people a specific localized competence that is rooted in place and time and that has its most important meanings and effects in local life. This knowledge is both the source and the result of what he also calls the 'generosity of community', the shared moral obligation to help and enhance that 'encompasses and supersedes the lines of difference that are such an integral part of everyday life' (Peace 2001: 67). This obligation to be generous in spirit and action has a great deal to do with the realization among Inveresk people that they, as a group, are faced with many forces and pressures external to the community, because as Peace sets out in quite some detail, all of them are part of complicated relations within the wider political economy of county, region, state, Europe and the world. To function as individuals and families, as skippers, farmers and publicans, and as the people of pier, country, village *and* Inveresk, they must transcend the discourse of domain to adopt the discourse of community. And the embodiment of that sense of community is their knowledge. In other words, the boundary of their community is the boundary of localized understandings, that stock of knowledge about themselves and each other through which their sense of belonging is produced and reproduced. The politics of place in Inveresk ultimately can be approached through the politics of discourse and knowledge. What, then, gives Inveresk the notion that it is a place apart, 'a different place altogether'? 'It is out of the exceptional familiarity which people have of one another, and the uses to which that information is put, that its sense of identity, a sense of its being a distinct and distinctive place in the world, is constituted' (Peace 2001: 84).

Telling Identity

The acts of recognizing members from non-members, of distinguishing your own from the others, of embracing those who share your identity rather than those who do not, are always acts of symbolic violence and selective knowledge. Place is one key factor in these personal politics of identity, and nowhere in Ireland are the politics of culture, place, identity and history more important than in Northern Ireland. In the six counties there, strangers are often and variously bemused, shocked and horrified to learn about the complexities involved in how the people of Northern Ireland socially read anyone and everyone they meet, particularly if they are from Northern Ireland, in terms of their religion, class and national identity. This is what Andrew Finlay (1999) has called the 'cultural protocols' that are observed, literally and figuratively, when strangers meet in Northern Ireland, where he grew up and where he wonders at its effects on him and his actions in interviews there as an ethnographer.

Finlay is not the first anthropologist to draw the attention of anthropologists to this practice of 'telling', which in essence is a recognition and appropriation of identity. In Rosemary Harris's (1972) study of a border community, she noted that Catholics and Protestants maintained often close but separate lives, in which their relationships were shadowed by the differences in religion and ultimately community. These differences were so important, yet so potentially incendiary to regular and peaceful social relations, that people and communities had to devise ways to tell the religious identity, and by extension national identity, of others by indirect means. As a result,

> Many Ulster people seem to have developed an extreme sensitivity to signs other than explicit badges that denote the affiliations of those that they meet. Each looks automatically for slight indications from another's name, physical appearance, expression and manner, style of dress and speech idiom to provide the clues that will enable the correct categorisation to be made. (R. Harris 1972: 148; see also Finlay 1999: 1.4)

The political ethnographer Frank Burton (1978: 37–67) later used the term 'telling' as shorthand for this process of social differentiation and identity marking. Because of the intense interest on the part of scholars, policy-makers, social critics and many others in ethnic conflict, sectarianism and nationalism, the processes of social identification which most matter are those that relate to religion, ethnicity, class and national identity. But the anthropologists Buckley and Kenney are correct to remind us all that 'telling' is but one way to approach the subject of recognizing and acting upon 'cultural cues', the everyday and often unconscious way humans everywhere recognize social sameness and difference in others: 'Cultural cues belong to the whole of social life, not just to ethnicity, and are used to differentiate between all sorts of types of person' (1995: 8).

'Telling' in the Northern Ireland context, however, cannot be analytically isolated from the social processes of distinguishing between individuals and groups in terms of their religion, political identity, ethnicity, class and 'home', in the sense of where they belong, in which place or locality. This telling has been recognized and examined by ethnographers in Northern Ireland for some time, and it is linked to the wider issues of cultural and social stereotyping (cf. Donnan and McFarlane 1986a). But telling in Northern Ireland often seems to be a complicated and extremely specific social interaction, often impossible for some visitors, and even some long-term residents, to fathom. That is because it is based on socialization, stereotyping and cultural categorizations that demand years of social experience in which the cues may seem slight, muted and petty, but their significance and impact are just the opposite.

So what do some, perhaps many, Northern Ireland people look for, and expect to see, when entering the public domain daily, when leaving home and locality where there is a high probability that there are many people who share religious and political identities with each other? How can people 'tell' what religion, national identity and ethnicity anyone else has or is, in the workplace, in school, when shopping, when in the pub and cinema?

Location and place are important cues: where one lives and where one was born, raised and educated are key indicators, principally because Northern Ireland is a society largely segregated by class, religion and ethnicity, particularly so since 1969 and the onset of the Troubles, during which there have been various attempts to intimidate people to shift residence (see Darby 1986). The names of certain neighbourhoods, housing estates, villages, and even parts of counties might in themselves indicate religion and national identity (just as their physical features are considered to indicate sectarian belonging; see Jarman 1993). One's primary and secondary school would almost certainly give an observer a fair chance at identifying the religious tradition in which someone was raised, since, on balance, Protestants attend the state 'national' schools and Catholics go to those run by the Catholic Church. In public agencies and institutions, such as Queen's University in Belfast, it is against the law to ask new employees their religion, but employment records do indicate one's secondary school, a sure giveaway to some.

Names also help people to tell identities. First (Christian) names when Irish/Gaelic (such as Kieran, Seamus, Siobhan, Sinead, Liam) or popular saints' names (such as Brigid, Dominic, Vincent) are often indicative of Catholic and Irish identity. 'Protestant' names include Elizabeth, Sammy, William, George and Charles, and surnames that are English or Scottish in origin are often signs of British identity (a surname beginning with 'Mac' is more likely to be Protestant than one beginning with 'Mc').

Language use overall can also provide clues to religion and ethnic identity. Of course, the easy identifier would be the Irish or the Ulster-Scots languages. In English, though, particular phrases, colloquialisms and epithets signal one community over another. 'Jesus, Mary and Joseph' would not trip lightly from the tongue of a good Protestant, and Catholics do not call each other 'Fenians' or 'Taigs', insults often heard in loyalist areas. Nationalists and republicans will often call Northern Ireland 'the North of Ireland' or 'the six counties', while unionists and loyalists might refer to it as 'Ulster'. The pronunciation of the alphabet also shows social difference. 'Catholics usually pronounce *a* as "ah" and *h* as "haitch", in contrast to Protestants, who say "ay" and "aitch"' (Buckley and Kenney 1995: 7).[3] And while this relates to class and where one was born and reared, these differences do reflect both enculturation within different communities and language teaching in schools. In a game of hangman which on a research visit in 2004 Wilson was playing with five primary school children in County Meath, in the

Republic, every time he spelled words with a, h and z (pronounced by him as 'zee' and not 'zed'), it elicited both laughter and attempts to teach him proper pronunciation of the letters in question!

Sport is another tell-tale sign of identity, in that the sports one plays, the games one watches, and the teams one supports are signs of national and class identity, as we considered at length in chapter five. To reiterate: cricket is British, hurling is Irish. Rugby is middle-class and (mostly) Protestant/British, football (soccer) is working-class and (mostly) Protestant/British, and Gaelic football is Irish. The only sports not sectarianized in Northern Ireland are those recently imported, such as ice hockey and baseball, which both communities can enjoy without negotiating the complexities of loyalty and identity (see Carter 2003b).

Telling is really a process of negotiating identity within the politics of place, work, home and leisure. The relatively minor differences that seem to separate Irish and British people and identities, what Buckley and Kenney consider to be the 'small differences' in culture between Catholics and Protestants in Northern Ireland (1995: 4-5; see also Akenson 1991; Cairns 2000: 442), that is, differences in regard to places, names, dress and leisure in a very small area, are actually major differences in social recognition and action, themselves part of the bedrock of the violent conflict. What may be small or insignificant to an outsider may be matters of extremely important historical and contemporary significance. In the case of Northern Ireland, the symbols that provide clues to social identification are the elements of social boundary, the cultural frontiers between Catholics and Protestants, nationalists and unionists, republicans and loyalists, that are the product of longstanding historical forces of colonialism, segregation, discrimination, racism and the conflicts of nation- and state-building. The cultural boundaries between the two major groups in Northern Ireland are national frontiers between the British and the Irish, wherein telling is a demonstration of the 'intellectual property' of each group, the cultural knowledge that is expressed and performed in myriad ways in everyday life, but also through more regularized and formal practices in the arts, music, dance, sport and parading (as discussed in chapter five; see also Buckley and Kenney 1995: 9; Harrison 1992). Just as we found in Inveresk, small differences have big meanings in what outsiders might see as relatively homogeneous communities. In rural Ireland, as in Belfast, small places can be extremely diverse social fields, where the minutiae of culture are the veritable stuff of the politics of identity.

Mary Catherine Kenney examined the forces at work in one small area of North Belfast, the Ardoyne, where she studied the interface between Catholics and Protestants, at so-called 'peace lines', walls set up between neighbourhoods of different religions that are meant to inhibit sectarian violence (Buckley and Kenney 1995: 73–98). Kenney explored the borders of the Ardoyne in physical and spatial senses, but also in terms of the social, political, cultural and economic boundaries between the people of the Ardoyne, Catholics and their neighbours (cf. Shirlow 2003b). She also looked at the boundaries of identity between young and old, nationalists and republicans, men and women, community activists and the IRA. Her ethnographic research was testament to the many types of the politics of identity that have involved the people of North Belfast for some time, as they have moved about within and beyond the Ardoyne, but also as they have shifted between various social and political roles.

Buckley and Kenney use the framework devised by Ruth Finnegan in her ethnography of the English city Milton Keynes to sharpen their focus on the negotiation of identity in both Belfast and rural County Londonderry, where Buckley conducted research (for a description of their two field sites, see Buckley and Kenney 1995: 15–19). Finnegan's (1989) analysis of music and culture in Milton Keynes led her to consider the various musical worlds in which people operated: some remained squarely within one world of music, while others travelled through many. This metaphor of worlds corresponds neatly to Peace's domains; both are evidence of the importance of social practice and place to the construction and negotiation of multiple identities. No *place* can contain culture fully, but culture has little meaning if it is not emplaced in some way. Individuals inhabit many worlds of identity and culture, and move often between them. These worlds of identity are domains of action and discourse, linked to place and locality in multiple ways. We have suggested that one way to approach the complexities of identity and place is through the motif of frontiers, in which cultural boundaries are created, sustained and subverted through social interaction.

Just as we saw for Inveresk, negotiating identity in Northern Ireland entails the enactment of social knowledge, linked to historical and cultural memory, but also based on the experiences of practice, the politics of telling. Telling is the Irish version of the universal practice of the cultural encoding and decoding of social identifications that find meaning in political encounter. Telling is a practice of negotiating frontiers, but it is also one of crossing and guarding one's borders. As William Kelleher (2003: 12) notes in his study of a border area in County Tyrone, telling is not only a process of watching and observing others, it is also about 'talking and participation', of engaging others who turn out to be from the same 'side of the house' as yourself. Telling is thus a process of self-identification, of 'watching yourself', and being aware that the story you are telling about yourself is an act of telling others about your own identities and identifications. In Northern Ireland there is a popular expression: 'whatever you say, say nothing'.[4] Telling proves that even if you keep your mouth shut in Northern Ireland, you can speak wonders. No matter how much you watch yourself when you watch others, you are still telling tales that cross the borders of identity.

Border Theory and Border Studies

Since the 1980s there has been increasing interest among anthropologists in the Northern Ireland borderlands, the land border between the United Kingdom and the Republic of Ireland that was created in the early 1920s when Ireland was partitioned. This partition created a twenty-six county Irish Free State (later made a Republic) and a six-county Northern Ireland, still a constituent part of the UK. Owing to the twin forces of European integration and the ethnonational and political conflict in Northern Ireland, which has the border as a central motif in the discourses among Irish nationalists and republicans, who see it as a marker of British imperialism, and among unionists and loyalists, who see it as a sign of British sovereignty, social anthropologists have sought to explore many issues of cultural and political change there. Among them have been conflict and cooperation, historical and other forms of social memory, sectarianism, ethnicity, justice and various types of policy.

Starting with the early work of Rosemary Harris (1972), a study that actually said very little about the border but which helped to establish some of the major themes in the ethnography of Northern Ireland that we reviewed in chapter two, anthropologists have turned increasingly to the issues of border life in Northern Ireland, where the borderline, the border as a political and social construction, and the notions of contest and dispute in a liminal frontier zone have all figured prominently as influential frames to local and national life. Coming after Harris, Joan Vincent has examined the histories of ethnicity, nationalism, sectarianism and violence in border areas of County Fermanagh (Vincent 1983, 1989, 1991, 1992, 1993, 1995). Thomas Wilson has investigated ways in which the South Armagh border is marked with nationalist and other symbols, and in turn symbolizes much more for border residents and border-crossers (Wilson 1993b, 1993c, 1994b, 1995, 1996, 2000). Hastings Donnan and William Kelleher have also conducted long-term research in the border regions of County Armagh and County Tyrone respectively; it is their work to which we will turn in the section following this one.

This attention to the border in Northern Ireland makes a great deal of sense because of the unfolding events there since 1969 when the Troubles erupted, throughout the waxing and waning issues of sovereignty, security and nationalism. The border events that reflected wider processes in Irish and British life, and sometimes triggered other actions which affected both the Troubles and efforts to end them, are too many to list here. A brief review can provide but a taste of how the border has been a motivating factor in many political and social issues in both political entities that it separates: the massing of the Irish army at the border in preparation for intervention in the North in the early Troubles; British helicopter and infantry incursions into the Republic, at many times and in many ways over the years, in the interests of the 'hot pursuit' of terrorists or of their interdiction;

efforts by both governments to close the border to smugglers and IRA action units; the removal of customs checks and immigration booths after the implementation of a 'Europe Without Frontiers' in 1992; and the selective closing of the border to deal with animal diseases, such as 'mad cow' and 'foot and mouth'. But interest by anthropologists in this border also makes a great deal of sense due to changes that have occurred in the field of anthropology over the same period, particularly in approaches to culture and ethnography, which swept the discipline from the mid-1980s on.

In fact, borders have come to the fore in many recent and innovative approaches in anthropology, particularly in new ways to theorize the de-coupling of space, time, culture and territory, and in attempts to reframe changing perspectives on nations and states.[5] Over the last twenty years the former approach has seen borders largely in metaphorical terms, as the perceptible but often obscured division between people and their 'others', and within the shifting terrains of gendered, sexual, ethnic and national identities. In these important themes within critical approaches to the conditions of post- and late-modern life,

> various scholars have adopted borders, border-crossings, and borderlands as focal metaphors that challenge conventional notions of culture, space, place and identity ... These writers de-emphasize borderlands as specific sites found near or around international borders and instead argue that they exist as zones to be found in all aspects of social life. (Cunningham and Heyman 2004: 290–1)

But the type of border studies that has most interested us, and to which we have contributed in various ways, has been that of a more empirical approach to structure, agency and narrative in the borderlands, border regions and frontier zones at and across the juridical borderlines that simultaneously separate and connect national states, or intra-state polities such as provinces or regions.[6] In this sort of border study political and social power are substantiated and articulated in often precise and particular ways that, while they have a great deal to do with the hierarchies of power that exist in all social relations (a principal concern of border theory), often have as much to do with the organs, agents and grand narratives of the state, which of course has national borders among its chief signifiers of sovereignty and citizenship.

Border studies and border theory are both represented in the ethnography of Ireland today, demonstrating yet again that the island should not be objectified by researchers in ways that make it different or special. Rather, it should be approached like any other place, as one that might yield information and insight into social, political, economic and cultural processes that may be found in abundance elsewhere, but perhaps not in the specific dimensions that can occur in a particular locality.

Home and Memory

People from both 'sides of the house' inhabit the Northern Ireland borderlands, and they all seek to sustain social and political boundaries that protect their homes and their communities in the face of remarkably potent national and global forces that encourage the transformation of borders into frontiers of communication and exchange. Holding on to the traditions of community while meeting the challenges of a transforming Northern Ireland is a problem for Protestant people in South Armagh. This is especially so when those changes turn you into an embattled minority in the borderlands of what was once *your* province, where the Protestant people have been the ethnic and religious majority, and enjoyed political, social and economic power for some time. Hastings Donnan (2005: 71–2) has noted that most anthropological studies have focused on ethnic *minorities*, thereby both stereotyping the majority and losing the opportunity to understand the ways in which majority and minority relations make both identities material.[7] In his study of Protestants in the Northern Ireland borderlands, where in County Armagh they are outnumbered by Catholics (by two to one overall in the border counties, see O'Dowd 1994: 36), Donnan (2005: 72–3) has chronicled the many reasons that Protestants give for feeling threatened, personally and as a community. State power has historically been weak in South Armagh due to the strong support among Irish nationalists and republicans for small and large acts of opposition to the British government and its agents. The region 'has one of the lowest rates of census return, television licences, vehicle insurance, and road taxation payments in the United Kingdom, routine acts of noncompliance taken by those subjected to decades of economic neglect and political disenfranchisement by a Protestant-dominated state' (Donnan 2005: 73). This relative weakness of the British state in the South Armagh borderlands is one of the factors that has led to the intimidation of Protestants from their homes. The threat of violence has been exacerbated by economic threats to their livelihood: industrial employment is almost nil, service employment is down, agriculture is dependent on European Union policies, and the Europeanization of the borderlands overall is resulting in more cross-border cooperation, which is itself a threat to unionists who decry any unnecessary cooperation with the Republic (see chapter seven). Despite their decreasing size, due to emigration, and shrinking political and economic bases, however, these border Protestants believe that 'in a very real sense it is *their* border and yet they feel they have little control over it' (Donnan 2005: 73, emphasis in original).

The significance of an ethnographic study of these increasingly powerless people, who once were members of a population whose pre-eminence was literally a matter of state power and sovereignty, and whose control over Northern Ireland was symbolized by a secure and unambiguous border, should be apparent to scholars of both border theory and border studies. The borderlands of South

Armagh are clearly a zone of shifting identities where the ties between people and place have been altered, sometimes weakened, at times even severed, creating conditions of dislocation and displacement. This ambiguity of identity and territory aside, the borderland Protestants continue to use the border to define themselves and to frame their relationships with others, in the border region, in Northern Ireland, and beyond. While their narratives of distress and dislocation are indications of their sense of loss, of their sense of a transformation of their social worlds, 'the trope of *dis*placement becomes a form of *em*placement' (Donnan 2005: 74, emphasis in original; see also Flynn 1997).

Like the people of Inveresk's domains, and the communities of the Ardoyne and London/Derry, the Protestants of the borderlands use narratives as key practices of identity and identification. The discourses of the loss of people and land, and of power and prestige, that have taken place from a distant idealized past to an unhappy present and into an uncertain future are all part of their wider narratives of belonging, tradition, territory and identity. These narratives 'enact' Protestant identity rather than result from it; telling the story of being Protestant, in constructing and passing on the narratives of individual and family and community, is itself an act of belonging. 'It is relating the narrative that makes them "Protestant" and not because they are a "Protestant" that they relate the narrative' (Donnan 2005: 75).

The enacting of Protestant identity, however, is not simply about belonging – as if belonging in individual and social senses could ever be simple, anywhere – because these narratives of victimization at the hands of the IRA, of government neglect and betrayal, of ethnic cleansing, of a steam-rolling EU, are also claims to social justice, in what is another way to make material Protestant identity. These border residents, like the community of Inveresk, as noted earlier, feel a 'threat of sameness': as their border becomes more porous, the boundaries of community also break down, making Protestants into something like their others, in the next village, in the Republic, or even in 'Europe'. They fear that the freedom to be different within their own community will be taken away from them, and that they will be forced to be diverse in ways that will change them irrevocably.

> They worry that their identity will leak away along its edges as the border opens up and they try to stem the flow discursively by recalling how they are written into the landscape's past, present, and future. As long as the border is fixed and stable, local ethnic boundaries may be muted and maybe even fluid. But as the border softens or begins to move around, people's identities are likely to be made hard and fast. (Donnan 2005: 96)

Thus they harden their identities as the national border becomes more permeable and the boundaries to their domains become less visible. The importance of remembering, of projecting their memories onto the physical landscape of their communities, of commemorating where people lived, worked and died, becomes the principal enactment of their identity, their most important political act.

Catholics and nationalists also struggle to make the spaces of the Northern Ireland borderlands into 'home places', despite what in their view has been a history of segregation and discrimination by the British state and the Northern Ireland Protestant majority. The nationalist people of County Tyrone whom Kelleher has studied for over twenty years are borderlanders too, with their own narratives of home, homeland, home-making and the 'home place'. This emphasis on the changing nature of the home in this Northern Ireland border region reflects a growing interest in anthropology in how people construct notions of home and belonging in the midst of post-modernity and the undermining of traditional ideas about the fixity of place, culture and identity (see, for example, Rapport and Dawson 1998). Much of this anthropology minimizes home as a place of rights, duties and social practice, and instead concentrates on home as a discursive accomplishment. Kelleher and Donnan are in many ways investigating the same things, in similar ways, but each in a different side of the house. Both clearly see narratives as political acts, a materialization of power and identity. To Kelleher, discourse is 'the material existence of linguistic and cultural practices that produce effects beyond and including the making of meaning' (2000: 142).

'Home' among the people whom Kelleher studied is about new narratives, new discourses of self and others, in a social and political world no longer stubbornly 'national' or state-centric, as was the case in the past modernist Ireland and Northern Ireland. Efforts to re-make home and homeland in the Northern Ireland border region today, after years of conflict and almost a decade of troubled peace, in a devolved Northern Ireland in a UK within an expanding EU, are efforts to reconceptualize relations within and across communities that are now on a global scale. The new global dimensions of transnationalism elasticize the boundaries of locality in this border region, reconfiguring local place and identity. According to Kelleher, this necessitates a reconceptualization of home, not in terms of ensuring fixed place within a fixed and stable community, 'but in terms of instituting a set of practices, routines, and everyday interactions that enable self recognition, make boundaries, and signify identity to others both within and outside its limits' (2000: 143).

Kelleher focuses on Mary McKeown (a pseudonym) and her family, and on the events and changes that have led cumulatively to her construction of a notion of home that is truly transnational. The many and important transformations she experienced over the last sixteen years reflect more general changes among many people, particularly women, in the nationalist community in the borderlands, but are also a complicated and individual narrative of change, a window on her life and that of her family. Mary's brother was killed by the British Army after crossing a border security checkpoint on his way to play Gaelic football in a field at the international borderline (see also Kelleher 1994). The British government said that it was an accident, but years of family investigation into the incident still leave many unanswered questions related to his and Mary's republican ties and sympathies, the general harassment of Catholics who crossed the border for work and leisure, and the unjust treatment of Catholics in a sectarian state. Mary's role in the investigation brought her to the United States, where, through the Gaelic Athletic Association, she met many other supporters of her cause, or of Irish republicans, or of anti-imperialism. Later Mary distanced herself from the republican movement, but grew in stature as a community activist. This all led to her leading a women's community protest against a global communications company setting up a mast on a hill overlooking the housing estate where they all lived (the company, ironically, was Orange Communications).

For Kelleher, these are processes of global forces of capitalism at work in Irish localities, forces that seek to rearrange local space and agency. Mary's narrative is one of action and reaction; the enactment of new identifications of home and community, and the articulation of new forms of local power. In this case the enactment of opposition and resistance is the performance of new forms of nationalist identity in the Catholic areas of Tyrone's borderlands, and as such these are worthy of scholarly attention, even by those who are too quick to privilege the politics of movement over the politics of place. In Kelleher's view, such critics 'should not cast the politics of home, place, and identity as a spatial false consciousness. Disempowered local people may likely turn critiques of local relations into critiques of global ones, and ethnographers ought to track that possibility' (2000: 166).

Mary McKeown's story demonstrates that attempts to reconstruct home by her and her family 'take place in a transnational field and that transnational relations are enabling for this woman and her female working class neighbors' (Kelleher 2000: 139). For Mary and her family and neighbours, remembering their family victims is but one act of resistance that ties them to other notions of home beyond their borderlands and even beyond Ireland.

Tales of Difference and Place

It is clear that at the heart of ethnographic research in Ireland today are the words and perspectives of Irish people. It is their tales about themselves, about their homes, about the people and places that are meaningful to them, that remain the most important forms of data that an anthropologist can discern.

The perspectives that we have reviewed in some detail in this chapter, of men and women from the rural West of Ireland, from inner-city Belfast, and from the borderlands of Tyrone and Armagh, demonstrate the importance of locality and place to their identities and in the identification of people with their neighbours, kin, co-nationals and others farther afield. These perspectives also show the diversity in local culture and identity, the polysemic dimensions to the practices of belonging in contemporary Ireland.

The processes of identity-making and remaking that we have reviewed suggest that notions of homogeneity in 'Irish' 'culture' need to be re-thought, if at times scrapped altogether, in favour of a model of reinvention and reproduction of diverse cultural forms, expressions, performances and everyday practices. Simply put, research templates, or assessments of local communities, that are supposed to reveal truths about Irish, Northern Irish or any other grand societal entity are no longer tenable as a research strategy or as a theoretical contribution. Precisely because of the increasing complexity and diversity of Ireland's people and their behaviours, in our view it is no longer feasible to discuss communities, or their cultures, as being 'pathological' or in a state of 'decline' (Scheper-Hughes 1979: 5), assertions that not only seemed reasonable to some, mostly foreign, readers at their time, but which formed the basis for some startling theorizations about Ireland in particular and anthropology in general (in chapter eight we consider how some Irish people reacted to these conclusions regarding their communities and culture). In fact, we do not think it possible for ethnographers in Ireland today to embark upon ethnographic research with the intention of studying community stability or decline, or notions of societal health or anomie; at the least, they could not do it with a straight face, or without linking communities to wider political economies in Ireland and beyond. Anthropologists would be foolish to wonder at the quaintness of Irish life in any respect, but perhaps particularly in respect of their ideas about slowly changing, post-peasant, homogeneous 'traditions' of Ireland.

This chapter, and this book, are testament to the complexity of Irish identities, cultures, communities and places. In Inveresk, Peace was struck by local people's fear that such forces that are often represented by terms like globalization, transnationalism and Europeanization would actually *reduce* their local communities' diversity and complexity, thereby making them all more alike. This 'threat of sameness' (Peace 2001: 5) flies in the face of the oft-asserted but seldom demonstrated, even less often disputed, notion that globalization will result in a decline in social barriers to heterogeneity, thereby liberating cultures from certain constraints that have prevented their diversification. Peace also laments the tendency of many anthropologists to construct a great deal of theorizing on shallow evidence, where 'modest ethnographic data is made to carry an exceptional meta-theorising load' (2001: 138). It is our hope that future ethnographers of Ireland will be less inclined to use its people in efforts to add to this ever-growing load of meta-theory, and be more attuned to listening to their hosts, whose own words might set new and innovative research agendas for the inquisitive, tactful and sensible researcher.

The social and cultural heterogeneity at the core of belonging in all of the localities and communities that we have examined in this chapter are proof of the lengths to which people in Ireland have gone to reinforce their senses of difference and distinction, to relish, and sometimes even disdain, their social variety, and to articulate continually their local notions of diversity. This is not to say that this is necessarily a benign process: the sectarianism and racism that are key ingredients in the diversity of Ireland are not laudable results of the processes we discuss here. But anthropologists in Ireland must be cognizant of one simple fact: Irish people are engaged in their own identity-making and reproduction. They not only read what we write, they write what we read. They know who they are, what they want, who they are not and what they do not want. As we have suggested throughout this book so far, these clear-headed projections of identity and culture make for dynamic social, political, economic and cultural relations, and tricky but exciting ground for anthropological fieldwork. And central to what people say about who they are, from where they have come, historically and geographically, and to where they are going, figuratively and literally, is the importance of place.

This fact does not allow us, however, to reduce ethnographic research to 'just' the words of our hosts and respondents. Anthropology is more than a narrative about narratives. Inextricably linked to what people tell us about themselves, their past and their 'others' are the participatory activities of the ethnographer, and the diverse sets of data that also can inform ethnographic analysis, such as historical documents, journalistic accounts, state records and the simple actions of witnessing and recording events, whether they be the grand rituals of church and government, or the mundane activities of everyday life. As Hervé Varenne concluded in his impressionistic and reflexive journey through a Dublin suburb, 'As far as I am concerned, the only justification for anthropology, the only reason why it should be supported by non-anthropologists, lies in its struggle to construct "holistic" accounts of the life of human beings in their local circumstances' (1993: 99).

In this chapter we have examined how the symbolic boundaries of community intersect with equally important perspectives on place and locality in certain locations in Ireland. 'Frontier' is a metaphor that appropriately captures the continual processes of negotiation of identity and culture that occur in the midst of the flows of people, ideas, goods, services and capital within localities, among domains of community, between communities, and across wider expanses of the political economies within which local places and communities are situated. With this chapter as a start, we seek to re-position place and locality within the anthropology of Ireland, to re-emplace it more firmly at the centre of what anthropologists do in Ireland. To accomplish this anthropologists must continue to interrogate the concepts of community, home, locality and culture, and not blithely accept them in the form that the meta-theorizing of post-modernity demands. Methods in anthropology are only as good as the questions asked, the problems raised, and the answers sought. We return again to Peace, who, like Varenne, sees the need for a continued dedication to anthropological methods in order to do justice to the social complexity that Ireland offers. In his discussion of the residents of Inveresk, whom we suggest are similar to many of the people of Ireland whom we have encountered in this book, Peace acknowledges that they

> fall far short of the perpetually mobile, increasingly rootless, identity-seeking migrants with which some anthropologists fill the category of the global ecumene. They know exactly where home is, they are aware with equal assertiveness to which community they belong, and they share these certainties with many others elsewhere in rural and urban western Europe. This makes it all the more imperative to do ethnography on solid, even conventional lines. (2001: 10)

To do this, anthropologists have to continue to listen, to observe, and to engage.

This chapter has presented, has 'made present', in Varenne's terms, ways in which Irish people act out their identities in the cultural and territorial frontiers of their lives. It has also explored many of the forces at work that have influenced or conditioned these actions, and in some cases have resulted from them. While these forces are decidedly local, regional and national in nature, these are not the only ones at play in framing Irish cultures, communities and identities, for all are caught up in various transnational and global relations. This has become particularly apparent in Ireland in recent years as the transnational and the global have been filtered increasingly through 'Europe'. It is these wider, supranational relations that are the focus of the next chapter.

–7–

Transnational and Global Ireland

There is no room anymore to define Irishness by what it is not.

Fintan O'Toole (1997b: 21)

In this book so far we have made a case for the need to view the past and present anthropology of Ireland as indicative of changes in Irish society and culture, of transformations in the theories, models and paradigms of social and cultural anthropology beyond Ireland, and of the scholarly and intellectual interests of ethnographers in Ireland, who for almost three-quarters of a century have engaged in dialogue with the fluctuating interests and needs of the academic world both inside of Ireland and in centres of knowledge farther afield. We do not want to suggest that the anthropology of Ireland is that of either a neatly bounded anthropology or a neatly bounded Ireland. We have sought to avoid the notion that the anthropology of Ireland takes its primary coherence solely from the place called 'Ireland', as if that is or was a clearly defined culture area, delineated in ways which make its spatial and temporal limits both clear and consistent. Nor do we seek to explore what some might see as a consistent or coherent body of anthropological knowledge, linked to and made intelligible by a readily discernible 'Ireland', which has a clear history and precise and neatly delimited contemporary dimensions.

On the contrary, the anthropology of Ireland is as complex, diverse and plural as have been the Irelands which anthropologists and other social scientists have investigated since 'modern' 'Ireland' came into existence. In this book we want to approach Ireland and Irishness (including the varieties of other identities among the new and old populations on the island who do not perceive themselves to be Irish, or to have Irishness) through the multiple means which anthropologists have utilized over the years, and which have resulted in multiple bodies of anthropological knowledge, and multivariate anthropological methods and practices. We see both Ireland and 'its' anthropology in their plural manifestations, as the 'anthropologies of Irelands'.

These anthropologies are multidimensional and multi-layered, and are as tied to international and global arenas as they are to the national. As an effect of this engagement with many levels of society and politics, the anthropology of Ireland is moving from the local to the global, perhaps as far and as fast as any other

137

'national' anthropology. So far it has not reached its potential, in that much more can and should be done to investigate the roles of culture and identity at every level of Irish peoples' articulation with transnational and global forces. The efforts made in this direction have encountered some interesting developments. We note, for example, that while Ireland and its anthropology are moving from more parochial concerns to more global ones, it is ironic that at least 'two Irelands' have switched places. The Republic, long seen as the less developed part of Ireland, dependent on agriculture, with a rural-orientated society dominated by the church and inefficient politics, has become the darling of modern and developed Europe. Northern Ireland, on the other hand, has gone from industrial zone of the first-world UK to provincial backwater, known globally over the last generation as the pre-modern site of tribal urban guerrilla warfare.

These stereotypical views are in great need of change, we suggest, because the reality is so much more complex, and this is a complexity which ethnographers are increasingly investigating. In this book we wish to bring these developments to the attention of a wider audience, beyond the past rather narrow confines of a region-ally and locally strategized 'anthropology of Ireland', which made Ireland into its own little 'culture area'. While our goal of widening interest in Irish society and culture might be seen to have good prospects because of changes in the terrain of culture globally, this change in a professional sense may be more apparent than real. Although it is arguable that no place in the world is now approached seriously as part of a 'culture area', and in fact there is little notion today in anthropology that culture areas drive theory, in ways which occurred in the past, nevertheless professional anthropology still approaches anthropologists on that basis, as might be witnessed in the American Anthropological Association placement advertise-ments, where, for example, posts are offered to Latin Americanists, or scholars with specialization in Africa or the Islamic world. Furthermore, although there is precious little consideration in anthropology today of bounded cultures or bounded peoples, national constraints still exist on the ways in which ethnographers design their research, and then go on to seek employment. And many anthropologists con-tinue to seek culture as the object and the subject of their professional investiga-tions. But what decidedly has changed has been the notion of the limits to that culture. Anthropology today, in and beyond Ireland, is interested in theorizing the flow of people and culture, and the movement of both across the global landscape.

While the anthropology of Ireland has throughout its history engaged most the-oretical shifts in international anthropology, it has not been found by scholars beyond Ireland to be a location of comparative significance. We think that this is lamentable, in that there is much to examine more globally which would have sig-nificance in an Irish context, and thus motivate and expand the limits of a narrowly defined 'Irish' anthropology. There is also much which happens in Ireland which is of comparative value to anthropologists elsewhere, who do not conduct research in Ireland, or teach there. In this chapter we examine changes in the social and political make-up of Ireland, changes which have fashioned a more diverse, multicultural Ireland, where the old ethnic composition of Irish and British, or settled and Traveller, has been transformed into a new mosaic of majority and minority, citizen and immigrant, Europeans and the others. It is an Ireland of 'new racism', of new ethnic conflict, of transnational peoples, practices and institutions. It is an Ireland where the new migrants from within and from outside the European Union are making the Irish, the British and the other residents and citizens of the island re-consider their roles as 'Europeans'. These processes of Europeanization are evidence of Ireland's new status as a transnational space, where the structures and actions of society and politics are linked in new, more and stronger ways to peoples, nations and states elsewhere.

The anthropology of Ireland which we seek to champion in this book must take into consideration those forces, practices, symbols and discourses which are not only meaningful to scholars, but are also meaningful to Irish people, who in various ways recognize them as significant in their pasts, presents and futures. And some of these forces are external to Ireland, emanating from such places as the centres of the European Union in Brussels and of the United Nations in New York. Because so much of transnationalism and Europeanization as processes in the transformation of identities is affected by national, international and supranational policy-making, we begin our examination of a more global Ireland with a look at an anthropology of political practice and policy processes, a theme which will occupy us in this and the subsequent chapter.

New Political Orders

New forms of governance are taking shape throughout Europe. New ways of deciding public policy, along with transformations in historical relations between political and civil society within and between European countries, are daily engaging global and local forces of resistance and subversion, on the one hand, and of support and enhancement, on the other. These processes are taking place within what scholars and others have labelled new social movements, new forms of subnationalism and identity politics, new perceptions of the old fixities of territory, sovereignty and citizenship, and new flows of peoples, capital, goods, ideas and information – all characterized through metaphors of space and place in such terms as 'ethnoscapes' (Appadurai 1996: 33–4). This new 'continental world order' reflects the creation of multiple and overlapping 'New Europes' (Bellier and Wilson 2000; see also Wilson 1998b) that are capturing the imagination of people at every level of politics and society both within the European Union and beyond its borders. 'Europeanization' is the term now widely used among scholars of European affairs who try to capture the mercurial elements of the day-to-day processes of greater European integration that are intended to involve the integration of institutions, behaviours and identities at every level of decision-making in each of the EU's current (2006) twenty-five member states, and among its present population of over 450 million.

One of the central motifs of governance propounded in the halls of power in the EU and its member states is that of 'social partnership', a term alien to many in other parts of the world and in differing political systems. As we noted in chapter one, Ireland is a leading proponent in Europe of the social partnership model, which includes government, business and trade union representatives, farmers' organizations, and leaders of the community and voluntary sectors in joint efforts to agree national social and economic policies. This model of social partnership, which entered the formal arena of Irish national policy-making in 1987, also figures prominently in local government in Northern Ireland, in large part due to the initiatives of the EU Special Support Programme for Peace and Reconciliation, which began in 1995 (Hughes et al. 1998). The idea and related practices of social partnership continue to figure prominently in the Europeanization of localities in Ireland, which we discuss later in this chapter. At this juncture, however, we note that Ireland is not only a land where European integration has been a significant aspect of public culture for more than thirty years, it is also a place where a good deal of work has been done in the anthropology of European integration, which sets it apart from most of the rest of the continent.

In fact, despite the importance of the European Union, relatively little research has been undertaken by anthropologists throughout Europe on the institutions and policies of the EU (although the number of such studies is growing; see, for example, Bellier and Wilson 2000; Shore 2000). This is partly the result of past and continuing ethnographic emphases on local communities or populations, and the methodological difficulties of conducting field research from a locality up and out to the centres of political and economic decision-making which are external to the community being studied. Perhaps surprising to some, however, the anthropological investigation of various aspects of the European Union – in terms of the ways its policies are experienced at local levels, and are defining and transforming a wide range of social identities – is becoming a strong theme in anthropological research in Ireland. This interest is resulting in a growing literature both on 'Europe' in Ireland and on an anthropology of the European Union in general (see, for example, Dilley 1989; Sheehan 1991; Shutes 1991, 1993; Wilson 1993a, 1993b, 1993c).

'Europe' in the guise of the European Union is very important to many Irish people, and thus is important in anthropology because of the discipline's goal of chronicling and understanding the social and cultural formations to everyday life. It is far from an exaggeration to say that the European Union has become an integral factor in everybody's daily life in Ireland, North and South, and it is generally perceived as such, welcomed by some, resisted by others. This is due to a number of factors which, although not peculiar to Ireland in the European Union, have given Ireland a unique configuration of 'Europeaness'.

There are many elements in the 'European' identities which Irish people have either adopted or rejected. A considerable number of workers in an economy which has long been dominated by farming and the food industries have benefited from the Common Agricultural Policy. There is a rich history in Ireland of historical ties to what is perceived to be the best of European culture. Among them are the connections fostered by emigration in the modern era; political republicanism shared with continental partners; the traditions of Christianity; colonialism and post-colonialism; and a shared Celtic past. Many Irish people look to the European Union as a possible arena within which to solve the problems of nationalism and sectarianism in Northern Ireland (cf. Kockel 1999). Some of the people just accept and even welcome their new citizenship in the EU as part of a wider process of European identity-making. Many other people in Ireland, however, deny a European identity precisely because the European Union may help to change the constitutional character of both the Republic of Ireland and Northern Ireland. Whatever the cause, the peoples of Ireland are aware of the moves, which originate at local, national and European levels, to one day have them acknowledge their European identity. Some support this, others oppose it. But the debate over European identity is growing in Ireland, and may be raging in the very near future when and if the peace dividend in Northern Ireland demands a larger role of the European Union, or when the special subsidies to the Irish Republic are ended, or whenever the issues of sovereignty are raised in the British parliament. While we have suggested above that both Ireland and its anthropology have undergone major changes over the years, one thing is certain today. The anthropology of the European Union in Ireland is already established, and will be both witness and analyst of the future impact of Europe in Ireland.

Although anthropological research in Ireland has increasingly turned to the study of public policy formation, we wonder if its most important contribution to comparative European ethnology in the future might be in the analysis of policy impact and reception at local levels. Because of their use of qualitative and quantitative methods, over relatively long periods of time, in localities, in order to contextualize the objective outcomes of policy within personalized, interested and symbolically charged local cultures and communities, anthropologists may be in the best position among all social scientists to provide the information necessary for the understanding of wider European social formations in the everyday lives of Europeans. Before we turn to ethnographic studies in Ireland that examine political policy and process at local levels, we wish to explore the issues of racism and immigration, which have captured the attention of millions of people across the continent, many of whom blame the EU's 'Europe without frontiers', and its integrated market without barriers to the legal movement of citizens and residents, goods, capital and information. We look next at the rise in racism in Ireland.

Resisting the New Racism

Racism is becoming an important topic in anthropological analyses of European societies, despite many forces which until recently had all but eliminated it as a research focus (Hervik 2004: 149). These forces include the political and humanitarian beliefs of anthropologists in general; the legal and moral codes which are intended to eliminate race as an organizing principle in many European countries, most notably those of northern Europe; and the overall turn in anthropology to issues of ethnicity and national identity in Europe over the last two intellectual generations (Gullestad 2004: 177). But this relative invisibility of race in the anthropological record is now a thing of the past, as anthropologists and other ethnographers have begun to see racism in its wider European dimensions, helping many scholars to focus on local and national manifestations of the problem (Modood and Werbner 1997). These European dimensions have a great deal to do with two processes. First, there is the new movement of peoples within a 'Europe without frontiers', a programme since 1992 of integrating the common market of the European Union. Second, there has been a related strengthening of the external borders of the EU, suggesting a growing support for a 'Fortress Europe', an entity of enforced inclusion and exclusion. As a result, anthropologists have been increasingly investigating and theorizing the changing roles of migrant peoples in each European country, as well as the transforming nature of movement in Europe as a whole, where new notions of home and away are developing within a transnational continental milieu. Verena Stolcke (1995) was among the first to draw our attention to the recent rise in racism in Europe and its intersections with new forms of nationalism and ethnic exclusion and conflict. Related research on international borders and national and regional identities in Europe has been stimulated by the pervasive and seemingly commonsense but astounding notions often to be found across the continent about 'others', from Asia, Africa and Eastern Europe, non-Europeans and non-EU Europeans, who seek employment and a better life in the EU (see, for example, Cole 1997; Driessen 1998; McDonogh 1993). As Marianne Gullestad (2004) shows for Norway, calls to recognize racism at home can be resisted, for good and bad reasons, even in countries that seek to eradicate racism in themselves as well as in others.

Peter Hervik (2004) reminds us of some things worth considering in the context of an increasingly transnational and global Ireland. Citing Malkki (1992), Hervik (2004: 151–2) notes that the new racism in Europe has moved away from the rhetoric of race and has unfolded in terms of culture, often in relation to the national order of things, and he warns that racism, even in the form of cultural identification and othering, can never be defined in the abstract. Racism is a social practice that is implicated in ethnic, gender, governmental and other orderings and dependent on the processes of social identification, and subsequent processes of making difference into hierarchies, of superior and inferior statuses. But racism is not only about recognizing and prioritizing difference, it is about 'the power to inferiorize, in particular the institutional power to control access to the labour market, political office, education, and the media, but also the power to use symbolic resources to engage institutional power' (Hervik 2004: 153). As we have reviewed so far in this book, the institutional and symbolic sources of power are changing in Ireland, and some of these changes are due to Ireland's new relationships within a Europeanizing and globalizing world.

Overall, we suggest that the social science of European integration and social change across the continent has begun to respond to the calls of these authors. Intellectual developments such as these are having an effect in Ireland, complementing in particular a growing literature in the sociology of the United Kingdom which has for some time investigated the interactions of racism and ethnic conflict, and changing national, regional and ethnic identities (see, for example, R. Cohen 1994; Gilroy 1991; S. Hall 1991, 1996; McCrone 1992, 1998; A. D. Smith 1995; Werbner and Anwar 1991). Anthropologists in Ireland have begun to examine in some detail the impact which the influx of new populations has had on traditional and contemporary social and political relations.

This new anthropology of race and ethnic conflict in Ireland – in a land which used to give people to the world, not receive them, and where most people have an abiding faith in the congruence of national culture and identity – is in fact evidence of a new transnationalism taking root on the island. The social boundaries of national and ethnic communities and identities are in flux (as we examined in chapter six), which is having a great effect on the widest range of social, economic, political and cultural relations, where the very nature of what it means to be Irish, British or Northern Irish is being questioned, and where all forms of governance and political, social and moral order are in transition. For the migrant in Ireland, the person of colour and the person who does not have English as a first language, this new Ireland is an experience of transnationalism along the lines documented and theorized in North America a decade ago (Basch, Glick Schiller and Szanton Blanc 1994). Ireland is their home, but not their only one. The Europe of the EU provides a terrain of opportunity, not necessarily a landscape of obstacles and confinement. And to the Irish and British citizens in Ireland, this new Europe is also a wonder of transnationalism, where they legally can work, go to school and even vote in twenty-four other countries!

That both Ireland and its people are in flux is clear; whether certain populations are in this dynamic state, in more or less degrees than in the past, is a matter both for empirical research and of theoretical perspective. One theme of this book, and something that has been clear to us for as long as we have been ethnographers in Ireland, is that Irish society has been in this state of flux for some time, and was never as static as some anthropologists have suggested, or have been purported to suggest. The Irelands of today have in fact departed from most of their stereotypical paths of tradition and stasis, in ways which make Ireland and the Irish as modern and post-modern, European and global, conservative and radical, as so many other more widely regarded societies, nations and states in the developed world. This is even true, we hasten to underscore, of Northern Ireland, despite the Troubles and apocryphal stories such as the airline pilot who advised his passengers, upon landing at Belfast's international airport: 'Welcome to Northern Ireland; please set your watches back two hundred years.'

In fact, the Republic and Northern Ireland are each beset with so many internally and externally influenced social and cultural alternatives, based in national and global economic and political change, that anthropologists and other ethnographers are, and will remain, hard-pressed to keep up. Simply put, demonstrating great changes in the fabric of Irish life, North and South, is not difficult; experiencing the changes of peace processes, immigration, rising crime, the expansion of the middle class, suburbanization, new social movements for human, civil and environmental rights, and the commodification of society are matters of daily life in Ireland. Explaining such changes, in ways which contribute to social and political understandings, and as part of the intellectual and policy discourses of Irish life, are the real challenges facing anthropologists as they reinvent themselves and their profession in line with some, but by no means all, of Ireland's reconstructions of self. Three areas in which the old inventions and new reinventions of Ireland converge and are put into stark relief are the new politics of race, ethnicity and gender.

'We're Not Racist Here'

Racism has long been a feature of Irish society, most notable in the past in the forms of anti-Irish, anti-Catholic and anti-Presbyterian policies and programmes. In recent generations such policies and practices of discrimination and exploitation have developed into some of the underlying causes of the current Troubles in Northern Ireland, as well as into clear strands of racism directed at various groups of people in the 'new Irelands' we have been considering. Among these victims of racism are the Travellers, a minority group of 25,000 or so in the Republic and 7,000 in Northern Ireland (Lentin 2001: 1.6, note 2), whose changing economic roles and social identities we discussed in chapter four; the ethnic minorities of the Republic and Northern Ireland, such as South and East Asians, Africans and Eastern Europeans; and smaller and more transitory groups, such as seasonal agricultural labourers, tourists and other visitors (as evidenced in the anti-English feelings which run high in some quarters of Dublin due to the influx of short-term working-class tourists who descend on that city to enjoy football internationals and hen and stag parties).

Of particular concern has been the rise in racist attacks on minority group members in almost all major urban centres, and most especially in Dublin and Belfast (the latter dubbed 'the race hate capital of Europe' in early 2004, see Doherty 2005). As Lentin demonstrates (2001), these attacks – ranging from major assaults to intimidation to selective exclusion in public venues such as restaurants – intersect neatly and unsettlingly with issues of gender, religion, refugee status and the need for skilled labour to sustain the economic boom of the Celtic Tiger. While the dimensions to this racism might appear to be new due to changes in Ireland's role in a world economy, it is clear that 'old' and 'new' racisms converge in many of the spaces of this changed Ireland, and that racism tells us much about Irish national and local identities. This racism in Ireland must be part of any new anthropological theorizing about the 'new' and the 'old' Irelands, because it touches a nerve connected to all aspects of Irish culture, power, history and identity. 'In theorising racism in Ireland, we need firstly to problematise Irishness itself and put paid to the notion of Ireland as a monoculture, a notion fostered by Ireland's strong sense of community and the commonsense equation of "Irishness" with "whiteness" ' (Lentin 2001: 1.5). Racism is not absent in Ireland, it is just that until recently it has been largely unacknowledged (McVeigh 1998: 12-14).

As we have seen, anthropology has been at the forefront of the social sciences in Ireland in reproducing some notions of traditional and modern Irish community. Racism has also long been of anthropological concern in Ireland, even if some of this concern has been muted, or overshadowed by other interests and concerns in the anthropology of the island which we reviewed in chapter two. Anthropology should now be at the forefront of problematizing those issues of multiculturalism, sexism, racism, patriarchalism, sectarianism and other forms of domination and exploitation which provide the cement that binds the notions of 'old' and 'new' Ireland, modern and post-modern Ireland, peripheral and global Ireland. The new racism provides a window on how Ireland deals with its new status as a transnational space.

At the core of the rising senses of racism in Ireland are various discourses and other practices (see Lentin 2001: 2.7–2.16, for a review of the various tropes in the discourse of racism in the Irish Republic). Racism is based on notions of Irish cultural traditions, heritage and authenticity, where the national homeland and the national culture are to be conserved and preserved against alien influence. Racism is perforce a process of 'othering', a dialectic between notions of self and home, and others and the foreign, where each reinforces the other's identity and ways of life. Thus racism in Ireland supports the notion that incomers, whether migrants, refugees or tourists, bring the causes of racism with them, along with the 'ills' of

Irish society such as secularism, sexual liberation, consumerism and alien religions. Other forms of racist projection blame immigrants for such things as litter, extramarital sex and avarice (Lentin 2001: 2.11), or for a lack of reciprocity in which they are believed to take more from society than they give (Peillon 2000). These discourses and exclusionary practices result in alternative and overlapping racisms in the Irish Republic, such as 'black' racism, anti-Semitism, anti-refugee movements and anti-Travellerism (Lentin 2001: 2.13), all of which are also present in Northern Ireland, along with racisms directed against other ethnic minorities and, some would suggest, against Catholics as well (Brewer 1992), in ways similar to those used against the Irish in Britain (Mac an Ghaill 1999, 2000).

Robbie McVeigh, in his analysis of contemporary racism in Northern Ireland, illustrates the implicit and accepted racialism at the heart of the perception of people of colour there, with this anecdote:

> In 1993, the former Manchester United and Northern Ireland soccer star George Best gave a speech at the Northern Ireland Football Writers' Dinner. Previously, the world-renowned African-Brazilian soccer player Pelé had been generous enough to suggest that Best was the greatest player of all time. Best's response to this modesty was to say that Pelé 'wasn't bad for a nigger'. (*Belfast Telegraph*, 24 May 1993, cited in McVeigh 1998: 11)

The comment is startling and illuminating in and of itself, but when one also considers the adulation that has been laid at Best's feet in Northern Ireland, where he is truly and widely perceived to be a hero, by both unionists and nationalists, and as a local boy who made good on a global stage (as was seen in the outpouring of tributes to Best following his death), then one must be forced to re-consider the codes of conduct regarding race and ethnic minorities that are acceptable in Northern Ireland. As McVeigh (1992, 1996, 1998) has concluded, the majority of people on the island do not see themselves as racist, and do not think that racism is a problem in Ireland. Throughout Ireland, people contend that they cannot be racist, 'because there aren't any Black people' there (McVeigh 1998: 13; O'Donnell 1995).

In this view, ironic and tragic as it is, the clear message is that people of colour are by their very presence the cause of racism. This racist logic would on its own be a worry, but it is also a referent to an empirical reality that is, quite frankly, inaccurate. While it has been difficult to estimate the number of people who are members of ethnic minorities in Northern Ireland today, due in part to the lack of census data since the census has historically been concerned with Protestant–Catholic ratios, their numbers are over 20,000, and more than 1.5 per cent of the population (McVeigh 1998: 18). And all predictions are that these figures will grow. For example, recent census and labour survey information shows a rise in the number of legal migrants to Northern Ireland. The 2001 Census records 26,659 people in Northern Ireland who were born outside of Ireland and the United Kingdom, with fewer than 7,000 of them from Western Europe, and a little over 6,000 from North America and the Caribbean (Bell, Jarman and Lefebvre 2004: 27). Point of origin of course says little about one's ethnic identification, and perhaps even less about what others may think of your ethnic or 'racial' identity based on your phenotypical appearance. But the figures attest to a fact of which many, if not most, people in Northern Ireland are aware: since the paramilitary cease-fires of the mid-1990s, there has been a noticeable increase in the numbers and diversity of people who have moved to Northern Ireland for work (most notably in nursing and health care, food processing, agriculture, and in other service roles, such as catering), education (particularly at higher levels, due to EU cultural and educational exchange programmes) and new domestic arrangements, where 'mixed marriage' can no longer simply refer to a partnership of Protestant and Catholic. This latter development is itself a product of the international mobility of Northern Ireland people, some of whom return from abroad with spouses who are not ethnically Irish or British. But while the numbers belie the fancy that there are no black people (and presumably other people of colour) in Northern Ireland, it is the underlying logic that is especially problematic to social scientists, social critics and many policy-makers in Northern Ireland. But not to all policy-makers.

As Hainsworth (1998: 38–50) shows, attitudes to ethnic minorities and charges of racism in Northern Ireland are often met with remarkably divergent responses by Northern Ireland's political parties, many of which cannot transcend their own policies regarding their political opponents in order to deal with wider social issues. A Member of Parliament from the Ulster Unionist Party (UUP), the largest unionist party in Northern Ireland, concluded that the proposed extension of British Race Relations legislation to Northern Ireland was a nonsense, presumably due in part to the protections such laws might accord to all Northern Ireland minorities, including nationalists; the same man wondered at all the fuss about anti-Asian bigotry in the province: according to him, 'his few Indian and Pakistani constituents "give no trouble to anybody. ... Nobody bothers about them. They are accepted as part of the scenery and I am not aware that they suffer any discrimination" ' (cited in Hainsworth 1998: 38–9). The Democratic Unionist Party (DUP), founded and led by the Reverend Dr Ian Paisley, has opposed legislation in support of Travellers on the basis that they are Irish, and should 'go back where they came from' (Hainsworth 1998: 47). The DUP have been in support of Race Relations legislation, just not its extension to include Travellers (Hainsworth 1998: 40). Nonetheless, on 4 August 1997 the Race Relations (Northern Ireland) Order was implemented, which named the Travellers as an ethnic group to be protected by law (McVeigh 1998: 13). But implicit and inherent racism is not the sole preserve of either side of the political conflict in Northern Ireland. In a public meeting in a

Belfast suburb in summer 2004, a local councillor of the Social Democratic and Labour Party (SDLP, a nationalist party which supports a more European and global approach to multiculturalism and human rights in Northern Ireland) complained that councillors were being 'treated like niggers' (*Belfast Telegraph*, 5 August 2004: 14).

Part of the fabric of racism in both Irelands is its denial, and the presumption that a passive ethnic minority population is a good one, because they 'give no trouble to anybody'. Denial of racism extends from a denial that people of colour, of ethnic difference, even exist, to a denial that anything bad ever really happens to them, to a denial that if bad things do occur, they are not due to 'us' (with an implicit assumption at work that racism is bred by the presence of its victims). Denial is not only a river in Egypt, as the old joke goes, but it is also a famous battle, won by Horatio Nelson, an admiral in the pantheon of British imperial history, a history which informs the streets and byways of Belfast and other locations in Northern Ireland. This imperial past, which has parallels in other European countries, and has ties to institutions and behaviours in the rest of the United Kingdom, is also remarkably opaque in Northern Ireland, unlike other European locales. Denial is a peculiarly obfuscating feature of ethnic and race relations in Northern Ireland and the Republic, for, as McVeigh concludes, 'There are minority ethnic people in Northern Ireland and they experience systematic racism. It is not the absence of racism but rather the relative absence of the discussion of racism which makes Ireland different from most European countries' (1998: 14). Irish racism is not a problem for the majority 'white' population, as long as the problem does not interfere with their lives. But systematic racism is certainly a problem for its victims, a problem to be resisted by some and to be avoided by others.

Sometimes the victimization of new immigrant groups is obscured by wider societal concerns with violence among majority populations, and thus the plight of such victims shrinks in importance to the bigger issue of the 'national questions'. In Northern Ireland, for example, the worst violence and discrimination is levelled at Catholics and Protestants; ethnic minorities there often have to keep their heads down, so as not to become implicated in a sectarianism which itself may mark the biggest difference between the 'new racism' of Northern Ireland and that of the Republic. As Donnan and O'Brien (1998) suggest, Northern Ireland Pakistanis often seek to avoid 'sticking out' in a social sense, so as to avoid being singled out for prejudicial acts, of bigots and sectarianists, but also to preclude implicitly communicated racist notions about difference in skin colour, dress and homeland which filter through the comments of neighbours and co-workers.

And while it is often difficult to avoid attention, due to the differentiations of skin colour, dress and language, these stereotypical cultural markers also make it difficult to present cultural heterogeneity to the wider Northern Ireland society.

The local white majority populations simply lump all Muslims and Asians into their own categories of race and religion (Donnan 1994). But the reality of cultural diversity among the transnational and migrant communities of Northern Ireland is much more complicated than the prejudicial constraints of others would allow. As Donnan and O'Brien indicate, the Pakistanis of Northern Ireland are not a homogeneous 'community'; to refer to them as such 'risks a sociological reductionism which flattens out their many differences' (1998: 200). Reference to bigger social groups on the island as coherent and homogeneous communities also smooths over the behavioural wrinkles and ideological identifications which give contemporary Ireland, North and South, its dynamic and multivariate character. The Pakistanis of Northern Ireland are in fact just one of the groups of people who have migrated to that part of the United Kingdom in search of economic security, peace and safety. In 1998 their numbers were estimated at between 600 and 700; at the same time there were approximately 1,000 to 1,500 Hindus and Sikhs in the province (Donnan 1991). Since the relative successes of the cease-fires, these numbers may have increased. All of these populations have experienced the transnationalism of new migratory movements across Europe; as part of these experiences they seek to celebrate their own cultural heritage while at the same time they wish to become integrated within local society and culture.

The transnationalism of these ethnic minorities, many of whom were born in Belfast and not Asia, must be seen in two important and related ways. The most commonly imagined perception in anthropological discourse is that of transnationals who have feelings of duty and belonging in two or more national contexts; in essence they are 'at home' in their land of origin and in their new land. As part of this transnationalism there is, secondly, the experience of diaspora, where in some cases migrants have had to settle, then move, often, thereby, establishing brief but important relationships with multiple 'homes', relationships commonly sustained through family networks. As Mark Maguire (2004: 97–8, 160) puts it in relation to the Vietnamese who arrived in Ireland twenty-five years ago, 'they belong, but differently so'; and though they may have a relationship to two 'homes', they are likely to feel 'strangers' in both. Many transnational populations have members who have a diluted sense of each of these homes. Often this is a generational characteristic, where the younger generation, born in the new homeland, has an ill-defined or tenuous connection to their parents' homeland. This too may reveal a hidden complexity, for, as Maguire explains, young Vietnamese-Irish people born outside Ireland 'often regard themselves as culturally different' from young Vietnamese-Irish born in Ireland, even when they are members of the same family. He quotes one young Vietnamese-Irish man:

> I see that most of the younger persons are going to get married to Irish people. Just because when they go to school they make friends with Irish people ... they behave like

Irish people, they act like Irish people, they even associate with the Irish people, every-thing they do is more like ordinary Irish people, because of the life and the integration they have has to be Irish. I think that Vietnamese people marrying Irish people is quite normal and that there is nothing wrong with that … But in my generation a couple of people married Irish people, but the marriages went bad. They not last long. It worries me. In my generation it's two different cultures. (cited in Maguire 2004: 135)

In Northern Ireland a similar view is expressed by many Pakistanis and other Muslims as being 'in-between' two worlds, that of Northern Ireland and Pakistan. As one young man told Donnan and O'Brien:

You're stuck in the middle because you're not truly Irish, you're never going to be accepted. The first thing that people are going to see is the colour of your skin before anything else. So you're not one of them and you're not a Pakistani either. Even over there [Pakistan] you're seen as a stranger as well. So you can't win, you're stuck in the middle. (1998: 217)

But being 'stuck in the middle' may have more connotations in Northern Ireland than this notion suggests, for Pakistanis and other ethnic minorities there are not only suspended between their 'old' and 'new' countries; they are also caught between the two sides of an ethno-national conflict. As the young man concluded, he is not truly Irish, but also not truly British, each of which functions as an essen-tial national identity in Northern Ireland. This young man is clearly walking the 'fuzzy frontiers' of national identity in today's United Kingdom (R. Cohen 1994), where the national identities of diasporic populations from the former British empire are mapped onto the often conflictual relations between the English, Welsh, Scottish and Irish, including the Northern Irish (unionists and nationalists).

In reaction to the sectarianism in which they have found themselves, Pakistanis in Northern Ireland have attempted to remain neutral, and to avoid being seen as either 'Catholic Muslims' or 'Protestant Muslims', according to the old joke (Donnan and O'Brien 1998: 197). This is not easy to do, because even the school which children attend can be seen as a way to take sides. But the effort and its message are clear, as was expressed by another Pakistani in discussion with Donnan and O'Brien:

Here it's not really politics, it's mostly local tribal differences and I think [for] someone who has come from another country or culture, that it is foolish to take sides. (1998: 208)

As a result, Pakistanis in Northern Ireland do not take political sides, but go about their daily routines in ways which do not interfere in the machinations of political parties and other legal and illegal political forces. Even when they vote, they do not do so on the basis of the issues of division which permeate the political culture of Northern Ireland. Pakistanis in Northern Ireland wish to become part of local society, not apart from it. They do not have separate ethnically defined neighbourhoods, schools and communities, and their businesses do not necessarily correspond to those with which other Muslims are identified in England (Donnan and O'Brien 1998: 203–4). Their goal is to keep a low profile, so low, some critics suggest, as to avoid bringing attention to the prejudice they suffer, for fear of making it worse.

This is not to say that local ethnic minorities will not stand up for what they believe. In August 2004, two local Chinese-born entrepreneurs tackled and disarmed a thief who stormed into their travel agency in the middle of the day on a busy Belfast thoroughfare and at the point of a gun demanded money. Explaining why he risked his life in this way, one of the brothers told us: 'we couldn't let them get away with that sort of thing; you have to protect your own'. What was left unsaid, but perhaps was not unclear, was what he meant by his 'own'.

The notion of being caught in the middle, no matter what you do, often leads to contradictory results. Among Pakistanis in Northern Ireland this may be illustrated in regard to the treatment of women and their selection of dress. Many continued to wear *shalwar-kamiz* in public, but when this attracted too much attention, some husbands put a stop to the practice. One Pakistani woman talked about the vulnerability she felt when wearing *shalwar-kamiz*:

> At the start, my husband didn't want me to wear English clothes, and then we went out and everybody was looking at me in these clothes [that is, *shalwar-kamiz*]. And then he says to me, no way are you wearing them. (Donnan and O'Brien 1998: 210)

Another woman noted that *shalwar-kamiz* was meant to deflect attention from women's bodies, but in Northern Ireland it had the opposite effect, where it seemed to increase visibility and vulnerability. For some younger Pakistanis in Northern Ireland, many of whom were born there, wearing *shalwar-kamiz* has become a form of cultural resistance, a sign both that I am different *and* that I am a native of Northern Ireland.

This changing role of traditional ethnic dress within patterns of assimilation and resistance highlights how transnationalism and racism cannot be separated from other forms of power and its abuse, particularly in terms of gender. For not only are racist attacks on the rise in Ireland, so too are attacks on women of colour. One such case, which horrified people in the Irish Republic, illustrates many of the concerns of this chapter. In July 2004, the headless corpse of a 25-year-old woman was found in a plastic bag in a scenic public area of Kilkenny. The head was not recovered. An investigation was immediately launched, in which press and police speculation centred on a belief that this was a tribal ritualistic murder, linked to longstanding practices in Nigeria, the homeland of the victim. The suggestion was that the woman's head had been taken as a trophy. To complicate matters, and to add both to its racist and prurient overtones, it was also alleged that the victim had been supporting herself and her family through the sex trade, as a dancer and prostitute in various locations across the Republic. It was further noted that since June 2004 four immigrants had been murdered in Ireland (*Sunday Independent*, 1 August 2004).

As this case illustrates, many in the new Irelands of the twenty-first century still perceive migrants as people who threaten the moral and political fabric of society. People of colour are especially vulnerable to this sort of assessment, particularly when they are women. Threats to immigrant women are just one of the costs that continue to be paid in an Ireland which is changing, but not changing fast enough to alleviate the sexism at the heart of public culture.

Patriarchal and State Dividends

Gender roles and inequalities have long been of interest to social scientists in Ireland, who for over a generation have examined gender in terms of various dimensions in Irish society, such as cultural reproduction, the institutions of the state and non-governmental organizations, labour, agriculture, and domestic cycles and everyday life (see Curtin, Jackson and O'Connor 1987b as the first attempt at a comprehensive and multidisciplinary approach to gender and social change in Ireland). Some of the early anthropology of gender was unsurprisingly influenced by Arensberg and Kimball's work, particularly in terms of a research preference for examining male roles, as suggested and provoked by Arensberg's *The Irish Countryman* (1937; Curtin, Jackson and O'Connor 1987a: viii; though see Salazar 1998). Much of this attention was part of the analysis of stability and change in farm life, especially among the small farmers who concerned the ethnographers who followed Arensberg and Kimball (see, for example, Curtin and Varley 1987), and who were indeed a large part of the population of the West and South of Ireland. Other anthropologists were concerned with women and their changing roles in Irish and Northern Irish life, whether at home, at work, or in public affairs (see, for example, Finlay 1987; Sheehan 1991, 1993; Throop 1999). Today increasing attention is being paid to how institutional and structural inequities persist in relation to the ways in which women are regarded and treated, in the midst of years of modernization and Europeanization, and despite legislation which at least in spirit is supposed to make sexism and prejudice a thing of the past. Some of this anti-women behaviour is experienced as part of the racism and ethnic bias of the patriarchalism of the polities of Ireland, North and South.

Pat O'Connor has been one of the pre-eminent critics of patriarchalism in Ireland. She uses the metaphor of 'changing places' (P. O'Connor 2000: 1.2) to understand how far Irish women have come in their efforts to resist a patriarchal society, but also how far they have still to go. More Irish women are now in paid employment, higher education and the professions, a 'change of places' that has also had an impact in their roles at home, with their partners and children. The social and political relations of the workplace, of education, of business and the professions, are also changing, in line with rights and liberation movements else-where in the EU and also more globally. Ireland, however, may still be seen as 'patriarchal' because of the low levels of married women's participation in paid work, the absence of abortion, the late introduction of divorce (1997), and the domination of the Roman Catholic Church and teachings (P. O'Connor 2000: 1.1; see also Mahon 1994). The Republic of Ireland is ranked seventeenth on the Human Development Index but only twenty-seventh on the Gender Development Index (P. O'Connor 2000: 2.5). In fact, according to O'Connor (2000: 2.1–2.2), Irish women have little access to structural power in Ireland, where certain types of privilege and authority are perceived to be natural and inevitable: 'the distribu-tion of power in Ireland reflects a gendered system of stratification which is as fun-damental as that of class' (2000: 2.2). Every advance made by women in terms of equal rights, pay and status is met by patriarchal reactions suggesting that men are under greater pressure than ever before to give up the structural powers they enjoy, in what O'Connor calls the Irish 'patriarchal dividend'.

> Nevertheless, in all sorts of ways power and privilege still remain very firmly concen-trated in male hands within the institutional church, the state and the economic system. Women are simultaneously depicted by such structures as all-powerful and invisible. I will argue that they are neither – but that they have played an important part in changing the society. (P. O'Connor 2000: 1.4)

The patriarchal dividend can be demonstrated in many ways in Ireland today, despite the moves to change places and provide alternative ideas, values and pat-terns of behaviour. In the Ireland of the Celtic Tiger, men's hourly wages are higher than women's; women are still most often employed in areas of 'female employ-ment' (primarily in the service sector) which are paid less and seen as less skilled; women are victims of vertical segregation, where they are under-represented among executives, administrators, managers and proprietors (despite their high educational levels); and women in leadership and management roles are consis-tently under-paid in relation to their male counterparts (P. O'Connor 2000: 3.1–3.7). This structural male advantage and power is supported by the Irish state, despite rhetoric and some governmental initiatives to the contrary.

However, women are no longer passive victims of such exploitation, if ever they were. O'Connor outlines how Irish women resist these structures of power, in the public and private arenas of political and civil society. This resistance, delineated in various ways through individual and collective consciousness and action, includes,

firstly, the challenging of male controlled structures within the world of paid employment and the state; secondly, the consolidation of an alternative power base for women
in the familial area; and thirdly, a transformational element (reflected for example, in
the creation of structures to meet needs which were ignored by a patriarchal society).
(P. O'Connor 2000: 2.9)

As part of these various types of resistance, women have formed their own
service organizations; they have been societal 'whistleblowers'; they have
appealed to supranational bodies (for example, the EU and the European Court
of Justice) in their efforts to change state privilege; and they have targeted
aspects of Irish culture which are not 'woman-friendly'. Overall, Ireland is a
landscape of remarkable and changing extremes of structural power and resistance, which takes it far beyond the simple notions of a traditional and relatively
unchanging small and poor nation at the edge of Europe. The Europe of the EU
has been one of the key forces in this reconfiguration of power, policy and practice.

Europeanization

Europeanization is an increasingly popular term in social science scholarship on
the EU, though used mainly in relation to governmental and policy adaptation to
EU legal and political structures and actions. Anthropologists, however, have
looked at Europeanization as a process of cultural integration and discord, an identification process with customs, symbols and political practices external to the
nation, yet somehow implicated in the past, present and future of the nation, along
with its attendant cities, regions and other significant localities.

Europeanization is in fact a process in the reconstruction of various forms of
identities in Europe (cf. Harmsen and Wilson 2000). John Borneman and Nick
Fowler see Europeanization 'as a strategy of self-representation and a device of
power', which is 'fundamentally reorganizing territoriality and peoplehood, the
two principles of group identification that have shaped the modern European
order' (1997: 487). From this perspective, Europeanization focuses on the issues
of culture and identity, both in terms of culture as a European Union project and
in terms of how EU policy has an impact on, and interacts with, local forms of
political and cultural identification throughout member states (Wilson 2000).
Anthropologists have viewed Europeanization in its relationship to regionalism,
deterritorialization and transnationalism, all of which combine to redefine relations of power within the EU and among peoples beyond its borders. And in the
midst of this globalization are the powerful forces of European integration which
have forged a political union and a common economic market of twenty-five states
and over 450 million citizen consumers.

In its broadest sense Europeanization is a process of making things and people 'more' 'European', but Europeanization is also a process of strategic political and economic change on the part of political, civic, business and transnational groups and institutions which are motivated by the programmes and ideas of the EU, and which are impelled by the need to adapt to the initiatives of others, in what is commonly known as a game of winners and losers (Wilson 1996). This form of Europeanization leads us to consider the strategic use of culture and identity by political and economic entities that seek an advantage in this game, particularly those who seek the funding and power which the EU can offer, whether directly from Brussels or indirectly through national and regional institutions.

Culture and identity are now important terms in European policy- and image-making. Culture can be used as a way to understand all types of Europeanization, whether it be in terms of institutional adaptation, the transformation of citizenship and identity, or the integration of transnational communities and social movements across national borders. This is especially apparent when policy-makers also perceive culture and identity to be key means to effect social change, in order to better 'Europeanize' and better compete on regional and national levels. This is what has been happening for some time in Ireland. In fact, the Republic of Ireland has become famous across Europe as a country which has not only adapted well to European integration, but has also mastered the game. It has a reputation for being an overall winner in terms of its Europeanization of policy, practice and image, which has made it a richer and more influential 'small nation'. And, as noted above, it has also been one of the few countries in Europe which has attracted ethnographic research into the nature and impact of the EU at local levels of society and culture.

Anthropologists in Ireland have recognized that they are among those best placed to investigate what the EU's economic and political programmes of integration do, and mean, in the everyday lives of its citizens and residents. But while the scholarship of the EU concentrates on the goals of an 'ever closer union' at EU and national levels of market integration and policy-making, it often overlooks, or takes for granted, the impact of EU-building at lower levels of society and polity. This is a shame, because European integration at any level will involve transformations in national and regional social structures, behaviours and values (Wilson 2000). The direct relationship between these transformations and the EU are often obscure, making it difficult for people to understand the sometimes rapidly changing circumstances of integration and Europeanization.

One arena within which local and regional transformation has taken place in Ireland has been that of the European Commission's Community Initiative, INTERREG, a programme that develops cross-border economic and political linkages between peripheral border regions of EU member states. In Ireland in general INTERREG is often touted as a successful EU programme, despite the fact that in some localities major difficulties are experienced. Ethnographic research in the small part of the Northern Ireland borderlands examined in the previous chapter, this time carried out in predominantly Catholic and nationalist areas, yielded a complex portrait of the national and local social and political barriers to the successful implementation of INTERREG in a region with some of the most disadvantaged areas of the two states, and one which has been ravaged by warfare and terrorism (Wilson 2000).

It was the EU's drive to create a Single European Market that led the European Commission, the executive body of the EU, to establish the INTERREG initiative. INTERREG supports cross-border cooperation; if a project is to be funded it must be based on cooperation among the government, voluntary and private sectors and among governments of the EU, member states, regions and localities. Such cooperation is crucial to the EU's project of integration, wherein political and social structures learn to cooperate across territorial, legal and cultural barriers in ways which will build a New Europe. At the start of the INTERREG programme in Ireland (1991–3) there was a real need for cross-border communication, cooperation and funding, because there had been little formal political and economic cross-border contact for seventy years. The programme's objectives and funding potential were welcomed in both Northern Ireland and the six border counties of the Irish Republic towards which it was directed, but the implementation of the programme presented a series of problems.

From the start it was agreed by the two national governments that INTERREG would be jointly managed by government departments in Belfast and Dublin. However, on the Northern Ireland side of the border it quickly became clear that the central government favoured local government projects, and that the state's plans to administer and implement the programme did not support the specific regional and cross-border aims of INTERREG. Nevertheless, the programme was pronounced a success by the governments, as a preliminary to the implementation of INTERREG II, scheduled for 1994–9. Central to the success of this new programme, at least as perceived from the vantage point of its architects in the EU, was its reliance on the building in border regions of political, administrative, economic and social partners, horizontally and vertically.

The EU's allocation to the Ireland/Northern Ireland INTERREG II Programme was £131 million sterling. However, applications were required to raise at least a quarter of their costs from state and private funding sources in order to be eligible for INTERREG aid. Thus the programme's impact was expected to be greater than the initial funds allocated, since INTERREG would only fund up to 75 per cent of total project costs. As one senior administrator of INTERREG assessed, the programme was expected to yield £250 million of total development aid, as it was set up to generate at least one pound for every two pounds spent (Wilson 2000). In fact, by 1998, funded projects in the second INTERREG initiative had averaged almost 40 per cent capital support from non-EU sources.

But there were obstacles to securing those funds according to many people in the borderlands. The most problematic administrative barrier to cross-border cooperation and economic development was the centralization of the Irish and British states. This centralization resulted in few effective regional structures ready to handle cross-border cooperation (this research took place before the Belfast Good Friday Agreement established a number of governmental cross-border bodies, which are still only modestly active while Northern Ireland awaits the return of the Northern Ireland Assembly, whose operations were suspended in October 2002). Centralization also meant a fair degree of mismatch and disagreement in terms of local and national economic and political priorities, and relatively little cross-border development planning. Local government in the border region had also failed to develop strong cross-border ties before the late 1990s, a reflection perhaps of the political barriers which had developed over seventy years of social and cultural divergence.

As a result, local councils in Northern Ireland did little to facilitate INTERREG, except in projects in which they themselves participated. However, most of these were meant to improve 'national' rather than cross-border infrastructure. These were 'safe' projects, generally supported by unionists who did not want to deal with local government in the Republic on more contentious social and political matters. Nevertheless, local government councils had important roles to play in INTERREG precisely because they applied for funds from central government under the initiative, in sub-programmes such as infrastructure and tourism. In the end, these local authorities became the most successful participants under the scheme, which made them both important agents in the economic development of the border region and key competitors to other bodies in the private and voluntary sectors.

The centralization of the INTERREG Programme was a problem for voluntary and community groups in the eastern border region of Northern Ireland, who from the beginning complained about the lack of information, the difficulty of obtaining and filling in the relevant forms, the confusion over application procedures and the secrecy about funding decisions. In interviews Wilson (2000) conducted with applicants for INTERREG funding, the government departments in Belfast were seen as distant and uninterested in local borderland concerns, despite the fact that the national government and its administration in Belfast publicly supported INTERREG and were only an hour's drive away. Many local people perceived that civil servants were often sympathetic, but the complexities of the application procedures and the programme's measures, many of which were administered by different government departments, all made the whole process murky and difficult to navigate. Perhaps this is not a surprising assessment among members of the nationalist community in the Northern Ireland borderlands, people long weary of what in their eyes was the oppression of a sectarian state. Yet many of these people had different and more positive impressions of this new funding policy, precisely because it was a *European* policy, which gave at least some of them an expectation of equity and efficiency.

Not only did local people continue to complain of a lack of adequate support regarding the application procedures, some also thought that their efforts went unrewarded because in their view local government controlled INTERREG funding in order to meet their own and central government needs. They concluded that central government's control of the application process and local government's partnership with central authorities made it difficult for community and voluntary sector groups to obtain INTERREG funding. Many also believed that the requirement to contribute at least 25 per cent matching funds was a government strategy to gain an advantage for local government bodies, which had much less trouble in acquiring such funds.

Many border people consequently felt excluded and marginalized. Their distrust of the government is a serious obstacle to any European funding scheme. While INTERREG II is supposed to be about partnership among the EU and local, regional and national governments, partnership is difficult to achieve with no history of effective regional government and a wide dissatisfaction with government in general. Such are the conditions in many communities in the predominantly nationalist and Catholic border region.

The EU's attempt to forge a 'Europe without frontiers' has only been partially successful in the Northern Ireland border region. Shared and contested culture both facilitates and impedes cross-border cooperation, in ways with parallels elsewhere in Europe (Anderson, O'Dowd and Wilson 2003). In the border areas of Northern Ireland, one's national identity, that is, whether one is Irish or British, inflects one's other identities, and while national identities may not always be good prescriptive models for certain types of behaviour, they are very good indicators of notions of community belonging – notions moulded by a generation if not more of sectarianism, war and prejudice (outlined in chapter six). National identities so dominate the cultural identifications of border people, perhaps of all people, in Northern Ireland that European identity is often perceived as a role to be played in order to secure a grant from the EU. As one farmer told Wilson: 'I know I am a European, but I do not think and act as a European. I am Irish and only have to be European when I want something from Europe.'

The cultural barriers to cooperation between nationalists and unionists within Northern Ireland are clear, and they extend to most aspects of cross-community relations, through church, sport, work, business and politics, which in the past were often strictly segregated by religion or political identity. The nationalist–unionist divide is also often played out in terms of local government cooperation across the borderline, when in the past, for example, a majority unionist district council in the North refused to work closely with local government in the Republic.

But just as those aspects of culture divide people in Northern Ireland one from the other, it would be wrong to assume that nationalists in Northern Ireland and in the Republic are a homogeneous lot. Political culture in the two constituencies has developed along separate lines since the partition of the island in the 1920s, in ways which have brought some aspects of the two nationalist traditions closer, but also in ways which have diverged considerably, especially in terms of the use of violence. As a result, two distinct political cultures have arisen on the island, that of the Republic of Ireland and that of Northern Ireland. This can be seen in a different border area, on the Irish Republic's side of the borderline, where a different culture of development offers a variant on Europeanization in Ireland.

Donegal is the most remote county in the Republic of Ireland, at least in terms of its distance from the capital, Dublin. It is one of the nine counties of the traditional province of Ulster, and one of the three which was kept in the Irish Free State when Ireland was partitioned, thereby guaranteeing a Protestant majority in the remaining six Ulster counties that formed Northern Ireland. While Donegal suffered from its alienation from the rest of Northern Ireland and its peripherality in the Irish Republic, it has revived with the development of the Celtic Tiger, due largely to substantial levels of Foreign Direct Investment (FDI) since the 1980s, including the support it has received from the EU through its Structural Funds. This has led to a new culture of development in Donegal, a transformation which has altered the materiality of social and political life considerably. Donegal has in fact become Europeanized:

> In County Donegal, as in most other parts of the country, the EU is everywhere; in signs displayed next to almost every infrastructure, building or development project, in shops, schools, hospitals and libraries, in the local media, in people's conversations. Quite simply, it has entered the fabric of life of the County. And in a less tangible way, the EU has also had a fundamental effect on the locus of power in Donegal, altering the relationship between local communities and the Irish state in quite profound ways. (Collinson 2005: 291)

This process of Europeanization has created alternative sources of power in the county, thereby changing the organization of local politics, and their overall articulation with Dublin. As Collinson has indicated, the establishment of new and influential local development structures in Donegal has challenged traditional forms of politics in a county long famous for its charismatic and personalistic patron–client politics (Sacks 1976). The new European-inspired and -directed culture of development has in fact created a 'new tier of mediation between local people and the state and EU' (Collinson 2005: 291).

The bases for these changes in Donegal political culture are similar to those in Armagh. EU development planning depends on the promulgation and acceptance of two principles, those of 'subsidiarity' and 'partnership', which in tandem are supposed to stimulate 'bottom-up' development planning. This empowerment of locality relies on the notion of a relatively equal representation from three distinct sectors in Irish public life: state bodies (government and civil service), 'social partners' (trade unions and employers) and local communities, elected by members of area-based development strategy groups that are themselves established through agreements made between the national government and the EU (see Collinson 2005: 293, for a better picture of this new EU development culture). These partners are an actualization of the EU's subsidiarity principle: decision-making and the exercise of power should be at the level of politics closest to the optimum solution to the problem. In short, subsidiarity means that whatever decisions need to be taken at the lowest levels of bureaucracy and government should be taken there.

These principles at work have undermined the historical domination of the 'Ruling Trinity' of local Donegal life, that of the priest, the politician and the shopkeeper, who are themselves a reproduction of church, state and business, which between them have determined the development of modern Ireland (as so strikingly demonstrated in Eipper's ethnographic study in Cork [1986]). Europeanization in Donegal, and elsewhere in Ireland we suspect, has undermined the relations between the members of the trinity, and in particular has diminished the power of local politicians. Because EU regulations demand a high degree of transparency and accountability in how development monies are acquired and allocated, local politicians can no longer guarantee that industrial, urban and rural development are theirs to command. In the early and middle years of the independent Irish state the opposite was true: development policies were decided in Dublin, and the government of the day determined where the money was to be spent. This was the backbone of the patronage politics which anthropologists have examined for generations (see, for example, Bax 1973, 1975; Komito 1984, 1989, 1993; Wilson 1989b, 1990). Today, this classic type of machine politics cannot control the material resources which allowed politicians to offer and grant the 'favours' that helped them to shore up support at the polls. On the contrary, not only have politicians been relegated from positions of control in the development process to just one group of interested actors, their current role is in some circles seen to be the least important. 'The fact that so few of the management boards and advisory committees which manage EU programmes in the county include any local politicians is cited by many of those working in this sector as one of its principal strengths' (Collinson 2005: 295). Among participants in European development programmes, which include INTERREG and LEADER (a rural development initiative), there has arisen a particular 'discourse of development', which reflects a philosophy of empowerment of local communities, as opposed to an empowerment of local government. As one community development worker complained to Paul Collinson, who was conducting doctoral research in Donegal in 1997:

They [politicians] don't consult with any community groups, they're not democratic, and they don't believe in Community Development at all. They believe it's only good for building a community hall, or organizing flower arranging classes, or whatever. All they're interested in are projects which will generate a profit. They're doing nothing about reconciliation and social exclusion. (cited in Collinson 2005: 296)

These notions of profit and economic development in Donegal should not be too surprising, despite the fact that reconciliation and social inclusion and exclusion are clearly and widely disseminated goals of European development. European integration is, after all, about the business of commerce, and about cultures of capitalist cooperation. While Europeanization has important institutional and policy dimensions, in Ireland and beyond, it is also about changing and converging practices and values in regard to such things as money, tourism, sex, sports and language (cf. Borneman and Fowler 1997), principal domains in the cultures of politics. As we have shown in this and previous chapters, these forces of transnational and global change have tied the Irish ever more closely to peoples and places elsewhere, thereby setting aside past notions of Ireland's peripherality.

'Ex-isle' in Europe

This chapter has reviewed some aspects of the new racism in Ireland, as they are linked to developing forces of transnationalism and globalization. The European Union has been a major element in these transformations, where refugee, 'economic immigrant' and 'illegal immigrant' have become new identifications for migrants and others in their efforts to preserve or resist the national dimensions to 'Fortress Europe' (Leontidou, Donnan and Afouxenidis 2005). Much as happened in Spain, the new statuses of Ireland, as Celtic Tiger, as winner in the game of European integration, as exemplar of an internationally respected sovereign state in UN affairs, have brought with them 'the creation of a new subjectivity for the non-European newcomers' (Merion 2004: 242). The EU is itself a transnational organization. By definition it aims to transcend national barriers to international state cooperation. To do this it has set itself on a course which demands ever-increasing integration, communication and cooperation at every major level and in every major sector of member states' economies, polities, societies and cultures. But this transnationalism of policy and political practice cannot be limited solely to public and state domains. The EU seeks to involve its citizens, and even many Europeans beyond its borders, in the wider processes of Europeanization, which in anthropological terms at least is a process of social identification and differentiation, linked to the various and often disputed notions of European identity. The new racism of Ireland, North and South, is a product of these transnational forces, of labour migration, of the commoditization of culture and identity, of the modernizing forces of the greatest trading bloc in world history. It is also a racism tied to old notions of differentiation and bigotry in Ireland, particularly as they are directed at Travellers, whose mobility has been used against them, both historically and today. And while the new transnational Ireland is clearly a more diverse and multicultural Ireland, it still demonstrates the patriarchalism and genderism which marked it in the past. Even given the successes of new political and moral orders, through new social movements of feminism, environmentalism and religious revivalism and liberation, there is still a great deal to achieve in the transformation of national hurdles to the transnationalism of Europeanization and globalization.

The important point to be made from all of this anthropological and other social scientific concern with racism, ethnic conflict, genderism and national and other identities in Ireland is that while in past years we and other anthropologists have attempted to set certain aspects of the anthropological record straight in order to redirect research agendas and to inform visiting scholars as to the diversity and depth of modern Irish life (see, for example, Curtin, Donnan and Wilson 1993a; Curtin and Wilson 1989a; Donnan and McFarlane 1989b; Peace 1989; Wilson 1984), we need, in our efforts to persevere in the integration of notions of Irish life and Irish anthropology, to clarify that Ireland is also as 'post-modern' as any other place and space in the globe today. The forces which mark post-modernity, post-colonialism and post-industrialism have been longstanding in the creation of Irish social and cultural alternatives. Transnationalism and globalization, in the guise of the transformations wrought by Europeanization, immigration and emigration, feminism and human rights legislation, are forcing the people of Ireland to consider their roles in what we called at the beginning of this book the reinvention of Ireland.

So many people are changing places, roles and perspectives in Ireland today that their very Irelands are changing around them too. Ireland is now many, with multiple and diverse alterities which give substance to the reinvented Irelands that are the focus of this book. Increasingly tied to the global and transnational processes explored in this chapter, Ireland can at last begin to see itself as more than just a stepping stone between London and New York, the twin poles between which it for so long imagined itself. As Fintan O'Toole has punned, 'After centuries of sending its people into exile, Ireland became itself an ex-isle' (1997: 11), in that it no longer conceives of itself only in relation to Britain, as marginal and cut off from where it believed lay the centres of power. In the next chapter by way of conclusion we consider the major themes which have driven the many different anthropologies that have sought to understand these new imaginings.

–8–

Ethnographic Experience and Engagement in the Anthropology of Ireland

> In Anthropology the essential facts of life must be stated simply and fully, though in scientific language, and such a plain statement cannot really offend the most delicately-minded nor the most prejudiced reader.
>
> Bronislaw Malinowski (1932: xlv)

This book has been about the construction and reinvention of Ireland, or the many Irelands, on the one hand, and the anthropology of Ireland, or the many anthropologies of Ireland, on the other. There have been diverse sources of the creation and reproduction of modern Ireland, and we have touched upon many of them in the pages above. Imperialism, colonialism, capitalism, rebellion and resistance have been prime economic and political movers, matched in various local, regional and national ways by sectarianism, nationalism, racism and sexism. Yet throughout these the idea of Ireland has taken shape, and has motivated the various Irish, British and other peoples on the island, and across the globe, to perceive and experience Ireland in ways which give form to the thoughts, actions and social structures that breathe life into Irish culture.

In fact, in Irish eyes, but in many more around the world, where the Irish people and Irish ways are held in both esteem and loving favour, Ireland is an integral part of the global scene. This is due of course to the reach of the Irish diaspora, and of the political, economic and social successes that Irish people have achieved, at home and in exile, on many local and global scales, which have in the last decades spurred on the Celtic Tiger miracle. But it also has a great deal to do with the cultures of Irishness that speak so clearly to the non-Irish peoples of the world, who have, through common experiences, of exile, of conquest, of post-coloniality, perceived Ireland and the Irish as both accessible and perhaps even integral to changing global notions of modernity and post-modernity. At the very least, it is difficult to imagine the other peoples of the British Isles without considering the roles which the Irish played in their development. As Declan Kiberd concluded in this book's opening epigraph, 'If Ireland had never existed, the English would have invented it' (1995: 9; though the reverse is also true, as Foster [2001: 26] suggests). And the English are not the only population to invent Ireland as an other to itself;

how many Irelands have been imagined by the overseas Irish, whose constructions of the 'old country' have each in their own ways helped to fashion their new country's vision of the old?

As we have indicated, the anthropology of Ireland has had as many sources to its construction as has the Ireland it seeks to understand. Among the forces that have shaped the anthropology of Ireland have been American cultural anthropology and British social anthropology, and their changing theoretical and methodological concerns and professional requirements.[1] But we have also sought to show that the anthropologies of Ireland are based on the changing notions of identity, society and culture in Ireland, especially as they are linked to each other and to other social, economic and political structures and forces. The anthropology of Ireland is also a historical record, and it reflects the changing histories of the peoples who inhabit Ireland. As we have emphasized throughout this book, all of these processes, at every level of Irish society and politics, have involved individual and small group agency. We have illustrated in the pages above, with reference to a wide range of anthropological and other ethnographic studies, that such agency occurs in local levels of Irish life, which have not traditionally been the focus or in some cases even of interest in many other academic disciplines. In a general and perhaps hegemonic view in anthropology, such local agency occurs at local levels in particular ways that inform other levels and locales in society – the anthropological perspective is on the connections and interactions among the social, economic and political fields, levels, arenas and institutions that tie peoples and places to each other (cf. Eipper 1986), and not solely, as is widely believed beyond the discipline, on the locality itself. Indeed, throughout this book we have tried to view Ireland not as a 'mere example' of wider issues, but as a site 'for the examination of how locality emerges in a globalizing world', as somewhere that the histories and cultural particularities are in the end always subject to the 'dynamics of the global' (Appadurai 1996: 18). And as we have seen, the three factors that Appadurai (1996: 198) identifies as currently most affecting the production of locality – the nation-state, electronic media and diasporic movement – have both expanded and constrained the space within which Ireland has been imagined, opening up new possibilities while closing down others and enabling the invention of 'Ireland' in ways that are sometimes subversive, sometimes resistant, and sometimes celebratory.

Consequently, our concern with social actors and the politics of agency does not end with how they operate in Irish society and culture. We also seek to provide windows on how the anthropology of Ireland might speak to anthropologies elsewhere, and how the study of Irish society and culture might prove useful beyond Ireland. To that end we have explored various aspects of anthropological identity and voice, but in this concluding chapter we wish to investigate further professional anthropological practice, and in particular examine anthropology in Ireland through a focus on ethnographic experience and engagement. Thus we return to the questions with which we began this book, questions about who invented Ireland, to ask 'who invented the anthropology of Ireland?' To answer this question, we must not only consider a bit more of the professional practice of anthropology but also a bit more of the state of anthropological theory and method today.

From Bog to Theory and Back Again

As we discussed in the introductory chapter, in the 1990s social anthropology as practised in Ireland was still burdened with the baggage of popular stereotypes and an often imprecise notion of what it had to say about Irish culture. While this may have been less true for researchers in Ireland who came from elsewhere, who often had a precise idea of what they wanted to say about Irish culture, even if in many instances it was to suit fashionable ideas that were important in their own countries (Wilson 1994a: 4), it is clear that the major theme in Irish ethnography before the 1970s was that of local community studies, an emphasis that persisted through to the 1990s. But as early as the 1980s, it had become evident to anthropologists and other ethnographers working in Ireland, and many more who were conducting or planning ethnographic research, that communities were no longer tenable as the object of ethnographic study, as they were increasingly regarded as social constructions based on outdated anthropological structural-functional models (see D. Bell 1981).

In 1989 the first major collection of ethnographic case studies of local Irish communities, *Ireland from Below*, was published (Curtin and Wilson 1989b), in what was significantly seen as a conscious effort to break with past theoretical models, to demonstrate, primarily for an anthropological and Irish readership, that ethnographers in and of Ireland had 'come a long way from their predecessors' views of static communities tied together through the forces of tradition, within frameworks of kinship and social structure, religion and myth, and isolation and egalitarianism' (Curtin and Wilson 1989a: xv). This collection, which served as a basic text in anthropology and ethnography for over a decade in most universities in Ireland, did not seek to transcend past anthropological models simply as a matter of professional progress; it was clear to its editors and contributors that Ireland had, by the 1980s, undergone radical social, economic and political transformations, and that ethnographic research was particularly well suited to chronicle and understand the important forces and events that were affecting local communities, forces which communities in turn sought to influence.

In the 1980s, for example, it was already apparent that the Republic of Ireland was experiencing de-industrialization and urbanization on an unprecedented scale, and, as we have shown above, these processes, while altered in focus and effect, are still active in Ireland, particularly in the form of consumerism, service economies, the decline in agriculture and rural communities, and the reassessments of class, race and ethnicity. The changes in the residence and living standards of Irish people were complicated by a remarkably new event in modern Irish history: in the 1980s the longstanding patterns of depopulation and migration had changed, with the advent of wide-scale participation in short-term emigration, the rise in the numbers of returned migrants, and the shift in population both to the East of Ireland and to the suburbs (for a more complete review of these developments, see Curtin and Wilson 1989a; for a review of how this affected the anthropology of cities, see Curtin, Donnan and Wilson 1993a). And anthropologists sought to keep up with these new departures in the make-up of Ireland, including those that were the result of communal violence in Northern Ireland, by providing case studies of specific communities, and the agents of short- and long-term change, as a partial complement to the macro-sociological analyses that were changing the nature of social science in Ireland at the time.

Ethnographers had a simple but important goal in mind then to examine 'the level of human day-to-day experience, the level which shapes the quality of people's lives', in order to document and analyse 'the complexities of social experience and discourse that go to make up, through the building blocks of communities within communities, the totalities of Irish society' (Curtin and Wilson 1989a: viii). *Ireland from Below* covered a great deal of ground that was new to ethnographic research, or at least to ethnographic research as it had been practised in Ireland up to that time, and it offered new approaches to such important themes in Ireland as religion, party politics and government, rural and urban economic development, class relations and other ways in which 'individuals and groups have adapted, or failed to adapt, to the new Ireland' (Curtin and Wilson 1989a: xv). But the anthropologists of the late 1980s knew there was much more to do to keep up with the transformations of that new Ireland, an Ireland which we have suggested throughout this book is still 'new', in what has been a succession of transformations and reinventions, necessitating that anthropology embrace its new role of studying all forms of social, economic and political change. Thus, since 1989, the anthropology of Ireland has increasingly turned its eye towards the critical analysis of culture, power and identity, in gender, ethnic, racial and other relations, in places and arenas of leisure and popular consumption as well as in new spaces of politics and economics. In the chapters above we have sought to illustrate the threads in theory, method and overall anthropological interest that connect ethnographers today to those who changed the dimensions of Anthropology Ireland in the late 1980s, and to those who framed anthropology in the generations before.

Thus this book also has been about the anthropology of change in Ireland, an anthropology insistent on keeping pace with the transformations that Northern Ireland and the Republic have undergone since the 1980s. In the previous chapters we have reviewed some of these anthropological transformations in theoretical and methodological approach (and we visit a few more in the pages below). Among them have been regional and national analysis, historical anthropology and anthropologies of the body, of subversion and dissidence, of supranationalism and globalization, all of which involve various forms of the politics of identity and the celebrations of old traditions and new cultural inventions. Throughout these radical changes in Irish life, and their related new departures in the professional field of anthropology, ethnographers have kept their focus on the everyday of localities and communities (even if today there is more of an emphasis on belonging to institutions and groups rather than on communities, whose limits and boundaries are more porous, or perhaps just more transparent, than ever), but they continue to recognize that more is needed. The metaphor used in the 1989 collection serves just as well today in regard to ethnographic research: Ireland is constructed from below, from the terra firma of locality, from the perspective of those who live and work in the marshland of the bog, on the shop floor, in the government office, and at the IT workstation, and that is where anthropologists need to go to do their own 'fieldwork'.

Over the last twenty years one of the most consistent and compelling voices working to persuade anthropologists in and of Ireland to change some of their direction has been that of Lawrence J. Taylor, who in particular has increasingly called upon anthropologists to engage the 'construction of the national self', along with their roles in that construction:

> the direction I favour is suggested by reflection not only on what anthropologists have done in Ireland, but on the Irish public's occasionally vituperative reaction to anthropology. That reaction is an element in the continuing construction of Ireland, a process with its own symbolic geography that defines Ireland internally and externally in relation to a limited number of significant and changing 'others'. (Taylor 1996: 215)

In this passage Taylor makes a clear case for seeing locality in Ireland from perspectives that allow anthropologists and others to approach the dialectical relations between local communities and their wider nations and states. By concentrating equally on national and local discourse, in a more interpretative anthropology that is sensitive to processes of identity and identification that are implicit in the notions of 'othering', anthropologists 'may throw a specifically anthropological light on issues important to both public and academic discourse and debate in Ireland' (Taylor 1996: 215). Taylor's evocation complements those of many contemporaries who have made similar entreaties to widen anthropological focuses in Ireland, to include regional, national and supranational constructions of self, and to consider analyses of the more global aspects of locality, culture and identity in Ireland (see, for example, Eipper 1986; Ruane 1994; Sheehan 1991; Shutes 1991, 1993; Tucker 1989; Vincent 1991, 1993; Wilson 1984, 1998a).

Taken together, these redirections in the anthropology of Ireland have guided us in this book, in our effort to shed more 'anthropological light' both on what matters to anthropologists and on what matters in Ireland, to the peoples of Ireland with whom we live and work. As we have suggested too, this illumination is not easy, in part because much anthropological theory, and certainly faddish and prescriptive theory, needs very little substantive data to test it, if any at all, since a great deal of contemporary social theory is philosophical in approach, universalist in character, and through its own first principles has excluded scientific testing and the rules of evidence.

Nevertheless, we reiterate that the anthropology of Ireland still has much to contribute to the ways in which anthropologists approach their professional field, not only in Ireland but beyond, and in so doing also contribute to both public and private social and political discourse in Ireland, as well as elsewhere in regard to Ireland. We agree with Taylor when he suggests that the more empirically based scholars of Ireland, who are grounded in more ways than one when it comes to matters theoretical and comparative, would 'benefit from raising their heads high enough to catch an occasional glimpse of cultural theory, but so too might post-modernist/postcolonialist theoreticians benefit from alighting on the sod long enough to learn something that they did not already know' (1996: 215). Pursuing the metaphor, we also assert that you can take the anthropologist out of the bog *and* you can take the bog out of the anthropologist, but we wonder why one would want to do either. As we have demonstrated repeatedly in the chapters above, empirically based anthropological studies of groups of people, within local, regional and national contexts, that are theoretically informed and that contribute in some quite sophisticated ways to theory, to method and to professional practice are not only possible; they have been accomplished often in Ireland, in a practice that continues.

In this book we thus seek to widen the anthropological focus, beyond even that called for by Taylor, and to elicit more anthropological voices, in order to challenge anthropologists to marry the needs of theory and method so that they might better provide informed anthropological perspectives on Ireland for anthropologists and for the peoples of Ireland. The national and supranational frames to this sort of anthropology, where 'an ethnographic attention to texts requires a corresponding attention to contexts' (Taylor 1996: 215), should enable anthropologists both to avoid the constraints of the reification of Ireland and its peoples as subject and object, and to elude nationalist discourse about the Irish and the British in Ireland. In its place anthropologists would continue to view Ireland in terms of its multiple geographical, economic and political fields, within which ethnographic 'fieldwork' would allow them to contextualize place and occasion in ways which are meaningful within and beyond Ireland. To Taylor such contextualization, and the linking of multiple fields of human experience in Ireland, is most successful and perhaps most relevant when there is a national focus on an event, person or set of actions which seems to crystallize public culture in meaningful ways, sparking a national dialogue that goes beyond the strict limits of its source: 'this national conversation focuses, heats up, and gathers definitive force whenever certain kinds of crises or cases erupt on the scene ... Anthropology can be useful at these moments as a tool for uncovering a culture in action, in reaction, in formation' (Taylor 1996: 221). Taylor's principal interest in this regard has been in religion in Ireland, and its role in the national affairs that have transformed public culture in the Republic over the last years, including such distressing events as bishops having love affairs, young girls emigrating to have abortions, and paedophilia within the Catholic Church. But before we turn to a fuller consideration of the changing nature of the anthropology of religion in Ireland, to illustrate some of the wider dimensions of changing approaches in the overall anthropology of Ireland, we think it prudent to examine how anthropology too has figured in wider public national debates about the nature of ethnographic research and who conducts it.

Whose Story? Whose Truth?

We have explored how the anthropology of Ireland was going through its own identity crisis in the 1980s and 1990s. This new reflexivity was partly a result of keeping up with the reflexive turn in all of anthropology, but it was also a response to the fact that the most popular perspectives in anthropology and in scholarship in general were those that painted a negative picture of Ireland and the Irish. At least this was how much of the most popular anthropology of Ireland in the United States and elsewhere was being received in Ireland, not least among the people who had been the hosts and friends to these 'foreign' ethnographers'.[2] As a reviewer put it in relation to one such publication, Nancy Scheper-Hughes' *Saints, Scholars and Schizophrenics*: 'Wait till they read that one in the pub in Ballybran!' (Callahan 1979: 311).

The ethical and professional issues at the heart of the debate about the nature of ethnography in Ireland also had something to do with popular and professional notions of who had the right to investigate and comment upon Irish culture and society. This perception of native and foreigner, insider and outsider, was never clear-cut or pervasive, but from the 1970s on not only were the published works of anthropologists coming under public scrutiny in Ireland to a degree unknown before then, but the national identity, or place of origin, of the ethnographer was also becoming a factor of criticism. It seemed to many that there was a 'long-standing asymmetry between theory and its Irish object', an asymmetry within which Ireland became 'the focus or object and interested outsiders [did] the work of analysing, while retaining most, if not all, of the critical agency and the discourses that enable it' (Thompson 2001: 4). The often acerbic debate thus revolved around research conducted in Ireland by outside anthropologists, most of whom were from the United States, and from the reception of the published results of that work. It was launched into public national consciousness when the issue of whose story was being told and by whom was featured in an article in *The Irish Times,* which warned of 'the Yank in the corner' (Viney 1983). There were other voices within and outside the academy that wondered too about the methods, goals and conduct of ethnographic research as practised by anthropologists. On publication of *Saints, Scholars and Schizophrenics* in 1979, Sidney Callahan, the reviewer cited above, wondered about the ethical propriety of quoting an informant 'who tells you something while waiting "in a slow moving line" to go to confession', reservations apparently played down by Scheper-Hughes, who in the end 'plowed on and probably got her doctorate out of it and was awarded a new research grant' (Callahan 1979: 311). Indeed, Callahan wryly concluded, 'After the English there's still the problem of the invading social scientist.'

Eileen Kane, the American anthropologist who founded the Department of Anthropology in the National University of Ireland, Maynooth (then St Patrick's College), was the first to bring these ethical and methodological issues to the attention of many visiting doctoral researchers, who were advised repeatedly by her that it is the responsibility of ethnographers everywhere to ensure that people and communities are not victimized by the ethnographers (for a sample of one person she influenced, see Wilson 1991). Kane did not just act as gatekeeper, as a 'more Irish than the Irish' convert to Irishness who sought to distance herself from the Americans who to some seemed to do more harm than good; she forcefully and consistently pushed anthropologists to contribute actively to the economic and social development of the communities they studied in Ireland. She also practised what she proposed, an effort that led to the largest, collaborative, comparative anthropological study of local community development in Ireland (Kane 1978). Despite the tremendous achievements of this applied anthropological work by Kane and her research associates, it is ironic that a quarter of a century later the works about Ireland that continue to capture the attention of audiences worldwide are those that see it as a place with peoples and culture in decline. As we noted in chapter three, the two American anthropologists whose work has drawn most of this attention are John C. Messenger and Nancy Scheper-Hughes.

John Messenger's works have for some merited the title of 'classics' in the field of Irish anthropology, as has Scheper-Hughes' book (1979), which was based on her doctoral dissertation. Messenger's long-term fieldwork in 'Inis Beag', one of the Aran Islands off the west coast of Ireland, which he conducted with his professional partner and wife Betty Messenger, was extremely influential outside of Ireland (their later research in Northern Ireland was less so, but that also resulted in a well-received historical folklore study, B. Messenger 1975, which was highly praised by local groups, unlike their work in the Aran Islands). However, the results of this initial fieldwork (J. C. Messenger 1969) were roundly condemned by many groups and institutions throughout Ireland, because of their perception of its attack on religion, the Catholic Church, local and national government, and education, among other important aspects of Irish society and culture, not least of which was the 'sacred cow' of the Gaeltacht (Inis Beag is an Irish-speaking region). Messenger, a forthright and implacable scholar, addressed both this reception and the importance of it for ethnographic ethics and politics, and for Ireland and the Irish, in a series of publications (J. C. Messenger 1983, 1984, 1989). In these works he lamented the fact that while many Irish people praised him for having the nerve to take on institutions of power in Irish society, and to confront the icons of Irish culture that may indeed be detrimental to Ireland, just as many other Irish people did not want to hear, and could not approach, the truth about Ireland, as he and Betty saw it. This ambivalence to what the anthropologist has to say about Ireland was also addressed in Lawrence Taylor's research in Donegal, where he noted that there are two things that the Irish do not want to hear about themselves, 'one of them is lies and the other's the truth' (Taylor 1996: 213). Ironically, as Messenger suggests, speaking the truth about Irish society may not be well received if it is voiced by American or other outside scholars, but it might be lauded if delivered by domestic critics:

> Foremost among the many topics addressed in my writings which have caused hurling sticks to be brandished on high are the social control techniques of priests, anti-clericalism, pagan retentions and reinterpretations in the folk Catholicism, sexual repression, disputes, the Gaelic Revival as a nativistic movement, primitivism, and impression management meant to fulfill the expectations of tourists. Yet most of these topics, among others equally controversial, have graced the plots of novels, plays, and short stories by Irish writers. (J. C. Messenger 1989: 124)

More recently, in 1999, Nancy Scheper-Hughes returned to the pseudonymous village of 'Ballybran', in southwest Ireland, twenty years after her ethnographic research there. That research had resulted in a famous book in psychological and medical anthropology (Scheper-Hughes 1979), which has also been the source of a longstanding debate in media and academic circles over anthropological ethics and individual, community and cultural privacy. When in 1999 Scheper-Hughes revisited the village, she was attempting to reconcile her responsibilities as ethnographer and scholar with those of guest and friend — she went to be heard and to listen. And there was a lot to discuss. As one ethnographer has summarized the central argument of Scheper-Hughes' book about Ballybran: 'a self-denying, nearly puritanical, ascetic strain of Irish Catholicism was creating mutual hostility between the sexes, repressing sexuality, and subverting warm maternal behaviour' (McFarlane 1994: 15). The villagers' response to this reconciliation was dramatic: Scheper-Hughes was all but shunned and expelled from Ballybran.

The response to Messenger and Scheper-Hughes may on some levels be surprising, but on others it is predictable, since it reflects the manner in which their research results were received as negative images by the people in the communities that offered their hospitality to these ethnographers so many years ago. However, it is also a response that on a more national level has for some time dogged anthropologists and other ethnographers, particularly those who are not natives of the Republic or Northern Ireland, and perhaps for good reason. For almost four decades 'the most quoted and referred to anthropologists of Ireland outside of Ireland have been those who have characterized (or been seen to characterize) Ireland and the Irish negatively', by presenting Ireland as 'a mentally ill, alcoholic, sexually repressed, clergy dominated, sexist, gerontocracy' (Wilson 1991: 9). And even if there is truth in these images – and there most certainly was when they were drawn first, and there is still in some quarters today – many other people in Ireland, including anthropologists and ethnographers professionally engaged there, argue that the labelling of 'Irish' culture and society in these ways does much to obscure the complexities of what occurs at local and national levels, of what is improving or deteriorating, of social and political change in processual and institutional matrices, and of what Irish people themselves consider to be the important problems that they face daily. As Eipper (1986) has suggested in his study of class, power and consciousness in the Bantry region of County Cork, micro and macro processes need to be studied so that the interlocking of levels of society can be examined, and in so doing the local and national can be seen in systemic structural and institutional terms, not as systems of different logic requiring different methods.

This interest in the national brings us back to Taylor's call for ethnographers to be scholars who rise up from the empirical domains of bog and boulevard to meet the more aerial demands of cultural and social theory head-on, within the same ethnographic experience. For Taylor, this had to be done when trying to understand how time and place were factors in the changing nature of religion in rural Donegal, in what amounted to a fresh approach in the anthropology of religion in Ireland.

'Soft' Voices, Places and Occasions

One of the key areas in which anthropologists have recently and convincingly approached the construction of the national self, across levels and domains of Irish society and culture, has been in their study of changing notions of religion. This has not always been so: for most of the development of anthropology in Ireland anthropologists did not study religion in depth. Religion certainly had figured in ethnographic analyses since the days of Arensberg and Kimball, and was a force in local life that was of concern to the scholars who speculated about cultural decline in Ireland, such as Messenger and Scheper-Hughes. But none of these placed religion at the centre of their analysis, as the principal focus of research, an omission that led some to conclude, as we noted in chapter one, that in relation to religion in Ireland, anthropology had spoken in a 'soft voice', one barely heard beyond the limits of the discipline (McFarlane 1994).

However, there were important exceptions to this rather implicit or indirect approach to religion in the anthropology of Ireland up to the 1990s, most notably that of Victor and Edith Turner, whose pioneering analysis of the Catholic pilgrimage to St Patrick's Purgatory in Lough Derg in County Donegal was the centrepiece in their hugely influential *Image and Pilgrimage in Christian Culture* (1978). This work was as significant worldwide as it was in the anthropology of religion in Ireland, and the application of the concepts of liminality and communitas – developed so powerfully in much of Victor Turner's earlier work (e.g. 1969) – to Marian apparitions in Ireland and elsewhere laid the groundwork for subsequent research on religious visions and charismatic emotion, as we outline below. Many of the issues that were to be taken up by a later generation of anthropologists researching religion in Ireland – particularly the relations between the local, national and global – are here first analysed in the context of Irish religion by the Turners (1978: 124) in their consideration of nationalism as a 'potent force' at Lough Derg, one that draws in large numbers of overseas Irish from Britain and further afield to participate in a devotion that many regard as peculiarly Irish. Pilgrimage, the Turners argue, is 'like a vertical shaft driven into the past, disclosing deep strata of ancient symbols, potent signifiers (sacred symbol-vehicles such as images, paintings, proper names, and places) which reinforce nationalistic sentiments' (Turner and Turner 1978: 106). It is through the study of such long-term socio-cultural processes as pilgrimage, they suggest, that we can begin to understand how ideology can change or persist.

As elsewhere, early anthropological interest in religion in Ireland often gathered around non-institutional forms of belief, in the realms of the magical and supernatural, such as witchcraft (Jenkins 1977) and *piseogery* or magical assault (Breen 1980), as well as around calendrical festivals like May Day and Halloween (see Breen 1980; Glassie 1982; Santino 1998) and the feast days that sometimes were the forerunners for the kinds of pilgrimage that occupied the Turners' attention. Interest also focused on the biblical imagery and theatricality of ritual in secret societies such as the Orange Order and Freemasons, and on 'faith healing' and the powers exercised by the seventh son of a seventh son (see Buckley 1982b, 1985-6, 2000, n.d.). Such 'folk' beliefs were rarely just quaint antiquarian curios left over from a bygone age, but were often the barometers and animators of ideological change, and the subject of acrimonious political debate within the church and, on occasion, of apparent political manipulation outside it too (as Jenkins [1993, 2004] shows in relation to allegations of black magic in 1970s Northern Ireland). Indeed, in the case of a series of Marian apparitions in the mid-1980s, such religious experiences could be seen as an element of contemporary cultural invention stimulated by Ireland's belated entry into modernity, as part of Irish Catholicism's response to the massive urban and secular transformations of the years immediately preceding (see M. Allen 2000). Nevertheless, anthropological expertise on the seemingly marginal and exotic was often too readily dismissed by other kinds of commentator, who were inclined to see such practices as colourful footnotes to the history of institutional religion, leading to anthropology's relative lack of influence in the wider study of religion that we have already mentioned.

As Eipper (1986: 93) has pointed out in his study of the local, national and international dimensions of power in the town of Bantry in the Republic of Ireland, the integration of church and state has led to a 'pervasive catholicity', where local culture and society were saturated with the iconography of religion and church, and where, 'in the very idioms of the language, a catholic imagery prevailed' (a point likely to hold throughout the Republic, where there is still a 'persistent popular Catholic religiosity' [O'Leary 2004: 91]). While it was clear, then, that religion's role in everyday life in Ireland had been changing, in a process of secularization that is at the heart of the reinventions of Ireland that we have been discussing, it is also clear that religion, and its associated belief systems and social regimes, remain indelible facets of Irish culture that anthropologists must examine if they want their voice to be heard in accounts of the island's changing relations of culture and power. Eipper's examination of Bantry was a definite step in that direction, for he shows how the local intersections of church, government and business in the creation of relationships of influence and power in peripheral County Cork were linked to *national* church and state, and *multinational* oil.

Northern Ireland has had a slightly different ethnographic record in regard to the study of religion, a record partly due to factors that set the North apart from the Republic, most notably those of communal conflict and religious diversity. While anthropologists working there had been relatively uninterested in religion *per se*, they had 'been preoccupied with how "religious" identities interact in complex ways with identities based on locality, class, kinship, age and gender' (McFarlane 1994: 15), as part of the wider anthropological scholarship on the Troubles which sought to understand the nature of the conflict (Cairns 2000; Jenkins 1986). This emphasis on such things as locality and class as they related to local religion and church (as found in Buckley 1982a, 1984; Bufwack 1982) certainly distinguished the anthropology of Northern Ireland from that of the Republic (although Eipper 1986 is an exception for its emphasis on culture and class in the South), and it reflected rich and diverse economic, political and religious histories.

McFarlane's research on religion and identity illustrates the heterogeneity of religious practice and expression in Northern Ireland, where there are many, and a growing number of, Christian churches and congregations, unlike the Republic, where as much as 95 per cent of the population has professed to be Roman Catholics, with historically no more than 5 per cent Protestants. As McFarlane

(1986, 1989) discovered in his field research in 'Ballycuan', a village of approximately 750 people in County Down, just outside of Belfast, the main social boundary in Northern Ireland is often not between Catholic and Protestant but between different types of Protestantism, followed closely by the social distinctions of class, residence and reputation that order local society. McFarlane recognized that there was a general notion in the village, whose residents were almost entirely Protestant, that there was little to distinguish one Catholic from another, but there was a great deal to consider when one wanted to understand the social forces at work among local Protestants. Chief among them were the matters of religious commitment and deportment among Protestants, related to issues of religion and church, and an individual's direct or indirect relation to God. 'For most people, it is clear that members of the Free Presbyterian and the small denominations are likely to be more given to religious fervour than, say, members of the Church of Ireland ... with its supposedly empty ritual' (McFarlane 1989: 31). For some locals the big divide is not between Catholics and Protestants – that of course is the biggest divide in Northern Ireland, but not one that matters much in the everyday life of Ballycuan. Rather, it is that between Free Presbyterians and Pentecostals at one end of the locally derived social scale of religion and churches, and the Church of Ireland (Anglican) congregation at the other. As one older Presbyterian woman concluded, 'there's only a paper wall between Catholics and the Church of Ireland, but a burning bush between us and them' (cited in McFarlane 1989: 31). This religious complexity is also matched by the political diversity of loyalists and unionists in Northern Ireland, where, for example, there are many and often divergent conceptions of the nation and the state which are at the heart of their political movements (Moore and Sanders 2002).

In this sort of approach, McFarlane demonstrates how a view of Protestantism 'from below' in Northern Ireland allows ethnographers to construct 'models of everyday practice' (1989: 41), which are primarily structured by day-to-day negotiations within local society. These models of everyday practice are more elaborate and perhaps more adaptable than those which seem to be constructed 'from above', at higher and more powerful levels of society, by people of influence in government, in the church, and in education. These top-down models, which McFarlane calls 'models of form', are of course also determinative of local practice and values, but it is in the ways these are represented locally, made meaningful, and acted upon that they are made more complicated, and adapted to local contemporary and historical frames of reference. What concerns us here, though, is the emphasis on local practices of negotiation and representation that make religion meaningful. McFarlane (1989: 28), like Eipper, shows how ethnographic methods can provide insights in local arenas that many macro-level analyses cannot, and furthermore that these ethnographic studies are much more than descriptive cases that provide interesting data; they are directly related to the formation and reproduction of larger social formations, and as such must be viewed as constitutive of social theory.

Taylor utilizes a similar approach to religion in Teelin and Carrick, County Donegal, his field sites for over twenty years. His research history, though, brought him to religion late, in that his doctoral research and later visits did not have religion as a principal focus. But local people's religious practices and beliefs were always apparent, and their importance in other public culture made religion an essential ingredient in his analyses, if a secondary one for some time. As Taylor suggests, he was not alone in this variable myopia: 'Although one would be hard pressed to suggest a feature of Irish culture more generally significant, Catholicism has received slight, and typically simplistic and reductive, treatment from anthropologists' (Taylor 1995: 28). But two specific field research events (Taylor 1995: 26-7), the first involving his discovery of an archive that held a record of a historical dispute between a priest and a landlord's agent, and the second involving a contemporary local priest who was known to have the ability to 'cure', opened a door onto locally practised religion that led Taylor, like McFarlane and Eipper before him, to theorize the nature of local and national religious action and beliefs through the ethnography of everyday relations at local levels: 'it was this coming together of archive and field, of religion and politics, of competing "representations" of a past – which in Ireland, as someone once said, is not dead, and not even past – that began to pull my interests in new directions' (Taylor 1995: 26).

These new directions were the stuff of the revitalization of theoretical and methodological practice that we have suggested is at the core of the reinventions of the anthropology of Ireland today. Taylor's starting point in his studies was to treat religion less as a body of knowledge, or a set of beliefs and values, and more as a set of relationships: 'An anthropological account of local religion begins not with a *religion* as definitive, theological texts define it, nor even a list of beliefs, but rather with people . . . acting, thinking, and speaking in a real if always contingent world' (Taylor 1995: 4; emphasis in original). And the frames for this experiential approach to religion were wide in temporal and spatial terms. Taylor has spent more than a decade of research in Donegal on this topic, and among Donegal people as they travel throughout Ireland in the course of their religious activities, and as far as Medjugorje on pilgrimage. He has analysed historical cases of local priests and landlords in dispute, and of changing geographies of power and domination, within and outside religious circles. He has also examined a variety of alternative religious experience, in such locations as local holy wells, in religious revitalization missions in Ireland, in pilgrimages to holy sites beyond Ireland, and in local charismatic prayer meetings (Taylor 1995). His goal was to provide an intimate view of religion that looks locally for the internal and external forces that shape the historical character of religion as power. In order to achieve this he

approached religion locally in terms of shared actions and beliefs, of a commu-
nality inscribed in 'fields of religious experience' that at macro levels of national
life might constitute religious regimes (Taylor 1995: 30–2; see also Bax 1987),
within which religious occasions might be complexly and divergently meaningful,
depending on one's role in both the fields and regimes of religious experience.

Taylor argues that the ethnographic method is a powerful tool in this context, for
it allows us to 'penetrate' the structure of religious experience, and to understand
how an event such as the healing mass 'both taps and creates power, building new
institutions as well as new religious world views' (1990: 98). In his account of the
spate of Marian apparitions and moving statues that swept rural Ireland in the mid-
1980s, Michael Allen (2000) is similarly interested in how new forms of power are
generated amongst those frustrated by institutional Catholicism, and who seek a
religious empowerment that does not require the mediation of a priest. These new
forms of power are brought about by the intensification of emotion that is experienced by visionary and devotee at these shrines, and that is transformed into
shared belief through their testimony and narrative elaboration (cf. Eipper 1996).
New forms of power are generated too among the charismatics studied by Liam
Murphy (2002), who describes how the Christian Fellowship Church stage an
annual 'March for Jesus' through the streets of Belfast as their local contribution
to what is a global event involving millions of people worldwide. The 'March' is
similar in structure to the politicized and divisive parades that we examined in
chapter five, but here the meaning is radically recontextualized within a transnational charismatic discourse that transforms the meaning of such movement, con-
verting it into a novel configuration of cosmic authority and power: 'This
harmonizing of global and local cultural logics is accomplished by charismatics
who resituate the purpose and effect of local parading traditions within a cosmic
framework. No longer about worldly authority, movement about the city is recast
as a performance of divine authority' (Murphy 2002: 28). In other ways too
charismatic rituals can be socially powerful in a Belfast divided between Catholic
and Protestant, and they dramatize reconciliation and dialogue in a manner that
reflects developments in the political field, such as the Good Friday Agreement,
over which they have no formal control (Murphy 2000).

In his study of the Charismatic Renewal Movement in Galway, Bohdan
Szuchewycz (1989), like Taylor and those described above, also relates the local to
the national, to see local religion as demonstrative of shifting power relations,
within the Catholic Church, but also between church and state, a theme which runs
through all of the new anthropology of religion, in Northern Ireland as well as in
the Republic, that we have examined here. Szuchewycz (1989) suggests that the
'silences' are the most important forms of piety, reflection and religiosity among
charismatics in Galway, which is unlike the emotional, public and spontaneous
forms of prayer that mark worldwide Protestant Pentecostalism, the movement

from which the Charismatics derive. According to Szuchewycz, this preference for silence may actually signify a reduced threat to the institutional Catholic Church, and thus constitutes an example of how an alternative local approach to religion may be less subversive to organized churches than might be the case elsewhere (Szuchewycz 1989: 53, 66–7).

Overall, these dynamic approaches to religion and the institutions of power as they relate to religion show how far ethnographic research has come since the days of Messenger and Scheper-Hughes, and suggest too how far ethnography has come in terms of its professional practice and its concern with the ethics and politics of fieldwork. Although anthropology may have spoken softly in relation to religion, as McFarlane (1994: 17) says, these new strengths in its approach to national discourses on religion, power and social change nevertheless make it a voice worth listening to, a sentiment that might be applied to the anthropology of Ireland more generally. While anthropological voices may have been muted, and anthropologists' profiles low-key, that situation has been changing, and needs to change more and more quickly, because anthropologists have much to offer public debate about the nature of culture and change in the Republic and in Northern Ireland, not least within the dynamic relations of identity and politics.

Identification and Explanation: The Politics and Practices of Identity

> We live in an age in which it is practically impossible to speak of politics without speaking also of identity. Identity provides us with a sense of who we are, where we have come from, and, more importantly, where we are going … identity offers itself, almost uniquely, as a means of ordering the chaos of our experience. It can assimilate the unlikely event, the crisis-wracked history, the piece of outrageous good fortune and find in this material not merely a story but an explanation. Perhaps more importantly, within this function identity is *forgiving*; it justifies the visceral response, smoothes over the contradictions of our prejudices and constitutes the final refuge from which we can argue our case and vindicate our position.
>
> (Kirkland 2002: 1)

Much of this book has been about Irish identities, and about identifications with class, gender, nation, locality, political party and territory. This is a reflection of the turn in anthropology away from culture as the object of analysis to a focus on how people perceive, use, celebrate, parade and dispute their cultures, and those of their neighbours, friends and enemies. This active process of using meaning to make sense of one's social world is simultaneously a process of individual and group identification, which is most often and perhaps best expressed as 'identity'. And since much of today's global anthropology emphasizes the action and agency explicitly and implicitly tied to such identifying, it has become almost impossible to do anthropology without doing identity. But we do not want identity as we have approached it here in this book to be seen in a manner similar to Samuel Johnson's reported notion of patriotism, as the last refuge of a scoundrel, as a category of ethnographic description and analysis that has been adopted worldwide in a final effort to give some coherence to an anthropology that is seen by many – many anthropologists included – as no longer the science of culture.

On the contrary, and as Kirkland shows in the excerpt above, identity has become the veritable stuff of politics and power in local, national and global societies and cultures precisely because it is so meaningful, malleable and adaptable. It would be hard to imagine any group of people anywhere in the world, certainly any large group of people with access to media, who have not witnessed the value of approaching selves and others in terms of their traditions, cultures and heritages, in ways which make claims to cultural identities into disarming strategies of acquiring rights, entitlements and privileges, the bases of political and other forms of power. As we have examined, in various ways and in each chapter, 'identity' and 'culture' are idioms in the expression of community, place, history, politics, economics, sexuality, class, nation and state, both within formal institutions and across multiple social fields and on potentially countless social occasions.

Thus in our conclusion we do not return to the issues of identity in order to practise the politics of identity within anthropology, or to reiterate the identifications of anthropologists, as a way of vindicating our approaches in this book. At least this is not our sole intention. More important than that in our return to identity as a motif in the inventions of Irishness and in the constructions of the anthropologies of Ireland is the emphasis which the peoples of Ireland today place on culture and identity, and which promises to last for some time. As Kirkland notes for Northern Ireland, for example, 'tradition, heritage, rights' are the 'triumvirate through which identity is paraded, or, to use the more accepted term, "celebrated"' (2002: 13).

Camille O'Reilly has been one of the ethnographers who has chronicled how the politics of culture and identity have grown in Northern Ireland, especially in regard to the politics of language (see also Kachuk 1994; McCoy 1997, 2005; for the Republic, see Coleman 2003). She has examined the growing importance of the Irish language in Catholic areas of West Belfast, where the language had to be revitalized, in large part in support of Irish nationalism, but in so doing helped to redefine community and culture within that part of Belfast among nationalists and republicans (O'Reilly 1998, 1999). While these politics of culture can be a liberating force in local life, they can also work to conceal relations of power that can support forms of domination, resistance and subversion. According to O'Reilly, the 'politics of culture' refers 'to a political idiom where action and belief are expressed, justified and explained in terms of culture, heritage and tradition, where culture is often understood in its popular sense as a quality that some people possess but others do not' (2003: 170). In this view, culture and tradition are claims to legitimacy, and ultimately political influence and power. Cathal McCall (2002) has shown how this has played out within the motifs and policy domains of partnership and parity of esteem within the new Northern Ireland. Unionists and loyalists have to a great extent reinvented the 'language' of Ulster Scots in Northern Ireland as a form of culture 'native' to certain regions of Ulster which were settled mainly by Presbyterian Scots (cf. D. Bell 2005; Radford 2001; for a review of other Scottish connections, see Strathern and Stewart 2001). This language movement was born as one way to balance the funding and other forms of public support that the Irish language has gained since the Belfast Good Friday Agreement was signed in 1998. As Máiréad Nic Craith (2002, 2003) has also demonstrated at length, the politics of language in Northern Ireland are at the heart of the two traditions model of life there, a model that permeates most if not all aspects of culture and community and obscures both the politics that underlie communal conflict and the cultural diversity of contemporary Northern Ireland.

But even if identity and culture are increasingly being used as explanations of social order and disorder, and as rationales for political action, anthropologists do not have the luxury of seeing identity as constitutive of social explanation, or of theoretical hegemony. Ultimately, what are we discovering if we are content with describing the day-to-day aspects of identity? Anthropologists must go beyond the 'identity' component of identity politics in order to recognize the historical forces at work in the fashioning of society, economy and polity, and in particular the institutional and behavioural contexts to local life.

There are many reasons why anthropologists must see beyond identity politics and the politics of identity.[3] Foremost among these are the limits to the notion of identity itself, in that identity 'never quite seems to coincide with the incoherences, the ambivalences and the gaps out of which we make ourselves' (Kirkland 2002: 1). As an explanation it is too neat and overarching, whether it be an explanation of an individual's or a group's actions. Identity is simply not messy enough as an analytical category, or, said a different way, it cannot account for the diversity and complexity that is apparent, and important, in the behaviours of people who use identity as an explanation, in what always has elements of essentialist argument. Another reason why identity alone is limited in anthropological practice and analysis is that it is too dependent on individual and group narratives: one simply cannot study identity, and certainly not understand it (within the obvious limits of what 'understanding' might mean in an academic context), unless one talks with people about their identities. At the same time, the importance of these narratives, beyond the importance set for them by our respondents, cannot be fully approached until other social, political, economic and cultural dimensions of those identities, and the manner in which they are expressed, are engaged. This is part of the historical practice of anthropology, and in Gavin Smith's (1999) terms it is an exercise in historical realism. All of these practices and processes in anthropology, in Ireland today and in the future, and in a more global anthropology, hinge on the tensions implicit in the anthropological approach to experience.

Ethnography and Experience

We have shown in this book that while anthropologists of Ireland address issues of concern to anthropologists when they conduct research, they also address many issues of concern to the peoples of Ireland, in all levels and domains of politics, economics, society and culture. We have offered many perspectives and examples of how the anthropology of Ireland, from below, at local levels of everyday life among people without particular power and influence, and from above, in the institutions of power of church, state and beyond, speaks in clear and accessible tones, and should no longer be considered the quiet voice of the past:

> no matter what theoretical wrapping anthropologists use to present their research on Ireland, the best texts are attractive because they are full of fine-grained descriptions of people saying and otherwise doing things, usually in the context of networks of relationships. In other words, the texts are not stripped of their essential humanity – we can all hear echoes of our own viewpoints or the viewpoints of people we know as we read them. (McFarlane 1994: 17)

In *The Anthropology of Ireland* we have explicitly sought to counter anthropological spin, and to contextualize some aspects of anthropological spin in the past. We approach this notion of spin with reference to Thomas Taaffe's (2003) research on representations of power among the media in Northern Ireland (see also K. Bell [2004], who conducted ethnographic research among political journalists covering the Troubles in Northern Ireland). According to Taaffe, ' "spin" is a constructed discursive formation, created to engage with, or reinforce the dominant hegemonic formation of a given moment. It is an explicitly conscious construction. It is the discursive part of an organised campaign to achieve a political objective' (2003: 122). In the chapters above we have consciously sought to subvert anthropological attempts to create hegemonic anthropological constructions. To us, it is preferable to let the people of Ireland guide us in our theoretical, methodological and professional constructions, and to allow their discourses to shape our professional objectives, and we have examined how the dynamic conditions today in the Republic and Northern Ireland make this a daunting and exciting challenge for anthropologists, not least because of the dynamism of global professional anthropology.

In fact, in these heady times of shifting bases to anthropological practice there seems precious little of a methodological and theoretical nature to define the field of anthropology as distinct from our cognate disciplines in the social sciences and humanities. In the United States in particular, there seems to be even less to provide a thread of professional coherence now that the icon of American anthropology, the 'four-field' approach, is increasingly seen to be vestigial, if not malignant. In the midst of all of this excitement of promise and turmoil, debates continue to rage as to whether culture is still the defining concept of anthropology, and if it is, is it because it is the object, the subject, and/or the medium of what anthropologists do?

Through all of these inventions and reinventions in anthropology, on both sides of the Atlantic, there has been a reluctance on the part of anthropologists to give up ethnographic research as the defining method of the field, and even more of a reluctance to subvert it as the defining experience of an anthropologist, the rite of passage to a doctorate to be certain, but also as the trope of professional and intellectual discourse, the validation of 'being there' (somewhere) where it, and its people, are 'other', in ways that the anthropologist recognizes and conveys.

This ethnography is in fact often referred to as 'fieldwork', in ways which also set anthropologists apart from others, in the academy, or non-academics 'at home'. And at the heart of both ethnography and fieldwork is the polysemic notion of 'experience', where anthropologists not only experience otherness while doing fieldwork, they also use field anecdotes, in the classroom but also increasingly in academic publications, to illustrate their own experiences *as* anthropologists. This process of validation depends to a great extent, and in increasingly important ways in professional anthropology, on a concentration on the experiences of the people we used to say we studied, but whom, in these more sensitive and respectful times, we now say we interviewed. This is because the empiricism of anthropology today relies increasingly on the documentation of the life experiences of our informants, hosts, guests, respondents and interviewees, and much less on other forms of empirical data collection, even that of straightforward observation. And as anthropology persists in privileging itself as a field that narrates narrations, it may increasingly desist from engaging the social and historical forces that affect those whose experiences we re-tell.

As Gavin Smith recently pointed out, in a work which explores how anthropologists can, and should, foster an anthropology of the present that is politically engaged:

> The stress on fieldwork has inevitably made experience almost a magic key for entering the world of adulthood among anthropologists ... But for anthropologists this highly intense and often quite anguished moment can mislead us into thinking that this exhausts the entire quotient of the social engagement required of us. (1999: 14)

This domain of anthropological experience has many levels. On the surface it is about the experience of fieldwork by an ethnographer: one goes, one does, one returns – without field experience one is not legitimized as an anthropologist. On another level it is about the content of what is experienced, of what is seen and heard and felt, which become the classroom arsenal of anecdotes that fortifies the university anthropologist. On still another level it is about the new empiricism in a more interpretative and reflexive anthropology. For some anthropologists, the primary professional and intellectual goal of research is to narrate the lived experiences of the people we live with and study, all the while within a reflexive mode of contextualizing the ethnographer's experience. All of these levels of experience are both necessary and warranted in anthropology today, but they mask other forces at work which cannot be subsumed under the mantle of experience. Certain historical, political, economic and social forces cannot be understood through reference to experience, in the sense of narratives of action and memory, or of the experiences of just the people with whom anthropologists interact. Such experiences are incomplete, and only a partial understanding of the historical forces at work in any locality.

We agree with Smith (1999: 9) when he suggests that some, maybe a majority of, anthropologists in some parts of the world see themselves as being engaged and political when in ethnographic research they assert that only by getting the best possible picture of their hosts' self-understanding of their social world can anthropologists contribute meaningfully to theory. This is also an incomplete view of an incomplete process, for there are many forces at work in social life that are imperfectly present in local lives. The celebrations of place, locality, tradition, identity and culture which we have reviewed in this book cannot be understood solely through the prism of 'experience' – they need too to be refracted through the lens of the 'explicit and detailed exposition of mechanisms of social reproduction' (G. Smith 1999: 9). The interpretative and reflexive approaches need to be balanced with an attention to the historical and political forces that frame the experiences of informant and fieldworker alike. These forces are discernible, comparable and approachable. In Smith's view, in which he calls this balance in approach 'historical realism', 'Neither the world as experienced phenomenologically nor the world as produced through historical fields of force has a greater "reality" the one over the other; yet their analysis does require quite self-conscious shifts of attention and of technique on the part of the analyst' (1999: 8).

Our examination of the anthropology of Ireland has sought to capture the complexity of the experiences both of Irish culture and of ethnography, and also to do justice to the diversity in ethnographic shifts of attention and technique over the last seventy-odd years. In our book we have privileged examples of ethnographic research that explore and seek to understand the realities of a changing Ireland. We have done this in support of a 'realist' approach in ethnography that will serve anthropology in and beyond Ireland:

> A realist ethnography needs to deal with experience ..., just as it needs to deal with
> practice: the one – experience – calls for the need to find means of investing interpre-

tative methods with ways of comprehending power and the situatedness of cultural perceptions, i.e.: the social distribution of knowledge; the other – practice – calls for the need to embed social practices and relationships in the historical shaping of institutions: not just institutions as the outcomes of accumulated practices or agency, but institutions in terms of the very inertia and concreteness of their existence. (G. Smith 1999: 11)

Institutions in this perspective are not things, or the objects of ethnographic research, but are processes of social and political reproduction. As Smith also suggests, once we see institutions 'less in terms of things and more in terms of forces', we will be better able to approach them as 'bridgeheads of power – facilitating certain practices, often by means of 'order' and regulation, and, just as surely, preventing other practices, closing certain social spaces, and inducing disorder and deregulation' (1999: 11).

We have shown how anthropologists in Ireland have been pursuing for some time, and are expanding their work on, institutions of policy and power. This is apparent in almost every aspect of ethnography in Ireland today, including those we have covered here in depth, such as the anthropologies of the body, identity, religion, economy, boundary making, community, and globalism and transnationalism. It is most apparent in the growing anthropology of policy, where this form of politically contextualized and realist anthropology is being increasingly heard. Only when the anthropology of Ireland speaks in these complementary registers, we suggest, will it fully realize the potential power of its voice.

Notes

Chapter 1 Anthropology Ireland: Identity, Voice and Invention

1. In this book 'Ireland' and 'Irish' refer to the whole island, while the 'Republic/the South' and 'Northern Ireland/the North' refer to its two component polities.

2. In the early 1990s, Ireland had only two university departments of anthropology. These were the Department of Social Anthropology in the Queen's University of Belfast and the Department of Anthropology in St Patrick's College, Maynooth (now the National University of Ireland, Maynooth). There were other departments with notable anthropological personnel, for example the Department of Political Science and Sociology in University College Galway, the Department of Sociology in University College Cork and the Department of Sociology at the University of Ulster in Coleraine, but for the most part at that time university anthropologists were solitary and often peripheral members of non-anthropological social science departments. The situation remains largely unchanged, at least in terms of numbers of anthropology departments on the island, though there are many more anthropologists professionally employed in Ireland today than just a decade ago, in universities, museums and the government and private sectors. In 1994, for example, there were approximately thirty social anthropologists employed on a full-time and permanent basis in universities and museums in all of Ireland (Wilson 1994a: 6); today there are almost thirty working in greater Belfast alone.

3. Graham McFarlane (1994) suggests that the anthropology of Ireland has had a 'soft voice' in the study of religion (see chapter eight). Until relatively recently the entire anthropology of Ireland has spoken with that same soft voice, with the exception of some ethnographies that were widely read and criticized in Ireland, a subject to which we also return in chapter eight.

4. These are examined at greater length in Wilson 1994a, which serves as an introduction to the first debate about anthropology's role in public culture in Ireland to appear in a popular periodical, the monthly political magazine *Fortnight*.

5. In a recent discussion about anthropological research among the permanent

sociocultural faculty in the Department of Anthropology at Binghamton University, State University of New York, and about the requirements needed for sound doctoral training, a consensus could not be reached over what was necessary and sufficient. One particular sore point of discussion was the old 'chestnut' that an anthropologist should conduct field research for at least one annual cycle, to witness social and cultural life through all the annual seasons. As one of the opponents to this position put it, this was an antiquated practice of an outdated anthropological tradition, linked to rural and agricultural studies, when old-fashioned anthropologists sought to chronicle the agricultural cycle: 'anthropologists do not do that anymore'.

6. While we recognize that for many historical and present intellectual and professional reasons there has been a bifurcation in anglophone anthropology, the principal domain for our analysis, between British and European-orientated social anthropology and North American-orientated cultural anthropology, in this book we shall use 'social anthropology' to refer to all forms of social anthropology, cultural anthropology and ethnology which have been utilized and addressed in Ireland.

7. This point is also made in Kirby et al. 2002a. Our discussion in this and the next two paragraphs owes much to the illuminating analyses of all of the authors in Kirby et al. 2002b.

Chapter 2 Locating the Anthropology of Ireland

This chapter draws on Curtin, Donnan and Wilson (1993a), Donnan and McFarlane (1986a, 1989b), and Wilson (1984, 1998a), and is informed by the recent fine critical historiographical essay by Byrne, Edmondson and Varley (2001).

1. This perspective on the two emphases in the ethnography of Ireland approximates the assessment of Crozier (1985: 12), who saw the ethnographic divide between the South and the North of Ireland as being that of 'dying peasant' and 'political and religious schism', respectively (see also Peace 1989).

2. For the clearest statement of support for the research findings of Arensberg and Kimball, see Hannan 1972; for the most damning indictment of Arensberg and Kimball's ethnography, see Gibbon 1973; see also Colin Bell and Howard Newby 1971, who seek to provide a mediatory view of Arensberg and Kimball's contribution to comparative community studies.

3. 'The Troubles' is the Irish term for the conflict which has raged in Northern Ireland since 1969. At the time of writing, the armed and overt conflict is in a state of cease-fire.

4. At one stage there were two departments of anthropology in Northern Ireland, one in Belfast, and the other at what was then the New University of Ulster

in Coleraine, where the British-trained Africanist, Peter Morton-Williams, occupied the chair until anthropology was incorporated into the sociology department. While a number of Americans have held posts in the North, the British social anthropological tradition has remained firmly established there, largely through the theoretical influence of anthropologists such as Ladislav Holy and Milan Stuchlik (both Czechs trained in British social anthropology), Reginald Byron (a British-educated American), Joyce Pettigrew, Andrew Sanders and Simon Harrison.

Chapter 5 Re-presenting 'Irishness'

1. With due acknowledgement to S. W. Pope (1997), whose monograph on sport and American identity has a similar title, and to Dominic Behan's song, an indictment of betrayal and violence, sung by a dying IRA volunteer.

2. Gaelic football, hurling (or hurley) and handball are the three main Gaelic sports. Camogie is the women's equivalent of hurling. The social science literature has focused mainly on *male* sporting Irishness, and has paid little attention to how sport is gendered (though see Liston 2002).

3. In rugby union Northern Ireland and the Republic of Ireland play as a single united national team against the English, Welsh and Scottish. Because of this, rugby players from the Republic of Ireland are eligible 'to represent Great Britain (of which they are not politically part)' in a touring side popularly known as the 'British Lions' but more properly called the 'Great British and Irish Lions' (see Tuck 2005: 108).

4. It did not always do so. In the 1970s, when sectarian violence was at its height in Northern Ireland, many national teams refused to play matches in Belfast. Between 1972 and 1978 the Northern Ireland national squad had to play ten of its 'home' fixtures in England (see Sugden and Bairner 1993: 70). We should also add that some Protestants are concerned about using leisure facilities in Catholic neighbourhoods in Belfast (Bairner and Shirlow 2003).

5. With acknowledgement to Kirkland (2002).

6. It is problematic to include the Protestant processions we consider below in a chapter entitled 'Re-presenting "Irishness"', even if we use inverted commas around 'Irishness'. Exactly what identity or identities these parades represent has changed historically and is subject to debate. Such identities have included 'Britishness', 'Ulster Protestant', 'Ulster Loyalist' and 'Northern Irish'. Others have suggested that the *Britishness* on display during the public processions on the Twelfth of July was expressed 'in a quintessentially *Irish* way' (see Glendinning 1997: 57, emphasis added); and there is, as Bairner (2001: 36) notes, 'a kind of unionism that takes on board the Irishness of Ulster Protestants' (for historical background on the Twelfth of July, or 'The Twelfth', as it is referred to in Northern

Ireland, see Bryan 2000; Larsen 1982b). In a conference on 'Varieties of Irishness' which included consideration of Protestant and Unionist as well as Catholic and Nationalist identities, David Trimble – then Senior Lecturer in Law at Queen's University Belfast and later leader of the Ulster Unionist Party and First Minister for Northern Ireland – cautioned against seeing Northern Ireland's 'Ulster-British people' as one of the 'varieties of Irishness' on the island (Trimble 1989: 50).

7. The Orange Order, which organizes the Twelfth of July processions and an average of 2,000 smaller parades annually in Northern Ireland (Bryan 2000: 182), is hierarchically organized into Private Lodges and District Lodges. According to Bryan (2000: 97–117), there are approximately 1,400 of the former and 126 of the latter, with District Lodges overseen by a County Grand Lodge, each of which sends representatives to the Grand Lodge of Ireland. Estimates of the Order's membership report 100,000, though this may have halved in recent years due to internal dissent (Bryan 2000: 111; Cecil 1993: 154). These figures include membership in the Association of Loyal Orange Women and the Junior Orange Institution for boys between the ages of 8 and 17. Two other organizations are also involved in parading, the Royal Black Institution and the Apprentice Boys of Derry, but these are not dealt with here. Nor are the Orange parades that take place in Canada, or those currently enjoying a revival in Ghana and Togo, where Rachel Naylor of the University of Ulster reports there are currently about twenty Orange lodges (*http://news.bbc.co.uk/go/pr/fr/-/1/hi/northern_ireland/4554863.stm*). Since 2001, Northern Irish expatriates in the Spanish coastal resort of Benidorm have organized a Twelfth of July parade that has attracted increasing numbers of participants (*The Irish Times*, 21 July 2005).

Chapter 6 Frontier Tales and the Politics of Emplacement

1. It is important to remember that even at the height of the popularity of community studies, in a period from the 1930s to the 1970s, many of its leading proponents saw its limits as theory, method and practice, and were aware that community boundaries were often arbitrarily drawn by local people as well as by scholars. For an overview of some of these concerns, see Arensberg 1961.

2. See Wolf (2001), who apologizes for using 'acculturation' to describe much more complex forces than could be satisfactorily accounted for through the use of the term; as he says, it was the best term available to him at the time, in the 1960s.

3. William Kelleher relates a story he was told in a border town about the time of the hunger strikers, when

> it was common for Catholics, when approaching a group of Protestants, to be accosted by a question that took variations on the form 'Where is Bobby Sands on hunger strike?' When the Catholics who were being questioned responded with 'the H-blocks,'

those questioning them could tell by the person's pronunciation of the letter h whether that person was Roman Catholic or not. Protestants and Catholics pronounced the letter h differently, and that difference could carry consequences. Some of the identified Catholics reported getting beaten up. (2003: 75–6)

4. See Kelleher (2003: 11) and Finlay (1999) for different perspectives on this phrase and its meaning for ethnographic practice.
5. For a review of the history and current state of border studies in anthropology, see *Borders: Frontiers of Identity, Nation and State* (Donnan and Wilson 1999). See also Donnan and Wilson 1994; Wilson and Donnan 1998.
6. The distinctions implied in the definition and use of terms such as 'border', 'borderlands' and 'frontier' are many and important, but a discussion of them would be too distracting here. For a more detailed treatment, see Wilson and Donnan 1998.
7. For a fuller discussion of the emphasis on ethnic minorities in border studies in anthropology, see Donnan 2005; see also Rabinowitz 1997, who analyzed minority and majority relations in Israel.

Chapter 8 Ethnographic Experience and Engagement in the Anthropology of Ireland

1. Much of the impact of North American academic and scholarly practices and interests must be discussed in terms of professional academic training: some of the most influential Irish and Northern Irish anthropologists and sociologists took at least one postgraduate degree in the USA or Canada, among them Joseph Ruane and the late Vincent Tucker in National University of Ireland (NUI), Cork, Liam O'Dowd in Queen's University Belfast, Anthony Varley in NUI, Galway, and Séamas Ó Síocháin and Mary Corcoran in NUI, Maynooth. Many other prominent Irish scholars, such as Chris Curtin in NUI, Galway, did their doctorates in Britain, thereby opening up more channels in the international and global dimensions to the anthropology of Ireland.
2. The general nature of the debate that revolved around what were mostly American anthropologists' published research results and their reception among various groups in Ireland can be traced through Feldman 1992; Jenkins 1992a, 1992b; J. C. Messenger 1983, 1984, 1989; Scheper-Hughes 1981a, 1981b, 1982, 1983b, 2000, 2001; Viney 1980, 1983.
3. We recognize that there are many approaches to identity politics in each of, and across, the academic disciplines. Here we refer to the distinctions between the two concepts which are drawn in Hill and Wilson 2003, where *identity politics* refers to 'how culture and identity, variously perceived to be traditional, modern, radical, local, regional, religious, gender, class and ethnic, are articulated, con-

structed, invented and commodified as the means to achieve political ends', and the *politics of identity* which has more to do with 'issues of personal and group power, found within and across all social and political institutions and collectivities, where people sometimes choose, and sometimes are forced, to interact with each other in part on the basis of their shared, or divergent, notions of their identities' (Hill and Wilson 2003: 2). Regardless of which approach is taken, what is important here is that all societies in a global world have identity as a key political factor, and all of these identities are expressions of the meanings, institutions and practices of culture.

References

Akenson, Donald Harman (1991), *Small Differences: Irish Catholics and Irish Protestants, 1815–1922*. Dublin: Gill and Macmillan.

Allen, Kieran (2000), *The Celtic Tiger? The Myth of Social Partnership in Ireland*. Manchester: Manchester University Press.

Allen, Michael (2000), From Ecstasy to Power: Marian Apparitions in Contemporary Irish Catholicism. In Adrian Peace (ed.), 'Britain Today: New Anthropological Perspectives', Special Issue of *Anthropological Journal on European Cultures* 9 (1): 11–35.

Anderson, James and Ian Shuttleworth (1998), Sectarian Demography, Territoriality and Policy in Northern Ireland. *Political Geography* 17: 187–208.

Anderson, James, Liam O'Dowd and Thomas M. Wilson (eds) (2003), *Culture and Cooperation in Europe's Borderlands*. Amsterdam and New York: Rodopi.

Appadurai, Arjun (1996), *Modernity at Large: Cultural Dimensions of Globalization*. Minneapolis, MN: University of Minnesota Press.

Arensberg, Conrad M. (1937), *The Irish Countryman,* Cambridge, MA: Macmillan.

—— (1961), The Community as Object and as Sample. *American Anthropologist* 63 (2): 241–64.

Arensberg, Conrad M. and Solon T. Kimball (1968) [1948], *Family and Community in Ireland*, Second Edition. Cambridge, MA: Harvard University Press.

—— (2001), *Family and Community in Ireland*, Third Edition. Ennis, County Clare, Ireland: CLASP Press.

Aretxaga, Begoña (1995), Dirty Protest: Symbolic Overdetermination and Gender in Northern Ireland Ethnic Violence. *Ethos* 23 (2): 123–48.

—— (1997), *Shattering Silence: Women, Nationalism and Political Subjectivity in Northern Ireland*. Princeton: Princeton University Press.

—— (2001a), The Sexual Games of the Body Politic: Fantasy and State Violence in Northern Ireland. *Culture, Medicine and Psychiatry* 25: 1–27.

—— (2001b), Engendering Violence: Strip-Searching of Women in Northern Ireland. In Dorothy Holland and Jean Lave (eds), *History in Person: Enduring Struggles, Contentious Practice, Intimate Identities*. Santa Fe: School of American Research Press.

Bairner, Alan (1997), 'Up to Their Knees'? Football, Sectarianism, Masculinity and Protestant Working-Class Identity. In Peter Shirlow and Mark McGovern (eds), *Who are 'The People'? Unionism, Protestantism and Loyalism in Northern Ireland*. London: Pluto Press.

—— (2001), *Sport, Nationalism, and Globalization: European and North American Perspectives*. New York: State University of New York Press.

—— (2003), Sport and the Politics of Irish Nationalism: The Struggle for Ireland's Sporting Soul. In Jörg Neuheiser and Stefan Wolff (eds), *Peace at Last? The Impact of the Good Friday Agreement on Northern Ireland*. New York: Berghahn Books.

—— (2005a), Introduction: Sport and the Irish. In Alan Bairner (ed.), *Sport and the Irish: Histories, Identities, Issues*. Dublin: University College Dublin Press.

—— (2005b), Sport, Irishness and Ulster Unionism. In Alan Bairner (ed.), *Sport and the Irish: Histories, Identities, Issues*. Dublin: University College Dublin Press.

Bairner, Alan and Peter Shirlow (1998), Loyalism, Linfield and the Territorial Politics of Soccer Fandom in Northern Ireland. *Space and Polity* 2 (2): 163–77.

—— (2003), When Leisure Turns to Fear: Fear, Mobility, and Ethno-Sectarianism in Belfast. *Leisure Studies* 22: 203–21.

Bakhtin, Mikhail M. (1984) [1968], *Rabelais and His World*. Bloomington: Indiana University Press.

Bartley, Brendan and Jamie A. Saris (1999), Social Exclusion in Cherry Orchard: Another Side of Suburban Dublin. In Andrew MacLaren and James Killen (eds), *Dublin Contemporaries: Trends and Issues for the Twenty-First Century*. Dublin: Geographical Society of Ireland.

Basch, Linda, Nina Glick Schiller and Cristina Szanton Blanc (1994), *Nations Unbound: Transnational Projects, Postcolonial Predicaments and Deterritorialized Nation-States*. London: Gordon and Breach.

Basegmez, Virva (2005), *Irish Scene and Sound: Identity, Authenticity and Transnationality among Young Musicians*. Stockholm Studies in Social Anthropology 57. Stockholm: Stockholm University.

Bax, Mart (1973), *Harpstrings and Confessions: Machine-Style Politics in the Irish Republic*. Amsterdam: van Gorcum.

—— (1975), The Political Machine and Its Importance in the Irish Republic. *Political Anthropology* 1: 6–20.

—— (1987), Religious Regimes and State Formation: Towards a Research Perspective. *Anthropological Quarterly* 60 (1): 1–11.

Bell, Colin and Howard Newby (1971), *Community Studies: An Introduction to the Sociology of the Local Community*. London: Allen and Unwin.

Bell, Desmond (1981), Community Studies: The Social Anthropological Heritage and Its Popularity in Ireland. *International Journal of Sociology and Social Policy* 1 (2): 22–36.

—— (1990), *Acts of Union: Youth Culture and Sectarianism in Northern Ireland*, London: Macmillan.

—— (2005), Loyalist Culture: A Litany of Blame. *The Vacuum* (Belfast), July: 17.

Bell, Jonathan (1978), Relations of Mutual Help Between Ulster Farmers. *Ulster Folklife* 24: 48–58.

—— (2005), *Ulster Farming Families 1930–1960*. Belfast: Ulster Historical Foundation.

Bell, Kathryn (2004), Competitors, Collaborators or Companions? Gossip and Storytelling among Political Journalists in Northern Ireland. *Journal of the Society for the Anthropology of Europe* 4 (1): 5–15.

Bell, Kathryn, Neil Jarman and Thomas Lefebvre (2004), *Migrant Workers in Northern Ireland*. Belfast: Institute for Conflict Resolution.

Bellier, Irène and Thomas M. Wilson (2000), Building, Imagining, and Experiencing Europe: Institutions and Identities in the European Union. In Irène Bellier and Thomas M. Wilson (eds), *An Anthropology of the European Union: Building, Imagining and Experiencing the New Europe*. Oxford: Berg Publishers.

Birdwell-Pheasant, Donna (1992), The Early Twentieth-Century Irish Stem Family: A Case Study from County Kerry, In Marilyn Silverman and Philip H. Gulliver (eds), *Approaching the Past: Historical Anthropology through Irish Case Studies*, New York: Columbia University Press.

—— (1999), The Home 'Place': Center and Periphery in Irish House and Family Systems. In Donna Birdwell-Pheasant and D. Lawrence-Zúñiga (eds), *House Life: Space, Place and Family in Europe*. Oxford: Berg.

Blacking, John R. (1987–8), *Dancing*, a series of six thirty-minute television programmes produced by Ulster Television Ltd, Belfast.

Blacking, John R., Kieran Byrne and Kate Ingram (1989), Looking for Work in Larne: A Social Anthropological Study. In Hastings Donnan and Graham McFarlane (eds), *Social Anthropology and Public Policy in Northern Ireland*. Aldershot: Avebury.

Borneman, John and Nick Fowler (1997), Europeanization. *Annual Review of Anthropology* 26: 487–514.

Bradby, Barbara (1994), Freedom, Feeling and Dancing: Madonna's Songs Traverse Girls' Talk. In Sara Mills (ed.), *Gendering the Reader*. Brighton: Harvester Wheatsheaf.

Breen, Richard (1980), The Ritual Expression of Inter-Household Relationships in Ireland. *Cambridge Anthropology* 6 (1–2): 33–59.

—— (1982), Naming Practices in Western Ireland. *Man* (N. S.) 17 (4): 701–13.

—— (1984), Dowry Payments and the Irish Case. *Comparative Studies in Society and History* 26 (2): 290–6.

Brennan, Helen (1999), *The Story of Irish Dance*. Dingle: Brandon.

Brewer, John D. (1992), Sectarianism and Racism, and Their Parallels and Differences. *Ethnic and Racial Studies* 15 (3): 352–64.

Brody, Hugh (1973), *Innishkillane: Change and Decline in the West of Ireland.* London: Allen Lane.

Bryan, Dominic (1998), 'Ireland's Very Own Jurassic Park': The Mass Media and the Discourse of 'Tradition' on Orange Parades. In Anthony D. Buckley (ed.), *Symbols in Northern Ireland*. Belfast: Institute of Irish Studies Press.

—— (1999), The Right to March: Parading a Loyal Protestant Identity in Northern Ireland. In Tim Allen and John Eade (eds), *Divided Europeans: Understanding Ethnicities in Conflict*. Leiden: E. J. Brill.

—— (2000), *Orange Parades: The Politics of Tradition, Ritual and Control*. London: Pluto Press.

—— (2003), Drumcree: Marching Towards Peace in Northern Ireland? In Jörg Neuheiser and Stefan Wolff (eds) *Peace at Last? The Impact of the Good Friday Agreement on Northern Ireland*. New York: Berghahn Books.

Bryan, Dominic, T. G. Fraser and Seamus Dunn (1995), *Political Rituals: Loyalist Parades in Portadown*. Coleraine: Centre for the Study of Conflict.

Bryan, Dominic and Neil Jarman (1997), Parading Tradition, Protesting Triumphalism: Utilising Anthropology in Public Policy. In Hastings Donnan and Graham McFarlane (eds), *Culture and Policy in Northern Ireland: Anthropology in the Public Arena*. Belfast: Institute of Irish Studies.

Bryson, John M. and Barbara C. Crosby (1992), *Leadership for the Common Good: Tackling Public Problems in a Shared-Power World*. San Francisco: Jossey-Bass Publishers.

Bryson, Lucy and Clem McCartney (1994), *Clashing Symbols: A Report on the Use of Flags, Anthems and Other National Symbols in Northern Ireland*. Belfast: Institute of Irish Studies.

Buckley, Anthony D. (1982a), *A Gentle People: A Study of a Peaceful Community in Northern Ireland*. Cultra: Ulster Folk and Transport Museum.

—— (1982b), Unofficial Healing in Ulster. *Ulster Folklife* 26: 15–34.

—— (1983), Playful Rebellion: Social Control and the Framing of Experience in an Ulster Community. *Man* (N. S.) 18 (2), 383–95.

—— (1984), Walls within Walls: Religion and Rough Behaviour in an Ulster Community. *Sociology* 18: 19–32.

—— (1985–6), The Chosen Few: Biblical Texts in the Regalia of an Ulster Secret Society. *Folk Life* 24: 5–24.

—— (1987), Bad Boys and Little Old Ladies: Youth and Old Age in Two Ulster Villages. *Ethnologia Europea* XVII: 157–63.

—— (ed.) (1998), *Symbols in Northern Ireland*. Belfast: Institute of Irish Studies.

—— (2000), Royal Arch, Royal Arch Purple and *Raiders of the Lost Ark*: Secrecy in Orange and Masonic Ritual. In T. M. Owen (ed.), *From Corrib to Cultra: Folklife Essays in Honour of Alan Gailey*. Belfast: Institute of Irish Studies.

—— (n.d.), 'Rise Up Dead Man, and Fight Again': Mumming, the Mass and the Masonic Third Degree. Unpublished paper.

Buckley, Anthony D. and Mary Catherine Kenney (1995), *Negotiating Identity: Rhetoric, Metaphor, and Social Drama in Northern Ireland*. Washington and London: Smithsonian Institution Press.

Bufwack, Mary S. (1982), *Village without Violence: An Examination of a Northern Irish Community*. Cambridge, MA: Schenkman.

Burton, Frank (1978), *The Politics of Legitimacy: Struggles in a Belfast Community*. London: Routledge and Kegan Paul.

Butler, Cathal (1985), *Travelling People in Derry and Tyrone*. Londonderry: World Development Group.

Byrne, Anne, Ricca Edmondson and Tony Varley (2001), 'Introduction to the Third Edition: Arensberg and Kimball and Anthropological Research in Ireland', in Conrad M. Arensberg and Solon T. Kimball, *Family and Community in Ireland*, Third Edition. Ennis, County Clare, Ireland: CLASP Press.

Byron, Reginald (1999), *Irish America*. Oxford: Clarendon Press.

Cairns, David (2000), The Object of Sectarianism: The Material Reality of Sectarianism in Ulster Loyalism. *Journal of the Royal Anthropological Institute* 6 (3): 437–52.

—— (2001), Moving the Immovable: Discursive Challenge and Discursive Change in Ulster Loyalism. *European Journal of Cultural Studies* 4 (1): 85–104.

Callahan, Sidney (1979), An Anthropologist in Ireland. *Commonweal*, 25 May: 310–11.

Carter, Thomas (2003a), In the Spirit of the Game? Cricket and Changing Notions of Being British in Northern Ireland. *Journal of the Society for the Anthropology of Europe* 3 (1): 14–26.

—— (2003b), Violent Pastime(s): On the Commendation and Condemnation of Violence in Belfast. *City & Society* XV (2): 255–81.

Carter, Thomas, Hastings Donnan and Huon Wardle (2003), *Global Migrants: The Impact of Migrants Working in Sport in Northern Ireland*. Belfast: Sports Council for Northern Ireland.

Casey, Ruth (2003), Defining the Local: The Development of an 'Environment Culture' in a Clare Village. In Michael Cronin and Barbara O'Connor (eds), *Irish Tourism: Image, Culture and Identity*. Clevedon: Channel View Publications.

Cecil, Rosanne (1989), Care and Community in a Northern Irish Town. In Hastings Donnan and Graham McFarlane (eds), *Social Anthropology and Public Policy in Northern Ireland*. Aldershot: Avebury.

—— (1993), The Marching Season in Northern Ireland: An Expression of Politico-Religious Identity. In Sharon Macdonald (ed.), *Inside European Identities: Ethnography in Western Europe*. Providence, RI: Berg.

Chapman, Charlotte Gower (1971), *Milocca: A Sicilian Village*. Cambridge, MA: Schenkman Publishing.

Clarke, Liam (1987), *Broadening the Battlefield: The H-Blocks and the Rise of Sinn Féin*. Dublin: Gill and Macmillan.

Cohen, Abner (1980), Drama and Politics in the Development of a London Carnival. *Man* (N. S.) 15 (1): 65–87.

Cohen, Anthony P. (1979), The Whalsay Croft: Traditional Work and Customary Identity in Modern Times. In Sandra Wallman (ed.), *Social Anthropology of Work*. London: Academic Press.

—— (ed.) (1982), *Belonging: Identity and Social Organisation in British Rural Cultures*. Manchester: Manchester University Press

—— (1985), *The Symbolic Construction of Community*. London: Routledge.

—— (ed.) (1986), *Symbolising Boundaries: Identity and Diversity in British Cultures*. Manchester: Manchester University Press.

—— (1987), *Whalsay: Symbol, Segment and Boundary in a Shetland Island Community*. Manchester: Manchester University Press.

—— (1994), *Self Consciousness: An Alternative Anthropology of Identity*. London: Routledge.

—— (ed.) (2000), *Signifying Identities: Anthropological Perspectives on Boundaries and Contested Values*. London: Routledge.

Cohen, Marilyn (1993), Urbanisation and the Milieux of Factory Life: Gilford/Dunbarton, 1825–1914. In Chris Curtin, Hastings Donnan and Thomas M. Wilson (eds), *Irish Urban Cultures*. Belfast: Institute of Irish Studies Press.

Cohen, Robin (1994), *Frontiers of Identity: The British and the Others*. London: Longman.

Cole, Jeffrey (1997), *The New Racism in Europe: A Sicilian Ethnography*. Cambridge: Cambridge University Press.

Coleman, Steve (2003), The Centralised Government of Liquidity: Community, Language and Culture under the Celtic Tiger. In Colin Coulter and Steve Coleman (eds), *The End of Irish History? Critical Reflections on the Celtic Tiger*. Manchester: Manchester University Press.

Collins, Martin (1994), The Sub-Culture of Poverty – A Response to McCarthy. In May McCann, Séamas Ó Síocháin and Joseph Ruane (eds), *Irish Travellers: Culture and Ethnicity*. Belfast: Institute of Irish Studies, Queen's University, Belfast.

Collinson, Paul (2005), Development, Democracy and the New Europe in the Irish Borderlands. In Thomas M. Wilson and Hastings Donnan (eds), *Culture and*

Power at the Edges of the State: National Support and Subversion in European Border Regions. Münster: LIT Verlag.

Connerton, P. (1989), *How Societies Remember*. Cambridge: Cambridge University Press.

Connolly, Sean J. (1997), Culture, Identity and Tradition: Changing Definitions of Irishness. In Brian Graham (ed.), *In Search of Ireland: A Cultural Geography*. London: Routledge.

Conrad, Kathryn (2001), Queer Treasons: Homosexuality and Irish National Identity. *Cultural Studies* 15 (1): 124–37.

Conway, John J. (1989), The Divergence of Public and Private Development in Two Kilkenny Neighbourhoods. In Chris Curtin and Thomas M. Wilson (eds), *Ireland from Below: Social Change and Llocal Communities*. Galway: Galway University Press.

Corcoran, Mary P. and Michel Peillon (eds) (2002), *Ireland Unbound: A Turn of the Century Chronicle*. Dublin: Institute of Public Administration.

Coulter, Colin (2003), The End of Irish History? An Introduction to the Book. In Colin Coulter and Steve Coleman (eds), *The End of Irish History? Critical Reflections on the Celtic Tiger*. Manchester: Manchester University Press.

Cresswell, Robert (1969), *Une communanté rurale d'Irlande*, Paris: Institut d'Ethnographie.

Cronin, Michael and Barbara O'Connor (eds) (2003), *Irish Tourism: Image, Culture and Identity*. Clevedon: Channel View Publications.

Cronin, Mike and Daryl Adair (2002), *The Wearing of the Green: A History of St Patrick's Day*. London: Routledge.

Crozier, Maurna (1985), Patterns of Hospitality in a Rural Ulster Community. Unpublished doctoral dissertation, Queen's University Belfast.

—— (ed.) (1989a), *Varieties of Irishness*. Belfast: Institute of Irish Studies.

—— (1989b), 'Powerful Wakes': Perfect Hospitality. In Chris Curtin and Thomas M. Wilson (eds), *Ireland from Below: Social Change and Local Communities*. Galway: Galway University Press.

—— (ed.) (1990a), *Varieties of Britishness*. Belfast: Institute of Irish Studies.

—— (1990b), Good Leaders and 'Decent Men': An Ulster Contradiction. In Myrtle Hill and Sarah Barber (eds), *Aspects of Irish Studies*. Belfast: Institute of Irish Studies.

—— (ed.) (1991), *All Europeans Now?* Belfast: Institute of Irish Studies.

Cunningham, Hilary and Josiah McC. Heyman (2004), Introduction: Mobilities and Enclosures at Borders. *Identities: Global Studies in Culture and Power* 11: 289–302.

Curtin, Chris (1988), Social Order, Interpersonal Relations and Disputes in a West of Ireland Community. In Mike Tomlinson, Tony Varley and Ciaran McCullough (eds), *Whose Law and Order? Aspects of Crime and Social*

Control in Irish Society. Belfast: Sociological Association of Ireland.

Curtin, Chris, Hastings Donnan and Thomas M. Wilson (1993a), Anthropology and Irish Urban Settings. In Chris Curtin, Hastings Donnan and Thomas M. Wilson (eds), *Irish Urban Cultures*. Belfast: Institute of Irish Studies Press.

—— (eds) (1993b), *Irish Urban Cultures*. Belfast: Institute of Irish Studies Press.

Curtin, Chris, Pauline Jackson and Barbara O'Connor (1987a), Introduction. In Chris Curtin, Pauline Jackson and Barbara O'Connor (eds), *Gender in Irish Society*. Galway: Galway University Press.

—— (eds) (1987b), *Gender in Irish Society*. Galway: Galway University Press.

Curtin, Chris and Colm Ryan (1989), Clubs, Pubs, and Private Houses in a Clare Town. In Chris Curtin and Thomas M. Wilson (eds), *Ireland from Below: Social Change and Local Communities*. Galway: Galway University Press.

Curtin, Chris and Anthony Varley (1982), Collusion Practices in a West of Ireland Livestock Mart. *Ethnology* 21 (4): 349–57.

—— (1986), Bringing Industry to a Small Town in the West of Ireland. *Sociologia Ruralis* 26: 170–85.

—— (1987), Marginal Men? Bachelor Farmers in a West of Ireland Community. In Chris Curtin, Pauline Jackson and Barbara O'Connor (eds), *Gender in Irish Society*. Galway: Galway University Press.

—— (1989), Brown Trout, 'Gentry' and Dutchmen: Tourism and Development in South Mayo. In Chris Curtin and Thomas M. Wilson (eds), *Ireland from Below: Social Change and Local Communities*. Galway: Galway University Press.

Curtin, Chris and Thomas M. Wilson (1989a), Introduction. In Chris Curtin and Thomas M. Wilson (eds), *Ireland from Below: Social Change and Local Communities*. Galway: Galway University Press.

—— (eds) (1989b), *Ireland from Below: Social Change and Local Communities*. Galway: Galway University Press.

Darby, John (1986), *Intimidation and the Control of Conflict in Northern Ireland*. Syracuse, NY: Syracuse University Press.

D'Arcy, Michael and Tim Dickson (1995), Editors' Introduction. In M. D'Arcy and T. Dickson (eds), *Border Crossings: Developing Ireland's Island Economy*. Dublin: Gill and Macmillan.

de Rosa, Ciro (1998), Playing Nationalism. In Anthony D. Buckley (ed.), *Symbols in Northern Ireland*. Belfast: Institute of Irish Studies Press.

Dilley, Roy (1989), Boat Owners, Patrons and State Policy in the Northern Ireland Fishing Industry. In Hastings Donnan and Graham McFarlane (eds), *Social Anthropology and Public Policy in Northern Ireland,* Aldershot: Avebury.

Dillon, Michele (1993), *Debating Divorce: Moral Conflict in Ireland*. Lexington: University Press of Kentucky.

Doherty, Gerry (2005), South Belfast Roundtable on Racism. (Northern Ireland Community Relations Council). *CRC News* 45: 10.

Donnan, Hastings (1990), Mixed Marriage in Comparative Perspective: Gender and Power in Northern Ireland and Pakistan. In Mark Hutter (ed.), 'Intermarriage', Special Issue of *Journal of Comparative Family Studies* XXI (2): 207–25.

—— (1991), *Other Faces: Indians in Northern Ireland.* BBC Northern Ireland, twenty-five-minute television programme.

—— (1994), 'New' Minorities: South Asians in the North. In Pól Ó Muirí (ed.), *The Unheard Voice: Social Anthropology in Ireland.* Belfast: Fortnight Educational Trust.

—— (1999), Shopping and Sectarianism at the Irish border. In Michael Rösler and Tobias Wendl (eds), *Frontiers and Borderlands: Anthropological Perspectives.* Frankfurt and New York: Peter Lang.

—— (2000), Private Acts and Public Violence: Interfaith Marriages in Northern Ireland. *Bulletin of the Royal Institute for Inter-Faith Studies* 2 (2), 15–32.

—— (2005), Material Identities: Fixing Ethnicity in the Irish Borderlands. *Identities: Global Studies in Culture and Power* 12 (1): 69–105.

Donnan, Hastings and Graham McFarlane (1983), Informal Social Organisation. In J. Darby (ed.), *Northern Ireland: The Background to the Conflict.* Belfast: Appletree Press and Syracuse, NY: Syracuse University Press.

—— (1986a), 'You Get On Better With Your Own': Social Continuity and Change in Rural Northern Ireland. In Patrick Clancy, Sheelagh Drudy, Kathleen Lynch and Liam O'Dowd (eds), *Ireland: A Sociological Profile.* Dublin: Institute of Public Administration.

—— (1986b), Social Anthropology and the Sectarian Divide in Northern Ireland. In Richard Jenkins, Hastings Donnan and Graham McFarlane, *The Sectarian Divide in Northern Ireland Today.* Royal Anthropological Institute of Great Britain and Ireland. Occasional Paper no. 41.

—— (eds) (1989a), *Social Anthropology and Public Policy in Northern Ireland.* Aldershot: Avebury Press.

—— (1989b), Introduction: Social Anthropology and Public Policy in Northern Ireland. In Hastings Donnan and Graham McFarlane (eds), *Social Anthropology and Public Policy in Northern Ireland.* Aldershot: Avebury.

—— (eds) (1997a), *Culture and Policy in Northern Ireland: Anthropology in the Public Arena.* Belfast: Institute of Irish Studies Press.

—— (1997b), Cultural Perspectives on Public policy in Northern Ireland. In Hastings Donnan and Graham McFarlane (eds), *Culture and Policy in Northern Ireland: Anthropology in the Public Arena.* Belfast: Institute of Irish Studies Press.

—— (1997c), Anthropology and Policy Research: The View from Northern

Ireland. In Cris Shore and Susan Wright (eds), *Anthropology of Policy: Critical Perspectives on Governance and Power*. London: Routledge.

—— (1997d), 'Counselling' the Unemployed in Belfast. In Hastings Donnan and Graham McFarlane (eds), *Culture and Policy in Northern Ireland: Anthropology in the Public Arena*. Belfast: Institute of Irish Studies Press.

Donnan, Hastings and Mairead O'Brien (1998), 'Because You Stick Out, You Stand Out': Perceptions of Prejudice among Northern Ireland's Pakistanis. In Paul Hainsworth (ed.), *Divided Society: Ethnic Minorities and Racism in Northern Ireland*. London: Pluto.

Donnan, Hastings and Thomas M. Wilson (1994), The Anthropology of Borders. In Hastings Donnan and Thomas M. Wilson (eds), *Border Approaches: Anthropological Perspectives on Frontiers*, Lanham, MD: University Press of America.

—— (1999), *Borders: Frontiers of Identity, Nation and State*. Oxford: Berg.

—— (2003), Territoriality, Anthropology, and the Interstitial: Subversion and Support in European Borderlands. *Focaal: European Journal of Anthropology* 41: 9–20.

Douglas, Mary (1966), *Purity and Danger: An Analysis of Concepts of Pollution and Taboo*. Harmondsworth: Penguin Books.

Driessen, Henk (1998), The 'New Immigration' and the Transformation of the European–African Frontier. In Thomas M. Wilson and Hastings Donnan (eds), *Border Identities*. Cambridge: Cambridge University Press.

Eipper, Chris (1986), *The Ruling Trinity: A Community Study of Church, State and Business in Ireland*. Aldershot: Gower.

—— (1989), *Hostage to Fortune: Bantry Bay and the Encounter with Gulf Oil*. Memorial University, St John's Newfoundland: Institute of Social and Economic Research.

—— (1996), The Voice of the Virgin: Irish Visionaries and their Testimony. In Richard Davis (ed.), *Irish-Australian Studies: Papers Delivered at the Eighth Irish-Australian Conference, Hobart July 1995*. Darlinghurst: New South Wales.

Fardon, Richard (1990), Localizing Strategies; The Regionalization of Ethnographic Accounts. In Richard Fardon (ed.), *Localizing Strategies: Regional Traditions of Ethnographic Writing*. Washington, DC: Smithsonian Institution Press.

Feld, Steven and Keith Basso (eds) (1996), *Senses of Place*. Santa Fe: School of American Research.

Feldman, Allen (1991), *Formations of Violence: The Narrative of the Body and Political Terror in Northern Ireland*. Chicago: University of Chicago Press.

—— (1992), On Formations of Violence. *Current Anthropology* 33 (5): 595–6.

Finlay, Andrew (1987), The Cutting Edge: Derry Shirtmakers. In Chris Curtin,

Pauline Jackson and Barbara O'Connor (eds), *Gender in Irish Society.* Galway: Galway University Press.

—— (1999), 'Whatever You Say Say Nothing': An Ethnographic Encounter in Northern Ireland and Its Sequel. *Sociological Research Online* 4 (3) (*www.socresonline.org.uk/socresonline/4/3/finlay.html*).

Finnegan, Ruth (1989), *The Hidden Musicians: Music Making in an English Town.* Cambridge: Cambridge University Press.

Fitzgerald, J. D., T. P. Quinn, B. J. Whelan and J. A. Williams (1988), *An Analysis of Cross-Border Shopping.* Dublin: Economic and Social Research Institute.

Flynn, Donna K. (1997), 'We Are the Border': Identity, Exchange, and the State along the Benin–Nigeria Border. *American Ethnologist* 24 (2): 311–30.

Foster, Roy F. (1989), Varieties of Irishness. In Maurna Crozier (ed.), *Varieties of Irishness.* Proceedings of the Cultural Traditions Group Conference, 3–4 March. Belfast: Institute of Irish Studies.

—— (2001), *The Irish Story: Telling Tales and Making it up in Ireland.* London: Penguin Books.

Foucault, Michel (1981), *The History of Sexuality: An Introduction.* Volume 1. Harmondsworth: Penguin Books.

—— (1991) [1977], *Discipline and Punish: The Birth of the Prison.* Harmondsworth: Penguin Books.

—— (1994) [1980], Two Lectures. In Nicholas B. Dirks, Geoff Eley and Sherry B. Ortner (eds), *Culture/Power/History: A Reader in Contemporary Social Theory.* Princeton: Princeton University Press.

Fox, Robin (1975), *Encounter with Anthropology.* Harmondsworth: Penguin Books.

—— (1978), *The Tory Islanders: A People of the Celtic Fringe.* Cambridge: Cambridge University Press.

—— (1979), The Visiting Husband on Tory Island. *Journal of Comparative Family Studies* X (2): 163–90.

Fraser, M. (1973), *Children in Conflict.* London: Secker and Warburg.

Fulton, Gareth (2005), Northern Catholic Fans of the Republic of Ireland Soccer Team. In Alan Bairner (ed.), *Sport and the Irish: Histories, Identities, Issues.* Dublin: University College Dublin Press.

Gaetz, Stephen (1992), Planning Community-Based Youth Services in Cork, Ireland: The Relevance of the Concepts 'Youth' and 'Community.' *Urban Anthropology* 21 (1): 91–113.

—— (1993), Who Comes First? Teenage Girls, Youth Culture and the Provision of Youth Services in Cork. In Chris Curtin, Hastings Donnan and Thomas M. Wilson (eds), *Irish Urban Cultures,* Belfast: Institute of Irish Studies Press.

—— (1997), *Looking Out for the Lads: Community Action and the Provision of Youth Services in an Urban Irish Parish.* St Johns, Memorial University of Newfoundland: Institute of Social and Economic Research.

Geertz, Clifford (1973), *The Interpretation of Cultures*. New York: Basic Books.

Gibbon, Peter (1973), Arensberg and Kimball Revisited. *Economy and Society* 2: 479–98.

Gibbon, Peter and Chris Curtin (1976), The Stem Family in Ireland. *Comparative Studies in Society and History* 20 (3): 429–53.

—— (1983a), Irish Farm Families: Facts and Fantasies. *Comparative Studies in Society and History* 25 (2): 375–80.

—— (1983b), Some Observations on 'The Stem Family in Ireland Reconsidered'. *Comparative Studies in Society and History* 25 (2): 393–5.

Gibbon, Peter and Michael D. Higgins (1974), Patronage, Tradition and Modernisation: The Case of the Irish 'Gombeenman'. *Economic and Social Review* 6 (1): 27–44.

—— (1977), The Irish 'Gombeenman': Re-incarnation or Rehabilitation? *Economic and Social Review* 8: 313–20.

Gilroy, Paul (1991), *'There Ain't No Black in the Union Jack': The Cultural Politics of Race and Nation*. Chicago: University of Chicago Press.

Glassie, Henry (1982), *Passing the Time in Ballymenone: Culture and History of an Ulster Community*. Philadelphia: University of Pennsylvania Press.

Glendinning, Robin (1997), The Twelfth. In Gordon Lucy and Elaine McClure (eds), *The Twelfth: What It Means to Me*. Belfast: Ulster Society (Publications) Ltd.

Gmelch, George (1977), *The Irish Tinkers: The Urbanization of an Itinerant People*. Menlo Park, CA: Cummings.

—— (1985). *The Irish Tinkers: The Urbanization of an Itinerant People*, Second Edition. Prospect Heights, IL: Waveland Press.

—— (1986), Return Migration to Rural Ireland. In R. L. King (ed.), *Return Migration and Regional Economic Problems*. London: Croom Helm.

Gmelch, George and Sharon Bohn Gmelch (1985), The Cross-Channel Migration of Irish Travellers. *Economic and Social Review* 16 (4): 287–96.

Gmelch, Sharon Bohn (1986), *Nan: The Life of an Irish Travelling Woman*. New York: W. W. Norton.

—— (1989), From Poverty Subculture to Political Lobby: The Traveller Rights Movement in Ireland. In Chris Curtin and Thomas M. Wilson (eds), *Ireland from Below: Social Change and Local Communities*. Galway: Galway University Press.

Gmelch, Sharon Bohn and George Gmelch (1976), The Emergence of an Ethnic Group: The Irish Tinkers. *Anthropological Quarterly* 49: 225–38.

Goffman, Irving (1961), *Asylums: Essays on the Social Situation of Mental Patients and Other Inmates*. Harmondsworth: Penguin Books.

Goody, Jack (1983), *The Development of the Family and Marriage in Europe*. Cambridge: Cambridge University Press.

Gottman, Jean (1951), Geography and International Relations. *World Politics* III: 153–73.

Graham, Brian (1997a), Ireland and Irishness: Place, Culture and Identity. In Brian Graham (ed.), *In Search of Ireland: A Cultural Geography*. London: Routledge.

—— (ed.) (1997b), *In Search of Ireland: A Cultural Geography*. London: Routledge.

Graham, Colin (2001), 'Blame it on Maureen O'Hara': Ireland and the Trope of Authenticity. *Cultural Studies* 15 (1): 58–75.

Gramsci, A. (1971), *Selections from the Prison Notebooks*. London: Lawrence and Wishart.

Grillo, Ralph (1999), Review of Culture and Policy in Northern Ireland: Anthropology in the Public Arena. *Social Anthropology* 7 (2): 203–4.

Gullestad, Marianne (2004), Blind Slaves of Our Prejudices: Debating 'Culture' and 'Race' in Norway. *Ethnos* 69 (2): 177–203.

Gulliver, Philip H. (1989), Doing Anthropological Research in Rural Ireland: Methods and Sources for Linking the Past and the Present. In Chris Curtin and Thomas M. Wilson (eds), *Ireland from Below: Social Change and Local Communities*. Galway: Galway University Press.

—— (1992), Shopkeepers and Farmers in South Kilkenny, 1840–1981. In Marilyn Silverman and Philip H. Gulliver (eds), *Approaching the Past: Historical Anthropology through Irish Case Studies*. New York: Columbia University Press.

Gulliver, Philip H. and Marilyn Silverman (1995), *Merchants and Shopkeepers: A Historical Anthropology of an Irish Market Town, 1200–1991*. Toronto: University of Toronto Press.

Haddon, Arthur C. and C. R. Browne (1891–3), Ethnography of the Aran Islands, Co. Galway. *Proceedings of the Royal Irish Academy* 18: 768–830.

Hainsworth, Paul (1998), Politics, Racism and Ethnicity in Northern Ireland. In Paul Hainsworth (ed.), *Divided Society: Ethnic Minorities and Racism in Northern Ireland*. London: Pluto.

Hall, Frank (1996), Posture in Irish Dancing. *Visual Anthropology* 8: 251–66.

—— (1999), Madness and Recall: Storied Data on Irish Dancing. In T. J. Buckland (ed.), *Dance in the Field: Theory, Methods and Issues in Dance Ethnography*. London: Macmillan Press.

Hall, Stuart (1991), The Local and the Global: Globalization and Ethnicity. In Anthony D. King (ed.), *Culture, Globalization and the World System*. Albany: State University of New York Press.

—— (1996), Introduction: Who Needs 'Identity'? In Stuart Hall and Paul du Gay (eds), *Questions of Cultural Identity*. London: Sage.

Hall, Stuart and Tony Jefferson (eds) (1976), *Resistance through Rituals*. London: Hutchinson.

Handelman, D. (1998) [1990], *Models and Mirrors: Towards an Anthropology of Public Events*. Oxford: Berghahn Books.

Hannan, Damian (1972), Kinship, Neighbourhood and Social Change in Irish Rural Communities. *Economic and Social Review* 3 (2): 163–88.

Harmsen, Robert and Thomas M. Wilson (2000), Introduction: Approaches to Europeanization. In Robert Harmsen and Thomas M. Wilson (eds), *Europeanization: Institutions, Identities and Citizenship*. Amsterdam: Rodopi B. V.

Harris, Lorelei (1984), Class, Community and Sexual Divisions in North Mayo. In Chris Curtin, Mary Kelly and Liam O'Dowd (eds), *Culture and Ideology in Ireland*. Galway: Galway University Press.

Harris, Rosemary (1961), The Selection of Leaders in Ballybeg, Northern Ireland. *Sociological Review* (N. S.) 9: 137–49.

—— (1972), *Prejudice and Tolerance in Ulster: A Study of Neighbours and 'Strangers' in a Border Community*. Manchester: Manchester University Press.

—— (1988), Theory and Evidence: The 'Irish Stem Family' and Field Data. *Man* (n. S.) 23 (3): 417–34.

Harrison, Simon (1992), Ritual as Intellectual Property. *Man* (N. S.) 27 (2): 224–44.

Hassan, David (2005), Sport, Identity and Irish Nationalism in Northern Ireland. In Alan Bairner (ed.), *Sport and the Irish: Histories, Identities, Issues*. Dublin: University College Dublin Press.

Hazelkorn, Ellen and Colm Murphy (2002), The Cultural Economy of Dublin. In Mary P. Corcoran and Michel Peillon (eds), *Ireland Unbound: A Turn of the Century Chronicle*. Dublin: Institute of Public Administration.

Helleiner, Jane (1993), Traveller Settlement in Galway City: Politics, Class and Culture. In Chris Curtin, Hastings Donnan and Thomas M. Wilson (eds), *Irish Urban Cultures*. Belfast: Institute of Irish Studies Press.

—— (2000), *Irish Travellers: Racism and the Politics of Culture*. Toronto: University of Toronto Press.

—— (2003), The Politics of Traveller 'Child Begging' in Ireland. *Critique of Anthropology* 23 (1): 17–33.

Helleiner, Jane and Bohdan Szuchewycz (1997), Discourses of Exclusion: The Irish Press and the Travelling People. In Stephen Riggins (ed.), *The Language and Politics of Exclusion: Others in Discourse*. Thousand Oaks, CA: Sage.

Henry, Stuart (ed.) (1981), *Can I Have It in Cash? A Study of Informal Institutions and Unorthodox Ways of Doing Things*. London: Astragal Books.

Herr, Cheryl (1990), The Erotics of Irishness. *Critical Inquiry* 17: 1–34.

—— (2004), Terrorist Chic and Marching Season Style. *The Vacuum* (Belfast), July: 2–3.

Hervik, Peter (2004), Anthropological Perspectives on the New Racism in Europe. *Ethnos* 69 (2): 149–55.

Hill, Jonathan and Thomas M. Wilson (2003), Identity Politics and the Politics of Identities. *Identities: Global Studies in Culture and Power* 10: 1–8.

Howe, Leo E. A. (1985), The 'Deserving' and the 'Undeserving': Practice in an Urban, Local Social Security Office. *Journal of Social Policy* 14: 49–72.

—— (1989a). 'Doing the Double' or Doing Without: The Social and Economic Context of Working 'On the Side' in Belfast. In Richard Jenkins (ed.), *Northern Ireland: Studies in Social and Economic Life*. Aldershot: Avebury.

—— (1989b), Unemployment, Doing the Double and Local Labour Markets in Belfast. In Chris Curtin and Thomas M. Wilson (eds), *Ireland from Below: Social Change and Local Communities*, Galway: Galway University Press.

—— (1989c), Social Anthropology and Public Policy: Aspects of Unemployment and Social Security in Northern Ireland. In Hastings Donnan and Graham McFarlane (eds), *Social Anthropology and Public Policy in Northern Ireland*. Aldershot: Avebury.

—— (1990), *Being Unemployed in Northern Ireland: An Ethnographic Study*. Cambridge: Cambridge University Press.

—— (1994), Ideology, Domination and Unemployment. *Sociological Review* 42 (2): 315–40.

—— (1998), Scrounger, Worker, Beggarman, Cheat: The Dynamics of Unemployment and the Politics of Resistance in Belfast. *Journal of Royal Anthropological Institute* 4 (3): 531–50.

Hughes, Joanne, Colin Knox, Michael Murray and Jonathan Greer (1998), *Partnership Governance in Northern Ireland*. Dublin: Oak Tree Press.

Humphreys, Alexander (1966), *New Dubliners: Urbanization and the Irish Family*. London: Routledge and Kegan Paul.

Inglis, Tom (1991), The Struggle for Control of the Irish Body: State, Church and Society in Nineteenth-Century Ireland. In Eric R. Wolf (ed.), *Religious Regimes and State Formation: Perspectives from European Ethnology*. Albany: State University of New York Press.

—— (1997), Foucault, Bourdieu and the Field of Irish Sexuality. *Irish Journal of Sociology* 7: 5–28.

—— (1998a) [1987], *Moral Monopoly: The Rise and Fall of the Catholic Church in Modern Ireland*. Dublin: University College Dublin Press.

—— (1998b), From Sexual Repression to Liberation. In Michel Peillon and Eamonn Slater (eds), *Encounters with Modern Ireland: A Sociological Chronicle 1995–1996*. Dublin: Institute of Public Administratiion.

Ingram, Kate (1997), Equal Opportunities, the Clothing Industry and the Law. In Hastings Donnan and Graham McFarlane (eds), *Culture and Policy in Northern Ireland: Anthropology in the Public Arena*. Belfast: Institute of Irish Studies.

Irwin, Colin (1997), Social Conflict and the Failure of Education Policies in Two Deeply Divided Societies: Northern Ireland and Israel. In Hastings Donnan and

Graham McFarlane (eds), *Culture and Policy in Northern Ireland: Anthropology in the Public Arena*. Belfast: Institute of Irish Studies.

Jarman, Neil (1992), Troubled Images: The Iconography of Loyalism. *Critique of Anthropology* 12: 133–65.

—— (1993), Intersecting Belfast. In Barbara Bender (ed.), *Landscape, Politics and Perspectives*. Oxford: Berg.

—— (1997), *Material Conflicts: Parades and Visual Displays in Northern Ireland*. Oxford: Berg.

—— (1998a), Material of Culture, Fabric of Identity. In Daniel Miller (ed.), *Material Cultures: Why Some Things Matter*. London: UCL Press.

—— (1998b), Painting Landscapes: The Place of Murals in the Symbolic Construction of Urban Space. In Anthony D. Buckley (ed.), *Symbols in Northern Ireland*. Belfast: Institute of Irish Studies Press.

—— (1999), Commemorating 1916, Celebrating Difference: Parading and Painting in Belfast. In Adrian Forty and Susanne Küchler (eds), *The Art of Forgetting*. Oxford: Berg.

—— (2000), For God and Ulster: Blood and Thunder Bands and Loyalist Political Culture. In T. G. Fraser (ed.), *The Irish Parading Tradition: Following the Drum*. London: Macmillan Press.

—— (2003), From Outrage to Apathy? The Disputes over Parades, 1995–2003. *Global Review of Ethnopolitics* 3 (1): 92–105.

—— (2004), From War to Peace? Changing Patterns of Violence in Northern Ireland, 1990–2003. *Terrorism and Political Violence* 16 (3): 420–38.

—— (2005), Teenage Kicks: Young Women and their Involvement in Violence and Disorderly Behaviour. *Child Care in Practice* 11 (3): 341–56.

Jarman, Neil and Dominic Bryan (1996), *Parade and Protest: A Discussion of Parading Disputes in Northern Ireland*. Coleraine: Centre for the Study of Conflict.

—— (1998), *From Riots to Rights: Nationalist Parades in the North of Ireland*. Coleraine: Centre for the Study of Conflict.

—— (2000a), Green Parades in an Orange State: Nationalist and Republican Commemorations and Demonstrations from Partition to the Troubles, 1920–1970. In T. G. Fraser (ed.), *The Irish Parading Tradition: Following the Drum*. London: Macmillan Press.

—— (2000b), *Stewarding Crowds and Managing Public Safety: Developing a Coordinated Policy for Northern Ireland*. Belfast: Community Development Centre.

Jarman, Neil, Dominic Bryan, Nathalie Caleyron and Ciro de Rosa (1998), *Politics in Public: Freedom of Assembly and the Right to Protest. A Comparative Analysis*. Belfast: Democratic Dialogue.

Jenkins, Richard (1977), Witches and Fairies: Supernatural Aggression and Deviance among the Irish Peasantry. *Ulster Folklife* 23: 33–56.

—— (1982), *Hightown Rules: Growing Up in a Belfast Housing Estate*. Leicester: National Youth Bureau.

—— (1983), *Lads, Citizens, and Ordinary Kids: Working-Class Youth Life-Styles in Belfast*. London: Routledge and Kegan Paul.

—— (1984), Ethnicity and the Rise of Capitalism in Ulster. In Robin Ward and Richard Jenkins (eds), *Ethnic Communities in Business*. Cambridge: Cambridge University Press.

—— (1986), Northern Ireland: In What Sense 'Religions' in Conflict? In Richard Jenkins, Hastings Donnan and Graham McFarlane, *The Sectarian Divide in Northern Ireland Today*. Royal Anthropological Institute of Great Britain and Ireland. Occasional Paper no. 4l.

—— (ed.) (1989), *Northern Ireland: Studies in Social and Economic Life*. Aldershot: Avebury.

—— (1992a), Doing Violence to the Subject. *Current Anthropology* 33 (2): 233–5.

—— (1992b), On Formations of Violence: Reply. *Current Anthropology* 33 (5): 596–7.

—— (1993), Beyond Ethnography: Primary Data Sources in the Urban Anthropology of Northern Ireland. In Chris Curtin, Hastings Donnan and Thomas M. Wilson (eds), *Irish Urban Cultures*. Belfast: Institute of Irish Studies Press.

—— (2004), Spooks and Spooks: Black Magic and Bogeymen in Northern Ireland, 1973–74. In Willem de Blécourt and Owen Davies (eds), *Witchcraft Continued: Popular Magic in Modern Europe*. Manchester: Manchester University Press.

Jenkins, Richard and Philip Harding (1986), Informal Economic Activity in Northern Ireland: A Review of the Literature. Unpublished paper. Swansea: University College Swansea, Department of Sociology and Anthropology.

Kachuk, Patricia (1994), A Resistance to British Cultural Hegemony: Irish-Language Activism in West Belfast. *Anthropologica* XXXVI: 135–54.

Kaeppler, Adrienne L. (1978), Dance in Anthropological Perspective. *Annual Review of Anthropology* 7: 31–49.

—— (1992), Dance. In Richard Bauman (ed.), *Folklore, Cultural Performances, and Popular Entertainments*. New York: Oxford University Press.

Kane, Eileen (1968), Man and Kin in Donegal: A Study of Kinship Functions in a Rural Irish and Irish-American Community. *Ethnology* 7 (3): 245–58.

—— (1978), *The Last Place God Made*. New Haven, CT: HRAFlex Books.

—— (1979a), The Changing Role of the Family in a Rural Irish Community. *Journal of Comparative Family Studies* 10 (2): 141–62.

—— (1979b), Is Rural Ireland Blighted? *Irish Press* (Dublin), 13 December.

—— (1986), Stereotypes and Irish Identity: Mental Illness as a Cultural Frame. *Studies* 75: 539–51.

Kane, Eileen, John Blacking, Hastings Donnan and Graham McFarlane (1988), A Review of Anthropological Research, North and South. In Liam O'Dowd (ed.), *The State of Social Science Research in Ireland,* Dublin: Royal Irish Academy.

Kearney, Richard (1997), *Postnationalist Ireland: Politics, Culture, Philosophy.* London: Routledge.

Kelleher, William (1994), Ambivalence, Modernity and the State of Terror in Northern Ireland. *PoLAR: Political and Legal Anthropology Review* 17 (1): 31–40.

—— (2000), Making Home in the Irish/British Borderlands: The Global and the Local in a Conflicted Social Space. *Identities: Global Studies in Culture and Power* 7 (2): 139–72.

—— (2003), *The Troubles in Ballybogoin: Memory and Identity in Northern Ireland.* Ann Arbor: University of Michigan Press.

Kenney, Mary C. (1998), The Phoenix and the Lark: Revolutionary Mythology and Iconographic Creativity in Belfast's Republican Districts. In Anthony D. Buckley (ed.), *Symbols in Northern Ireland.* Belfast: Institute of Irish Studies Press.

Kertzer, David I. (1988), *Ritual, Politics, and Power.* New Haven, CT: Yale University Press.

Kiberd, Declan (1995), *Inventing Ireland.* London: Jonathan Cape.

Kierans, Ciara and Philip McCormack (2002), Elmdale: A Search for an Understanding of Community through Protest and Resistance. *Irish Journal of Anthropology* VI: 113–29.

Kirby, Peadar, Luke Gibbons and Michael Cronin (2002a), Introduction: The Reinvention of Ireland: A Critical Perspective. In Peadar Kirby, Luke Gibbons and Michael Cronin (eds), *Reinventing Ireland: Culture, Society and the Global Economy.* London: Pluto Press.

—— (eds) (2002b), *Reinventing Ireland: Culture, Society and the Global Economy,* London: Pluto.

Kirk, John M. and Donal P. Ó Baoill (eds) (2002), *Travellers and Their Language.* Belfast: Queen's University Belfast.

Kirkland, Richard (2002), *Identity Parades: Northern Irish Culture and Dissident Subjects.* Liverpool: Liverpool University Press.

Kneafsey, Moya (2003), 'If it Wasn't for the Tourists We Wouldn't Have an Audience': The Case of Tourism and Traditional Music in North Mayo. In Michael Cronin and Barbara O'Connor (eds), *Irish Tourism: Image, Culture and Identity.* Clevedon: Channel View Publications.

Knox, Colin (2001), The 'Deserving' Victims of Political Violence: 'Punishment' Attacks in Northern Ireland. *Criminal Justice* 1 (2): 181-99.

Kockel, Ullrich (ed.) (1994), *Culture, Tourism and Development: The Case of Ireland.* Liverpool: Liverpool University Press.

—— (ed.) (1995), *Landscape, Heritage and Identity: Case Studies in Irish Ethnography*. Liverpool: Liverpool University Press.

—— (1999), Nationality, Identity and Citizenship: Reflecting on Europe at Drumcree Parish Church. *Ethnologia Europea* 29 (2): 97–108.

—— (2002), *Regional Culture and Economic Development: Explorations in European Ethnology*. Aldershot: Ashgate.

Komito, Lee (1984), Irish Clientelism: A Reappraisal. *Economic and Social Review* 15 (3): 173–94.

—— (1989), Dublin Politics: Symbolic Dimensions of Politics. In Chris Curtin and Thomas M. Wilson (eds), *Ireland from Below: Social Change and Local Communities*. Galway: Galway University Press.

—— (1993), Personalism and Brokerage in Dublin Politics. In Chris Curtin, Hastings Donnan and Thomas M. Wilson (eds), *Irish Urban Cultures*. Belfast: Institute of Irish Studies Press.

Kristeva, Julia (1982), *Powers of Horror: An Essay on Abjection*. New York: Columbia University Press.

Laffan, Brigid and Rory O'Donnell (1998), Ireland and the Growth of International Governance. In William Crotty and David E. Schmitt (eds), *Ireland and the Politics of Change*. London: Longman.

Lanclos, Donna M. (2003), *At Play in Belfast: Children's Folklore and Identities in Northern Ireland*. New Brunswick: Rutgers University Press.

Larsen, Sidsel S. (1982a), The Two Sides of the House: Identity and Social Organisation in Kilbroney, Northern Ireland. In Anthony P. Cohen (ed.), *Belonging: Identity and Social Organisation in British Rural Cultures*. Manchester: Manchester University Press.

—— (1982b), The Glorious Twelfth: The Politics of Legitimation in Kilbroney. In Anthony P. Cohen (ed.), *Belonging: Identity and Social Organisation in British Rural Cultures*. Manchester: Manchester University Press.

Lentin, Ronit (2001), Responding to the racialisation of Irishness: Disavowed multiculturalism and its discontents. *Sociological Research Online* 5 (4) (*www.socresonline.org.uk/5/4/lentin.html*).

LeMaster, Barbara (1993), When Women and Men Talk Differently: Language and Policy in the Dublin Deaf Community. In Chris Curtin, Hastings Donnan and Thomas M. Wilson (eds), *Irish Urban Cultures*. Belfast: Institute of Irish Studies Press.

Leontidou, Lila, Hastings Donnan and Alex Afouxenidis (2005), Exclusion and Difference along the EU Border: Social and Cultural Markers, Spatialities and Mappings. *International Journal of Urban and Regional Research* 29 (2): 389–407.

Lewis, Oscar (1966), The Culture of Poverty. *Scientific American* 215 (4): 19–25.

Leyshon, Andrew and Roger Lee (2003), Introduction: Alternative Economic

Geographies. In Andrew Leyshon, Roger Lee and Colin C. Williams (eds), *Alternative Economic Spaces*. London: Sage.

Leyton, Elliott (1966), Conscious Models and Dispute Regulation in an Ulster Village. *Man* (N. S.) 1: 534–42.

—— (1970), Spheres of Inheritance in Aughnaboy. *American Anthropologist* 72: 1378–88.

—— (1974), Opposition and Integration in Ulster. *Man* (N. S.) 9: 185–98.

—— (1975), *The One Blood: Kinship and Class in an Irish Village*. St John's Institute of Social and Economic Research: Memorial University of Newfoundland.

—— (1976), Studies in Irish Social Organization: The State of the Art. Paper delivered at the American Anthropological Association meetings, Washington, December.

Liston, Katie (2002), The Gendered Field of Irish Sport. In Mary P. Corcoran and Michel Peillon (eds), *Ireland Unbound: A Turn of the Century Chronicle*. Dublin: Institute of Public Administration.

Lloyd, David (2001), Regarding Ireland in a Post-Colonial Frame. *Cultural Studies* 15 (1): 12–32.

Loughran, Christina (1986), Armagh and Feminist Strategy: Campaigns Around Republican Women Prisoners in Armagh Jail. *Feminist Review* 23: 59–79.

Lowie, Robert (1920), *Primitive Society*. New York: Boni and Liveright.

Mac an Ghaill, Máirtín (1999), *Contemporary Racisms and Ethnicities: Social and Cultural Transformations*. Buckingham: Open University Press.

—— (2000), The Irish in Britain: The Invisibility of Ethnicity and Anti-Irish Racism. *Journal of Ethnic and Migration Studies* 26 (1): 137–47.

McCafferty, Nell (1984), It is My Belief that Armagh is a Feminist Issue. In Nell McCafferty, *The Best of Nell: A Selection of Writings over Fourteen Years*. Dublin: Attic Press. First published in *The Irish Times*, 17 June 1980.

McCall, Cathal (2002), Political Transformation and the Reinvention of the Ulster-Scots Identity and Culture. *Identities: Global Studies in Culture and Power* 9 (2): 197–218.

McCann, May (1994), A Woman's Voice: A Feminist Looks at Irish Anthropology. In Pól Ó Muirí (ed.), *The Unheard Voice: Social Anthropology in Ireland*, Belfast: Fortnight Educational Trust.

McCann, May, Séamas Ó Síocháin and Joseph Ruane (1994), *Irish Travellers: Culture and Ethnicity*. Belfast: Institute of Irish Studies, Queen's University Belfast.

McCarthy, P. (1994), The Sub-Culture of Poverty Reconsidered. In M. McCann, S. Ó Síocháin and J. Ruane (eds), *Irish Travellers: Culture and Ethnicity*. Belfast: Institute of Irish Studies.

MacClancy, Jeremy (1996), Sport, Identity and Ethnicity. In Jeremy MacClancy (ed.), *Sport, Identity and Ethnicity*. Oxford: Berg.

McCormick, Jonathan and Neil Jarman (2005), Death of a Mural. *Journal of Material Culture* 10 (1): 49–71.

McCoy, Gordon (1997), Rhetoric and Realpolitik: The Irish Language Movement and the British Government. In Hastings Donnan and Graham McFarlane (eds), *Culture and Policy in Northern Ireland: Anthropology in the Public Arena*. Belfast: Institute of Irish Studies Press.

—— (2005), Irish Language Culture. *The Vacuum* (Belfast), July: 4–5.

McCrone, David (1992), *Understanding Scotland: The Sociology of a Stateless Nation*. London: Routledge.

—— (1998), *The Sociology of Nationalism*. London: Routledge.

McCrone, David, Angela Morris and Richard Kiely (1995), *Scotland – the Brand: The Making of Scottish Heritage*. Edinburgh: Edinburgh University Press.

McDonogh, Gary W. (1993), The Face behind the Door. In Thomas M. Wilson and M. Estellie Smith (eds), *Cultural Change and the New Europe*, Boulder CO: Westview.

McFarlane, Graham (1979), Mixed Marriages in Ballycuan, Northern Ireland. *Journal of Comparative Family Studies* 10: 191–205.

—— (1986), 'It's Not as Simple as That': The Expression of the Catholic and Protestant Boundary in Northern Irish Rural Communities. In Anthony P. Cohen (ed.), *Symbolising Boundaries: Identity and Diversity in British Cultures*. Manchester: Manchester University Press.

—— (1989), Dimensions of Protestantism: The Working of Protestant Identity in a Northern Irish Village. In Chris Curtin and Thomas M. Wilson (eds), *Ireland from Below: Social Change and Local Communities*. Galway: Galway University Press.

—— (1994), A Soft Voice: The Anthropology of Religion in Ireland. In Pól Ó Muirí (ed.), *The Unheard Voice: Social Anthropology in Ireland*. Belfast: Fortnight Educational Trust.

MacGaffey, Janet (1991), *The Real Economy of Zaire: The Contribution of Smuggling and Other Unofficial Activities to National Wealth*. Philadelphia: University of Pennsylvania Press.

McGovern, Mark (2003), 'The Cracked Pint Glass of the Servant': The Irish Pub, Irish Identity and the Tourist Eye. In Michael Cronin and Barbara O'Connor (eds), *Irish Tourism: Image, Culture and Identity*. Clevedon: Channel View Publications.

McLaughlin, Eithne (1989), In Search of the Female Breadwinner: Gender and Unemployment in Derry City. In Hastings Donnan and Graham McFarlane (eds), *Social Anthropology and Public Policy in Northern Ireland*, Aldershot: Avebury.

—— (1991), Work and Welfare Benefits: Social Security, Employment and

Unemployment in the 1990s. *Journal of Social Policy* 20 (4): 485–508.

—— (1997), Unemployment, Labour Supply and the Meaning of Money. In Hastings Donnan and Graham McFarlane (eds), *Culture and Policy in Northern Ireland: Anthropology in the Public Arena.* Belfast: Institute of Irish Studies.

McLaughlin, Eithne and Kate Ingram (1991), *All Stitched Up: Sex and Skill in the Northern Irish Clothing Industry.* Belfast: Equal Opportunities Commission.

MacLaughlin, Jim (1995), *Travellers and Ireland: Whose Country? Whose History?* Cork: Cork University Press.

McLean, Stuart (1999), 'With Death Looking Out of Their Eyes': The Spectropoetics of Hunger in Accounts of the Irish Famine. *Social Analysis* 43 (3): 40–67.

—— (2003), Céide Fields: Natural Histories of a Buried Landscape. In Pamela J. Stewart and Andrew Strathern (eds), *Landscape, Memory and History: Anthropological Perspectives.* London: Pluto Press.

—— (2004), *The Event and Its Terrors: Ireland, Famine, Modernity.* Stanford: Stanford University Press.

McVeigh, Robbie (1992), The Specificities of Irish Racism. *Race and Class* 33 (4): 31–45.

—— (1996), *The Radicalization of Irishness: Racism and Anti-racism in Ireland.* Belfast: Centre for Research and Documentation.

—— (1998), 'There's No Racism Because There's No Black People Here': Racism and Anti-racism in Northern Ireland. In Paul Hainsworth (ed.), *Divided Society: Ethnic Minorities and Racism in Northern Ireland.* London: Pluto Press.

Maguire, Mark (2004), *Differently Irish: A Cultural History Exploring 25 Years of Vietnamese-Irish Identity.* Dublin: The Woodfield Press.

Mahon, Evelyn (1994), Ireland: A Private Patriarchy? *Environment and Planning A* 26: 1277–96.

Malinowski, Bronislaw (1932), *The Sexual Life of Savages in North-Western Melanesia.* London: Routledge and Kegan Paul Ltd.

Malkki, Liisa H. (1992), National Geographic: The Rooting of People and the Territoriality of National Identity among Scholars and Refugees. *Cultural Anthropology* 7 (1): 24–44.

—— (1995), *Purity and Exile: Violence, Memory, and National Cosmology among Hutu Refugees in Tanzania.* Chicago: University of Chicago Press.

Manning, Frank E. (1992), Spectacle. In Richard Bauman (ed.), *Folklore, Cultural Performances, and Popular Entertainments: A Communications-Centered Handbook.* Oxford: Oxford University Press.

Marger, M. (1989), Asians in the Northern Ireland Economy. *New Community* 15 (2): 203–10.

Marston, Sallie A. (2002), Making Difference: Conflict over Irish Identity in the New York City St Patrick's Day Parade. *Political Geography* 21: 373–92.

Merion, Asunción (2004), Politics of Identity and Identity Policies in Europe: The Case of Peruvian Immigrants in Spain. *Identities: Global Studies in Culture and Power* 11 (2): 241–64.

Messenger, Betty (1975), *Picking up the Linen Threads.* Austin: University of Texas Press.

Messenger, John C. (1964), Literacy vs. Scientific Interpretation of Cultural 'Reality' in the Aran Islands of Eire. *Ethnohistory* 11: 41–55.

—— (1967), The 'Black Irish' of Montserrat. *Éire-Ireland* II (1): 27–40.

—— (1968), Types and Causes of Disputes in an Irish Folk Community. *Éire-Ireland* III (1): 27–37.

—— (1969), *Inis Beag: Isle of Ireland.* New York: Holt, Rinehart and Winston.

—— (1971), Sex and Repression in an Irish Folk Community. In Donald Marshall and R. Suggs (eds), *Human Sexual Behavior.* New York: Basic Books.

—— (1983), *An Anthropologist at Play: Balladmongering in Ireland and Its Consequences for Research*, Lanham, MD: University Press of America.

—— (1984), Problems of Irish Ethnography. *Royal Anthropological Institute Newsletter* 3: 2–13.

—— (1989), *Inis Beag Revisited: The Anthropologist as Observant Participator.* Salem, WI: Sheffield Publishing Company.

—— (1994), St Patrick's Day in 'The Other Emerald Isle'. *Éire-Ireland* XXIX (1): 12–23.

Milton, Kay (1990), *Our Countryside, Our Concern: The Policy and Practice of Conservation in Northern Ireland.* Belfast: Northern Ireland Environment Link.

—— (1993), Belfast: Whose City? In Chris Curtin, Hastings Donnan and Thomas M. Wilson (eds), *Irish Urban Cultures.* Belfast: Institute of Irish Studies Press.

—— (1994), An Environmentalist's Science: An Examination of Social Science and Social Change. In Pól Ó Muirí (ed.), *The Unheard Voice: Social Anthropology in Ireland.* Belfast: Fortnight Educational Trust.

—— (1996), *Environmentalism and Cultural Theory: Exploring the Role of Anthropology in Environmental Discourse.* London: Routledge.

—— (1997), Modernity and Postmodernity in the Northern Irish Countryside. In Hastings Donnan and Graham McFarlane (eds), *Culture and Policy in Northern Ireland: Anthropology in the Public Arena.* Belfast: Institute of Irish Studies.

—— (2002), *Loving Nature: Towards an Ecology of Emotion.* London: Routledge.

Mitchell, J. Clyde (1956), *The Kalela Dance: Aspects of Social Relationships among Urban Africans in Northern Rhodesia.* Manchester: The Rhodes-Livingstone Institute.

Modood, Tariq and Pnina Werbner (eds) (1997), *The Politics of Multiculturalism in the New Europe: Racism, Identity and Community.* London: Zed Books.

Moore, Ronnie and Andrew Sanders (2002), Formations of Culture: Nationalism and Conspiracy Ideology in Ulster Loyalism. *Anthropology Today* 18 (6): 9–15.

Murphy, Liam D. (2000), The Name of Our God is Dialogue: Millennial Visions in Northern Ireland. *Journal of Ritual Studies* 14 (2): 4–15.

—— (2002), Demonstrating Passion: Constructing Sacred Movement in Northern Ireland. *Journal of the Society for the Anthropology of Europe* 2 (3): 22–30.

Murtagh, Brendan (1996), *Community and Conflict in Rural Ulster: A Summary Report*. Belfast: Northern Ireland Community Relations Council.

—— (1998), Community, Conflict and Rural Planning in Northern Ireland. *Journal of Rural Studies* 14 (2): 221–31.

Nagle, John (2005a), *Is 'Everybody Irish on St Paddy's'? Ambivalence and Conflict on St Patrick's Day: A Research Report into People's Attitudes into St Patrick's Day 2004*. Queen's University Belfast: Institute of Irish Studies.

—— (2005b), 'Everybody is Irish on St Paddy's': Ambivalence and Alterity at London's St Patrick's Day 2002. *Identities: Global Studies in Culture and Power* 12: 563–83.

National Economic and Social Council (1999), *Opportunities, Challenges and Capacities for Choice*. Report No. 105. Dublin: NESC.

Negra, Diane (2001), Consuming Ireland: Lucky Charms Cereal, Irish Spring Soap and 1-800-Shamrock. *Cultural Studies* 15 (1): 76–97.

Nic Craith, Máiréad (2002), *Plural Identities, Singular Narratives: The Case of Northern Ireland*. New York and Oxford: Berghahn Books.

—— (2003), *Culture and Identity Politics in Northern Ireland*. Houndmills: Palgrave Macmillan.

Ní Shúinéar, Sinéad (1994), Irish Travellers, Ethnicity and the Origins Question. In May McCann, Séamas Ó Síocháin and Joseph Ruane (eds), *Irish Travellers: Culture and Ethnicity*. Belfast: Institute of Irish Studies, Queen's University Belfast.

—— (n.d.), Hegemony and Heterogeneity: Othering in the Western European Isles. Unpublished paper.

O'Brien, M. (2004), Selling Soccer. In Michel Peillon and Mary P. Corcoran (ed.), *Place and Non-place: The Reconfiguration of Ireland*. Dublin: Institute of Public Administration.

O'Carroll, Cliona (2005), 'Cold Beer, Warm Hearts': Community, Belonging and Desire in Irish Pubs in Berlin. In Thomas M. Wilson (ed.), *Drinking Cultures: Alcohol and Identity*. Oxford: Berg.

O'Connor, Barbara (1997), Safe Sets: Women, Dance and 'Communitas'. In Helen Thomas (ed.), *Dance in the City*. London: Macmillan Press.

—— (1998), Riverdance. In Michel Peillon and Eamonn Slater (eds), *Encounters with Modern Ireland: A Sociological Chronicle 1995–1996*. Dublin: Institute of Public Administration.

—— (2003), 'Come and Daunce with Me in Irlande': Tourism, Dance and Globalisation. In Michael Cronin and Barbara O'Connor (eds), *Irish Tourism:*

Image, Culture and Identity. Clevedon: Channel View Publications.

O'Connor, Barbara and Michael Cronin (eds) (1993), *Tourism in Ireland: A Critical Analysis*. Cork: Cork University Press.

O'Connor, Pat (2000), Changing Places: Privilege and Resistance in Contemporary Ireland. *Sociological Research Online* 5 (3) (*www.socresonline.org.uk/5/3/o'connor.html*).

O'Donnell, Rory (1995), Ireland: Myths of Innocence. In Bernd Baumgartl and Adrian Favell (eds), *New Xenophobia in Europe*. The Hague: Kluwer Law International.

—— (1999), Reinventing Ireland: From Sovereignty to Partnership. Jean Monnet Inaugural lecture, University College Dublin, National University of Ireland, 29 April.

—— (2000), The New Ireland in the New Europe. In Rory O'Donnell (ed.), *Europe: The Irish Experience*. Dublin: Institute of European Affairs.

O'Dowd, Liam (1994), *Whither the Irish Border? Sovereignty, Democracy and Economic Integration in Ireland*. Belfast: Centre for Research and Documentation.

O'Dowd, Liam and Thomas M. Wilson (eds) (1996), *Borders, Nations, and States: Frontiers of Sovereignty in the New Europe.* Aldershot: Avebury Press..

O'Faolain, Nuala (1996), *Are You Somebody? The Life and Times of Nuala O'Faolain*. Dublin: New Island Books.

Ogle, Shaun (1989), Housing Estate Improvements: An Assessment of Strategies for Tenant Participation. In Hastings Donnan and Graham McFarlane (eds), *Social Anthropology and Public Policy in Northern Ireland*. Aldershot: Avebury.

O'Hearn, Denis (1998), *Inside the Celtic Tiger: The Irish Economy and the Asian Model.* London: Pluto.

—— (2003), Macroeconomic Policy in the Celtic Tiger: A Critical Reassessment. In Colin Coulter and Steve Coleman (eds), *The End of Irish History? Critical Reflections on the Celtic Tiger*. Manchester: Manchester University Press.

Okely, Judith (1983), *The Traveller-Gypsies*. Cambridge: Cambridge University Press.

O'Leary, Richard (2004), The Relics of St Thérèse. In Michel Peillon and Mary P. Corcoran (eds), *Place and Non-Place: The Reconfiguration of Ireland*. Dublin: Institute of Public Administration.

O'Malley, Padraig (1990), *Biting at the Grave: The Irish Hunger Strikes and the Politics of Despair*. Belfast: Blackstaff Press.

O'Reilly, Camille (1998), The Irish Language as Symbol: Visual Representations of Irish in Northern Ireland. In Anthony D. Buckley (ed.), *Symbols in Northern Ireland,* Belfast: Institute of Irish Studies Press.

—— (1999), *The Irish Language in Northern Ireland: The Politics of Culture and Identity*. London: Macmillan.

—— (2003), The Politics of Culture in Northern Ireland. In Jörg Neuheiser and Stefan Wolff (eds), *Peace at Last? The Impact of the Good Friday Agreement on Northern Ireland*. New York: Berghahn Books.

O'Sullivan, Eoin (1993), Identity and Survival in a Hostile Environment: Homeless Men in Galway. In Chris Curtin, Hastings Donnan and Thomas M. Wilson (eds), *Irish Urban Cultures*. Belfast: Institute of Irish Studies Press.

O'Toole, Fintan (1997a), Unsuitables from a Distance: The Politics of *Riverdance*. In Fintan O'Toole, *The Ex-Isle of Erin*. Dublin: New Island Books.

—— (1997b), *The Ex-Isle of Erin: Images of a Global Ireland*. Dublin: New Island Books.

Peace, Adrian (1986), 'A Different Place Altogether': Diversity, Unity and Boundary in an Irish Village. In Anthony P. Cohen (ed.), *Symbolising Boundaries: Identity and Diversity in British Cultures*. Manchester: Manchester University Press.

—— (1989), From Arcadia to Anomie: Critical Notes on the Constitution of Irish Society as an Anthropological Subject. *Critique of Anthropology* 9 (1): 89–111.

—— (1992), No Fishing Without Drinking: The Construction of Social Identity in Rural Ireland. In Dimitra Gefou-Madianou (ed.), *Alcohol, Gender and Culture*. London: Routledge.

—— (1993), Environmental Protest, Bureaucratic Closure: The Politics of Discourse in Rural Ireland. In Kay Milton (ed.), *Environmentalism: The View From Anthropology*. London: Routledge.

—— (1996) When the Salmon Comes: The Politics of Summer Fishing in an Irish Community. *Journal of Anthropological Research* 52: 85–106.

—— (1997), *A Time of Reckoning: The Politics of Discourse in Rural Ireland*. St John's, Newfoundland: Institute of Social and Economic Research.

—— (2001), *A World of Fine Difference: The Social Architecture of a Modern Irish Village*. Dublin: University College Dublin Press.

Peillon, Michel (2000), Strangers in Our Midst. In Eamonn Slater and Michel Peillon (eds), *Memories of the Present: A Sociological Chronicle of Ireland 1997–1998*. Dublin: Institute of Public Administration.

Peillon, Michel and Mary P. Corcoran (eds) (2004), *Place and Non-Place: The Reconfiguration of Ireland*. Dublin: Institute of Public Administration.

Peillon, Michel and Eamonn Slater (eds) (1998), *Encounters with Modern Ireland: A Sociological Chronicle of Ireland 1995–1996*. Dublin: Institute of Public Administration.

Pope, S. W. (1997), *Patriotic Games: Sporting Traditions in the American Imagination, 1876–1926*. Oxford: Oxford University Press.

Rabinowitz, Dan (1997), *Overlooking Nazareth: The Ethnography of Exclusion in Galilee*. Cambridge: Cambridge University Press.

Radford, Katy (2001), Creating an Ulster Scots Revival. *Peace Review* 13 (1): 51–7.

Rapport, Nigel (2002), 'Best of British!': An Introduction to the Anthropology of Britain. In Nigel Rapport (ed.), *British Subjects: An Anthropology of Britain*. Oxford: Berg.

Rapport, Nigel and Andrew Dawson (eds) (1998), *Migrants of Identity: Perceptions of Home in a World of Movement*. Oxford: Berg.

Robb, H. M. (1995), The Border Region: A Case Study. In Michael D'Arcy and Tim Dickson (eds), *Border Crossings: Developing Ireland's Island Economy*. Dublin: Gill and Macmillan.

Roche, Rosellen (2003), The Inheritors: An Ethnographic Exploration of Stress, Threat, Violence, Guts, Fear and Fun among Young People in Contemporary Londonderry, Northern Ireland. Unpublished doctoral dissertation, University of Cambridge.

Rolston, Bill (1991), *Politics and Painting: Murals and Conflict in Northern Ireland*. London: Fairleigh Dickinson, Associated University Press.

Rosaldo, Renato (1988), Ideology, Place, and People without Culture. *Cultural Anthropology* 3 (1): 77–87.

Roseberry, William (1988), Political Economy. *Annual Review of Anthropology* 17: 161–85.

Ruane, Joseph (1989), Success and Failure in a West of Ireland Factory. In Chris Curtin and Thomas M. Wilson (eds), *Ireland from Below: Social Change and Local Communities*. Galway: Galway University Press.

—— (1994), Nationalism and European Community Integration: The Republic of Ireland. In Victoria A. Goddard, Josep R. Llobera and Cris Shore (eds), *The Anthropology of Europe: Identities and Boundaries in Conflict*. Oxford: Berg.

Ryder, Chris and Vincent Kearney (2001), *Drumcree: The Orange Order's Last Stand*. London: Methuen.

Sacks, Paul (1976), *Donegal Mafia*. New Haven, CT: Yale University Press.

Salazar, Carles (1996), *A Sentimental Economy: Commodity and Community in Rural Ireland*. Oxford: Berghahn.

—— (1998), Gender Relationships and the Domestic Sphere in Rural Ireland: Reflections on a Personal Experience. *Europea: Journal of the Europeanists* IV (1): 27-43.

—— (1999), On Blood and Its Alternatives: An Irish History. *Social Anthropology* 7 (2): 155–67.

Santino, Jack (1998), *The Hallowed Eve: Dimensions of Culture in a Calendar Festival in Northern Ireland*. Lexington: University Press of Kentucky.

—— (1999), Public Protest and Popular Style: Resistance from the Right in Northern Ireland and South Boston. *American Anthropologist* 101 (3): 515–28.

Saris, Jamie A. (1996), Mad Kings, Proper Houses, and an Asylum in Rural Ireland. *American Anthropologist* 98 (3): 539–54.

—— (1997), The Asylum in Ireland: A Brief Institutional History and Some Local

Effects. In Anne Cleary and Margaret P. Tracy (eds), *The Sociology of Health and Illness in Ireland*. Dublin: University College Dublin Press.

—— (1999), Producing Persons and Developing Institutions in Rural Ireland. *American Ethnologist* 26 (3): 690–710.

—— (2000), Culture and History in the Halfway House: Ethnography, Tradition, and the Rural Middle Class in the West of Ireland. *Journal of Historical Sociology* 13 (1): 10–36.

Saris, Jamie A. and Brendan Bartley (2002), The Arts of Memory: Icon and Structural Violence in a Dublin 'Underclass' Housing Estate. *Anthropology Today* 18 (4): 14–19.

Saris, Jamie A., Brendan Bartley, Ciara Kierans, Colm Breathnach and Philip McCormack (2000), Horses and the Culture of Protest in West Dublin. In Eamonn Slater and Michel Peillon (eds), *Memories of the Present: A Sociological Chronicle of Ireland, 1997–1998*. Dublin: Institute of Public Administration.

Schechner, Richard (1995), *The Future of Ritual: Writings on Culture and Performance*. London: Routledge.

Scheper-Hughes, Nancy (1979), *Saints, Scholars and Schizophrenics: Mental Illness in Rural Ireland*. Berkeley: University of California Press.

—— (1981a), Reply to Ballybran. Weekend Supplement, *The Irish Times*, 21 February, pp. 9-10.

—— (1981b), *Cui Bonum* – For Whose Good? A Dialogue with Sir Raymond Firth. *Human Organization* 40 (4): 371–2.

—— (1982), Ballybran – Reply to Eileen Kane. *Royal Anthropological Institute Newsletter* 51: 12–13.

—— (1983a), Deposed Kings: The Demise of the Rural Irish Gerontocracy. In Jay Sokolovsky (ed.), *Growing Old in Different Societies: Cross-Cultural Perspectives*. Belmont, CA: Wadsworth Publishing Company.

—— (1983b), From Anxiety to Analysis: Rethinking Irish Sexuality and Sex Roles. *Women's Studies* 10: 147–60.

—— (1987), The Best of Two Worlds, the Worst of Two Worlds: Reflections on Culture and Field Work among the Rural Irish and Pueblo Indians. *Comparative Studies in Society and History* 29 (1): 56–75.

—— (2000), Ire in Ireland. *Ethnography* 1: 117–40.

—— (2001), *Saints, Scholars and Schizophrenics: Mental Illness in Rural Ireland*, Anniversary Edition, revised and expanded, Berkeley: University of California Press.

Scott, James C. (1990), *Domination and the Arts of Resistance: Hidden Transcripts*. New Haven, CT: Yale University Press.

Shanklin, Eugenia (1980), The Irish Go-Between. *Anthropological Quarterly* 53: 162–72.

—— (1982), *Donegal's Changing Traditions: An Ethnographic Study*, New York: Gordon and Breach.

Shanks, Amanda (1987), The Stem Family Reconsidered: The Case of the Minor Gentry of Northern Ireland. *Journal of Comparative Family Studies* 18 (3): 339–61.

—— (1988), *Rural Aristocracy in Northern Ireland*. Aldershot: Avebury.

—— (1990), Northern Irish Gentry Culture: An Anomaly. In Myrtle Hill and Sarah Barber (eds), *Aspects of Irish Studies*. Belfast: Institute of Irish Studies.

—— (1994), Cultural Divergence and Durability: The Border, Symbolic Boundaries and the Irish Gentry. In Hastings Donnan and Thomas M. Wilson (eds), *Border Approaches: Anthropological Perspectives on Frontiers*. Lanham, MD: University Press of America.

Sheehan, Elizabeth A. (1991), Political and Cultural Resistance to European Community Europe: Ireland and the Single European Act. *Socialism and Democracy* 13: 101–18.

—— (1993), The Academic as Informant: Methodological and Theoretical Issues in the Ethnography of Intellectuals. *Human Organization* 52 (3): 252–9.

Sherlock, Joyce L. (1999), Globalisation, Western Culture and Riverdance. In Avtar Brah, Mary J. Hickman and Mairtin Mac an Ghaill (eds), *Thinking Identities: Ethnicity, Racism and Culture*. London: Macmillan.

Shirlow, Peter (2003a), Northern Ireland: A Reminder from the Present. In Colin Coulter and Steve Coleman (eds), *The End of Irish History? Critical Reflections on the Celtic Tiger*. Manchester: Manchester University Press.

—— (2003b), 'Who Fears to Speak?' Fear, Mobility and Ethno-Sectarianism in the Two 'Ardoynes'. *Global Review of Ethnopolitics* 3 (1): 76–91.

Shore, Cris (2000), *Building Europe: The Cultural Politics of European Integration*. London: Routledge.

Shutes, Mark T. (1989), Changing Agricultural Strategies in a Kerry Parish. In Chris Curtin and Thomas M. Wilson (eds), *Ireland from Below: Social Change and Local Communities*. Galway: Galway University Press.

—— (1991), Kerry Farmers and the European Community: Capital Transitions in a Rural Irish Parish. *Irish Journal of Sociology* 1: 1–17.

—— (1993), Rural Communities without Family Farms? Family Dairy Farming in the Post-1993 EC. In Thomas M. Wilson and M. Estellie Smith (eds), *Cultural Change and the New Europe*. Boulder, CO and Oxford: Westview Press.

Silverman, Marilyn (1989), 'A Labouring Man's Daughter': Constructing 'Respectability' in South Kilkenny. In Chris Curtin and Thomas M. Wilson (eds), *Ireland from Below: Social Change and Local Communities*. Galway: Galway University Press.

—— (1992), From Fisher to Poacher: Public Right and Private Property in the Salmon Fisheries of the River Nore in the Nineteenth Century. In Marilyn

Silverman and Philip H. Gulliver (eds), *Approaching the Past: Historical Anthropology through Irish Case Studies*. New York: Columbia University Press.

—— (1993), An Urban Place in Rural Ireland: An Historical Ethnography of Domination, 1841–1989. In Chris Curtin, Hastings Donnan and Thomas M. Wilson (eds), *Irish Urban Cultures*. Belfast: Institute of Irish Studies.

—— (2001), *An Irish Working Class: Explorations in Political Economy and Hegemony, 1800–1950*. Toronto: University of Toronto Press.

Silverman, Marilyn and Philip H. Gulliver (eds) (1992a), *Approaching the Past: Historical Anthropology through Irish Case Studies*, New York: Columbia University Press.

—— (1992b), Historical Anthropology and the Ethnographic Tradition: A Personal, Historical, and Intellectual Account. In Marilyn Silverman and Philip H. Gulliver (eds), *Approaching the Past: Historical Anthropology through Irish Case Studies*, New York: Columbia University Press.

Singer, Milton (1972), *When a Great Tradition Modernizes*. New York: Praeger.

Skinner, Jonathan (2004), *Before the Volcano: Reverberations of Identity on Montserrat*. Kingston, Jamaica: Arawak Publications.

—— (2006), Modernist Anthropology, Ethnic Tourism and National Identity: The Contest for the Commoditization and Consumption of St Patrick's Day, Montserrat. In Kevin Meethan, Alison Anderson and Steven Miles (eds), *Tourism, Consumption and Representation: Narratives of Place and Self.* Wallingford: CABI Publishing.

Slater, Eamonn (1998), Dependent Rugby. In Michel Peillon and Eamonn Slater (eds), *Encounters with Modern Ireland: A Sociological Chronicle 1995–1996*. Dublin: Institute of Public Administration.

—— (2000a), The Archaeology of Irish Golfscapes. In Eamonn Slater and Michel Peillon (eds), *Memories of the Present: A Sociological Chronicle of Ireland 1997–98*. Dublin: Institute of Public Administration.

—— (2000b), When the *Local* goes Global. In Eamonn Slater and Michel Peillon (eds), *Memories of the Present: A Sociological Chronicle of Ireland 1997–1998*. Dublin: Institute of Public Administration.

Slater, Eamonn and Michel Peillon (eds) (2000), *Memories of the Present: A Sociological Chronicle of Ireland 1997–1998*. Dublin: Institute of Public Administration.

Sluka, Jeffrey (1989), *Hearts and Minds, Water and Fish: Support for the IRA and INLA in a Northern Irish Ghetto*. Greenwich: JAI Press.

—— (1992a), The Anthropology of Conflict. In Carolyn Nordstrom and JoAnn Martin, (eds), *The Paths to Domination, Resistance, and Terror.* Berkeley: University of California Press.

—— (1992b), The Politics of Painting: Political Murals in Northern Ireland. In

Carolyn Nordstrom and JoAnn Martin (eds), *The Paths to Domination, Resistance, and Terror.* Berkeley: University of California Press.

—— (1992c), Review of Allen Feldman, Formations of Violence. *Anthropology Ireland* 2 (1): 33–40.

—— (1995), Domination, Resistance and Political Culture in Northern Ireland's Catholic-Nationalist Ghettos. *Critique of Anthropology* 15 (1): 71–102.

—— (1999), Review of Culture and Policy in Northern Ireland: Anthropology in the Public Arena. *American Anthropologist* 101 (2): 449–51.

Smith, Anthony D. (1995), *Nations and Nationalism in a Global Era.* Cambridge: Polity Press.

Smith, Gavin (1999), *Confronting the Present: Towards a Politically Engaged Anthropology.* Oxford: Berg.

Smith, Noel D. (1998), 'Being Me Own Person': Diverse Lifestyles among Young Women in the Irish Midlands. Unpublished doctoral dissertation, Queen's University Belfast.

Spencer, Paul (ed.) (1985), *Society and the Dance: The Social Anthropology of Process and Performance.* Cambridge: Cambridge University Press.

Stahl, Ellen J. (1979), A New Explanation of Sexual Repression in Ireland. *Central Issues in Anthropology* 1 (1): 37–67.

Stewart, Pamela J. and Andrew Strathern (2002), *Violence: Theory and Ethnography.* London: Continuum.

Stolcke, Verena (1995), Talking Culture: New Boundaries, New Rhetorics of Exclusion in Europe. *Current Anthropology* 36 (1): 1–24.

Strathern Andrew and Pamela J. Stewart (2001), *Minorities and Memories: Survivals and Extinctions in Scotland and Western Europe.* Durham, NC: Carolina Academic Press.

Sugden, John and Alan Bairner (1993), *Sport, Sectarianism and Society in a Divided Ireland.* Leicester: Leicester University Press.

Sugrue, Karen (2002), Sex in the City. In Mary P. Corcoran and Michel Peillon (eds), *Ireland Unbound: A Turn of the Century Chronicle.* Dublin: Institute of Public Administration.

Sweeney, George (1993a), Self-Immolation in Ireland: Hungerstrikes and Political Confrontation. *Anthropology Today* 9 (5): 10–14.

—— (1993b), Irish Hunger Strikes and the Cult of Self-Sacrifice. *Journal of Contemporary History* 28: 421–37.

Szuchewycz, Bodhan (1989), The Meanings of Silence in the Irish Catholic Charismatic Movement. In Chris Curtin and Thomas M. Wilson (eds), *Ireland from Below: Social Change and Local Communities.* Galway: Galway University Press.

Taaffe, Thomas (2001), Claiming the King's Highway: Assertions of Power, Domination and Territory During the Marching Season in Northern Ireland.

Journal of the Society for the Anthropology of Europe 1 (2): 16–27.

—— (2003), Images of Peace: The News Media, Politics and the Good Friday Agreement. In Jörg Neuheiser and Stefan Wolff (eds), *Peace at Last? The Impact of the Good Friday Agreement on Northern Ireland.* New York: Berghahn Books.

Taylor, Lawrence J. (1980a), Colonialism and Community Structure in Western Ireland. *Ethnohistory* 27: 169–81.

—— (1980b), The Merchant in Peripheral Ireland: A Case from Donegal. *Anthropology* 4: 63–76.

—— (1981), 'Man the Fisher': Salmon Fishing and the Expression of Community in a Rural Irish Settlement. *American Ethnologist* 8: 774–88.

—— (1989a), Bas i-nEirinn: Cultural Constructions of Death in Ireland. *Anthropological Quarterly* 62 (4):175–87.

—— (1989b), The Mission: An Anthropological View of an Irish Religious Occasion. In Chris Curtin and Thomas M. Wilson (eds), *Ireland from Below: Social Change and Local Communities.* Galway: Galway University Press.

—— (1990), The Healing Mass: Fields and Regimes of Irish Catholicism. *Archives de Science Sociales des Religions* 71: 93–111.

—— (1992), The Languages of Belief: Nineteenth-Century Religious Discourse in Southwest Donegal. In Marilyn Silverman and Philip H. Gulliver (eds), *Approaching the Past: Historical Anthropology through Irish Case Studies.* New York: Columbia University Press.

—— (1993a), Peter's Pence: Catholic Discourse and Nationalism in Nineteenth-Century Ireland. *Journal of the History of European Ideas* 16: 103–8.

—— (1993b), Review of Allen Feldman, *Formations of Violence. Irish Journal of Sociology* 3: 148–54.

—— (1995), *Occasions of Faith: An Anthropology of Irish Catholics.* Philadelphia: University of Pennsylvania Press

—— (1996), 'There are Two Things that People Don't Like to Hear About Themselves': The Anthropology of Ireland and the Irish View of Anthropology. *The South Atlantic Quarterly* 95 (1): 213–26.

Thomas, Helen (1995), *Dance, Modernity and Culture: Explorations in the Sociology of Dance.* London: Routledge.

—— (2003), *The Body, Dance and Cultural Theory.* Houndmills: Palgrave Macmillan.

Thompson, Spurgeon (2001), Introduction: Towards an Irish Cultural Studies. *Cultural Studies* 15 (1): 1–11.

Throop, Elizabeth A. (1999), *Net Curtains and Closed Doors: Intimacy, Family, and Public Life in Dublin.* Westport, CT: Bergin and Garvey.

Trimble, David (1989), Addresses and Discussion. In Maurna Crozier (ed.), *Varieties of Irishness.* Proceedings of the Cultural Traditions Group Conference,

3–4 March. Belfast: Institute of Irish Studies.

Tuck, Jason (2005), Rugby Union and National Identity Politics. In Alan Bairner (ed.), *Sport and the Irish: Histories, Identities, Issues*. Dublin: University College Dublin Press.

Tucker, Vincent (1989), State and Community: A Case Study of Glencolumbkille. In Chris Curtin and Thomas M. Wilson (eds), *Ireland from Below: Social Change and Local Communities*. Galway: Galway University Press.

Turner, Victor (1969), *The Ritual Process*. Harmondsworth: Penguin Books.

—— (1982), *From Ritual to Theatre: The Human Seriousness of Play*. New York: Performing Arts Journal Publications.

—— (1988), *The Anthropology of Performance*. New York: Performing Arts Journal Publications.

Turner, Victor and Edith Turner (1978), *Image and Pilgrimage in Christian Culture: Anthropological Perspectives*. Oxford: Blackwell.

Varenne, Hervé (1993), Dublin 16: Accounts of Suburban Lives. In Chris Curtin, Hastings Donnan and Thomas M. Wilson (eds), *Irish Urban Cultures*. Belfast: Institute of Irish Studies Press.

Varley, Anthony (1983), 'The Stem Family in Ireland' Reconsidered. *Comparative Studies in Society and History* 25: 381–91.

Vincent, Joan (1983), Marriage, Religion and Class in South Fermanagh, 1846–1920. In Owen Lynch (ed.), *Emergent Structures and the Family*. Delhi: Hindustan Publishing Corporation.

—— (1989), Local Knowledge and Political Violence in County Fermanagh. In Chris Curtin and Thomas M. Wilson (eds), *Ireland from Below: Social Change and Local Communities*. Galway: Galway University Press.

—— (1991), Irish Border Violence and the Question of Sovereignty. In M. D. Zamora, B. B. Erring and A. L. LaRuffa (eds), *The Anthropology of War and Peace*. St. Mary's College of Bayonbong, Nueva Vizcaya: Rex Book Store.

—— (1992), A Political Orchestration of the Irish Famine: County Fermanagh, May 1847. In Marilyn Silverman and Philip H. Gulliver (eds), *Approaching the Past*, New York: Columbia University Press.

—— (1993), Ethnicity and the State in Northern Ireland. In Judith D. Toland (ed.), *Ethnicity and the State*. New Brunswick: Transaction Publishers.

—— (1995), Conacre: A Reevaluation of Irish Custom. In Jane Schneider and Rayna Rapp (eds), *Articulating Hidden Histories: Exploring the Influence of Eric R. Wolf*. Berkeley: University of California Press.

Viney, Michael (1980), Geared for a Gale. *The Irish Times*, 24 September, p. 12.

—— (1983), The Yank in the Corner: Why the Ethics of Anthropology are a Worry for Rural Ireland. Weekend Supplement, *The Irish Times*, 6 August 1983, p. 1.

Walsh, Patricia (1971), Itinerancy and Poverty: A Study in the Sub-culture of Poverty. Unpublished Masters dissertation. University College Dublin. (cited by

McCarthy 1994: 129 as 'McCarthy, Patricia 1972, *Itinerancy and Poverty: A Study in the Sub-Culture of Poverty*, unpublished M.Soc.Sc. Thesis, Dublin: University College').

Werbner, Pnina and Muhammad Anwar (eds) (1991), *Black and Ethnic Leaderships in Britain: The Cultural Dimensions of Political Action*. London: Routledge.

Wilk, Richard R. (1996), *Economics and Cultures: Foundations of Economic Anthropology*. Boulder, CO: Westview.

Williams, Drid (2003) [1991], *Anthropology and the Dance*. Urbana, IL: University of Illinois Press.

Wilson, Thomas M. (1984), From Clare to the Common Market: Perspectives in Irish Ethnography. *Anthropological Quarterly* 57 (1): 1–15.

—— (1987), Mythic Images of the Irish Family in the Works of Flaherty, deValera, and Arensberg and Kimball. *Working Papers in Irish Studies Northeastern University* 87 (2/3): 14–31.

—— (1988), Culture and Class among the 'Large' Farmers of Eastern Ireland. *American Ethnologist* 15 (4): 680–95.

—— (1989a), Large Farms, Local Politics, and the International Arena: The Irish Tax Dispute of 1979. *Human Organization* 48 (1): 60–70.

—— (1989b), Broker's Broker: The Chairman of the Meath County Council. In Chris Curtin and Thomas M. Wilson (eds), *Ireland from Below: Social Change and Local Communities*. Galway: Galway University Press.

—— (1990), From Patronage to Brokerage in the Local Politics of Eastern Ireland. *Ethnohistory* 37 (2): 158–87.

—— (1991), On Characterisation and Identity: Further Reflections on Long Term Research in Ireland. *Anthropology Ireland* 1 (1–2): 6–10.

—— (1993a), An Anthropology of the European Community. In Thomas M. Wilson and M. Estellie Smith (eds), *Cultural Change and the New Europe: Perspectives on the European Community*. Boulder, CO and Oxford: Westview Press.

—— (1993b), Frontiers Go But Boundaries Remain: The Irish Border as a Cultural Divide. In Thomas M. Wilson and M. Estellie Smith (eds), *Cultural Change and the New Europe: Perspectives on the European Community*. Boulder, CO and Oxford: Westview Press.

—— (1993c), Consumer Culture and European Integration at the Northern Irish Border. In W. Fred van Raaij and Gary J. Bamossy (eds), *European Advances in Consumer Research*. Volume 1. Provo, UT: Association for Consumer Research.

—— (1994a), A Question of Identity: Problems of Social Anthropology in Ireland. In Pól Ó Muirí (ed.), *The Unheard Voice: Social Anthropology in Ireland*. Belfast: Fortnight Educational Trust.

—— (1994b), Symbolic Dimensions to the Irish Border. In Hastings Donnan and Thomas M. Wilson (eds), *Border Approaches: Anthropological Perspectives on Frontiers*. Lanham, MD: University Press of America.

—— (1995), Blurred Borders: Local and Global Consumer Culture in Northern Ireland. In Janeen Arnold Costa and Gary J. Bamossy (eds), *Marketing in a Multicultural World: Ethnicity, Nationalism and Cultural Identity*. London: Sage.

—— (1996), Sovereignty, Identity and Borders: Political Anthropology and European Integration. In Liam O'Dowd and Thomas M. Wilson (eds), *Borders, Nations and States: Frontiers of Sovereignty in the New Europe*. Aldershot: Avebury.

—— (1998a), Themes in the Anthropology of Ireland. In Susan Parman (ed.), *Europe in the Anthropological Imagination*. Upper Saddle River, NJ: Prentice-Hall.

—— (1998b), An Anthropology of the European Union, From Above and Below. In Susan Parman (ed.), *Europe in the Anthropological Imagination*. Upper Saddle River, NJ: Prentice-Hall.

—— (1998c), 'Doing the Double' Twice Over: The Subversive Informal Economy at the Irish–British Border. Unpublished paper presented at the annual meetings of the American Anthropological Association, as part of a panel on 'Class and Identities At and Across Borders of Deterritorializing Nation-States', organized and chaired by Michael Kearney and Thomas M. Wilson, Philadelphia.

—— (2000), The Obstacles to European Union Regional Policy in the Northern Ireland Borderlands. *Human Organization* 59 (1): 1–10.

Wilson, Thomas M. and Hastings Donnan (1998), Nation, State and Identity at International Borders. In Thomas M. Wilson and Hastings Donnan (eds), *Border Identities: Nation and State at International Frontiers*. Cambridge: Cambridge University Press.

—— (2005a), Territory, Identity and the Places In-Between: Culture and Power in European Borderlands. In Thomas M. Wilson and Hastings Donnan (eds), *Culture and Power at the Edges of the State: National Support and Subversion in European Borderlands*. Münster: Lit Verlag.

—— (eds) (2005b), *Culture and Power at the Edges of the State: National Support and Subversion in European Borderlands*. Münster: Lit Verlag.

Wolf, Eric R. (1999), *Envisioning Power: Ideologies of Dominance and Crisis*. Berkeley: University of California Press.

—— (2001), *Pathways of Power: Building an Anthropology of the Modern World*. Berkeley: University of California Press.

Women Against Imperialism (1980), *Women Protest for Political Status in Armagh Gaol*. No publication details given.

Wulff, Helena (2002), Yo-Yo Fieldwork: Mobility and Time in a Multi-Local Study of Dance in Ireland. *Anthropological Journal on European Cultures* 11: 117–37.

—— (2003a), The Irish Body in Motion: Moral Politics, National Identity and Dance. In Noel Dyck and Eduado P. Archetti (eds), *Sport, Dance and Embodied Identities*. Oxford: Berg.

—— (2003b), Steps and Stories about Ireland. In Mary Brady (ed.), *Choreographic Encounters*. Cork: Institute for Choreography and Dance.

—— (2003c), Steps on Screen: Technoscapes, Visualization and Globalization in Dance. In Christina Garsten and Helena Wulff (eds), *New Technologies at Work: People, Screens and Social Virtuality*. Oxford: Berg.

—— (2005), Memories in Motion: The Irish Dancing Body. In Bryan S. Turner (ed.), 'Dancing Bodies'. Special issue of *Body & Society* 11 (4): 45–62.

—— (in press), *Dancing at the Crossroads: Memory and Mobility in Ireland*. Oxford: Berghahn Books.

Index

5805 213